APPLICATION OF THE MANAGEMENT SYSTEM FOR FACILITIES AND ACTIVITIES

THE MANAGEMENT SYSTEM FOR FACILITIES AND ACTIVITIES

APPLICATION OF THE
MANAGEMENT SYSTEM FOR
FACILITIES AND ACTIVITIES

Safety standards survey
The IAEA welcomes your response. Please see:
http://www-ns.iaea.org/standards/feedback.htm

The following States are Members of the International Atomic Energy Agency:

AFGHANISTAN	GHANA	PAKISTAN
ALBANIA	GREECE	PANAMA
ALGERIA	GUATEMALA	PARAGUAY
ANGOLA	HAITI	PERU
ARGENTINA	HOLY SEE	PHILIPPINES
ARMENIA	HONDURAS	POLAND
AUSTRALIA	HUNGARY	PORTUGAL
AUSTRIA	ICELAND	QATAR
AZERBAIJAN	INDIA	REPUBLIC OF MOLDOVA
BANGLADESH	INDONESIA	ROMANIA
BELARUS	IRAN, ISLAMIC REPUBLIC OF	RUSSIAN FEDERATION
BELGIUM	IRAQ	SAUDI ARABIA
BELIZE	IRELAND	SENEGAL
BENIN	ISRAEL	SERBIA
BOLIVIA	ITALY	SEYCHELLES
BOSNIA AND HERZEGOVINA	JAMAICA	SIERRA LEONE
BOTSWANA	JAPAN	SINGAPORE
BRAZIL	JORDAN	SLOVAKIA
BULGARIA	KAZAKHSTAN	SLOVENIA
BURKINA FASO	KENYA	SOUTH AFRICA
CAMEROON	KOREA, REPUBLIC OF	SPAIN
CANADA	KUWAIT	SRI LANKA
CENTRAL AFRICAN	KYRGYZSTAN	SUDAN
REPUBLIC	LATVIA	SWEDEN
CHAD	LEBANON	SWITZERLAND
CHILE	LIBERIA	SYRIAN ARAB REPUBLIC
CHINA	LIBYAN ARAB JAMAHIRIYA	TAJIKISTAN
COLOMBIA	LIECHTENSTEIN	THAILAND
COSTA RICA	LITHUANIA	THE FORMER YUGOSLAV
CÔTE D'IVOIRE	LUXEMBOURG	REPUBLIC OF MACEDONIA
CROATIA	MADAGASCAR	TUNISIA
CUBA	MALAYSIA	TURKEY
CYPRUS	MALI	UGANDA
CZECH REPUBLIC	MALTA	UKRAINE
DEMOCRATIC REPUBLIC	MARSHALL ISLANDS	UNITED ARAB EMIRATES
OF THE CONGO	MAURITANIA	UNITED KINGDOM OF
DENMARK	MAURITIUS	GREAT BRITAIN AND
DOMINICAN REPUBLIC	MEXICO	NORTHERN IRELAND
ECUADOR	MONACO	UNITED REPUBLIC
EGYPT	MONGOLIA	OF TANZANIA
EL SALVADOR	MOROCCO	UNITED STATES OF AMERICA
ERITREA	MYANMAR	URUGUAY
ESTONIA	NAMIBIA	UZBEKISTAN
ETHIOPIA	NETHERLANDS	VENEZUELA
FINLAND	NEW ZEALAND	VIETNAM
FRANCE	NICARAGUA	YEMEN
GABON	NIGER	ZAMBIA
GEORGIA	NIGERIA	ZIMBABWE
GERMANY	NORWAY	

The Agency's Statute was approved on 23 October 1956 by the Conference on the Statute of the IAEA held at United Nations Headquarters, New York; it entered into force on 29 July 1957. The Headquarters of the Agency are situated in Vienna. Its principal objective is "to accelerate and enlarge the contribution of atomic energy to peace, health and prosperity throughout the world".

IAEA SAFETY STANDARDS SERIES No. GS-G-3.1

APPLICATION OF THE MANAGEMENT SYSTEM FOR FACILITIES AND ACTIVITIES

SAFETY GUIDE

INTERNATIONAL ATOMIC ENERGY AGENCY
VIENNA, 2006

COPYRIGHT NOTICE

© IAEA, 2006

Printed by the IAEA in Austria
July 2006
STI/PUB/1253

IAEA Library Cataloguing in Publication Data

Application of the management system for facilities and activities : safety
    guide. — Vienna : International Atomic Energy Agency, 2006.
        p. ; 24 cm. — (IAEA safety standards series, ISSN 1020–525X ;
    no. GS-G-3.1)
    STI/PUB/1253
    ISBN 92–0–106606–6
    Includes bibliographical references.

    1. Nuclear facilities — Management. 2. Radiation — Safety
measures. I. International Atomic Energy Agency. II. Series: Safety
standards series ; GS-G-3.1.

IAEAL   06–00443

FOREWORD

by Mohamed ElBaradei
Director General

The IAEA's Statute authorizes the Agency to establish safety standards to protect health and minimize danger to life and property — standards which the IAEA must use in its own operations, and which a State can apply by means of its regulatory provisions for nuclear and radiation safety. A comprehensive body of safety standards under regular review, together with the IAEA's assistance in their application, has become a key element in a global safety regime.

In the mid-1990s, a major overhaul of the IAEA's safety standards programme was initiated, with a revised oversight committee structure and a systematic approach to updating the entire corpus of standards. The new standards that have resulted are of a high calibre and reflect best practices in Member States. With the assistance of the Commission on Safety Standards, the IAEA is working to promote the global acceptance and use of its safety standards.

Safety standards are only effective, however, if they are properly applied in practice. The IAEA's safety services — which range in scope from engineering safety, operational safety, and radiation, transport and waste safety to regulatory matters and safety culture in organizations — assist Member States in applying the standards and appraise their effectiveness. These safety services enable valuable insights to be shared and I continue to urge all Member States to make use of them.

Regulating nuclear and radiation safety is a national responsibility, and many Member States have decided to adopt the IAEA's safety standards for use in their national regulations. For the Contracting Parties to the various international safety conventions, IAEA standards provide a consistent, reliable means of ensuring the effective fulfilment of obligations under the conventions. The standards are also applied by designers, manufacturers and operators around the world to enhance nuclear and radiation safety in power generation, medicine, industry, agriculture, research and education.

The IAEA takes seriously the enduring challenge for users and regulators everywhere: that of ensuring a high level of safety in the use of nuclear materials and radiation sources around the world. Their continuing utilization for the benefit of humankind must be managed in a safe manner, and the IAEA safety standards are designed to facilitate the achievement of that goal.

IAEA SAFETY STANDARDS

SAFETY THROUGH INTERNATIONAL STANDARDS

While safety is a national responsibility, international standards and approaches to safety promote consistency, help to provide assurance that nuclear and radiation related technologies are used safely, and facilitate international technical cooperation, commerce and trade.

The standards also provide support for States in meeting their international obligations. One general international obligation is that a State must not pursue activities that cause damage in another State. More specific obligations on Contracting States are set out in international safety related conventions. The internationally agreed IAEA safety standards provide the basis for States to demonstrate that they are meeting these obligations.

THE IAEA STANDARDS

The IAEA safety standards have a status derived from the IAEA's Statute, which authorizes the Agency to establish standards of safety for nuclear and radiation related facilities and activities and to provide for their application.

The safety standards reflect an international consensus on what constitutes a high level of safety for protecting people and the environment.

They are issued in the IAEA Safety Standards Series, which has three categories:

Safety Fundamentals
—Presenting the objectives, concepts and principles of protection and safety and providing the basis for the safety requirements.

Safety Requirements
—Establishing the requirements that must be met to ensure the protection of people and the environment, both now and in the future. The requirements, which are expressed as 'shall' statements, are governed by the objectives, concepts and principles of the Safety Fundamentals. If they are not met, measures must be taken to reach or restore the required level of safety. The Safety Requirements use regulatory language to enable them to be incorporated into national laws and regulations.

Safety Guides
—Providing recommendations and guidance on how to comply with the Safety Requirements. Recommendations in the Safety Guides are expressed as 'should' statements. It is recommended to take the measures stated or equivalent alternative measures. The Safety Guides present international good practices and increasingly they reflect best practices to

help users striving to achieve high levels of safety. Each Safety Requirements publication is supplemented by a number of Safety Guides, which can be used in developing national regulatory guides.

The IAEA safety standards need to be complemented by industry standards and must be implemented within appropriate national regulatory infrastructures to be fully effective. The IAEA produces a wide range of technical publications to help States in developing these national standards and infrastructures.

MAIN USERS OF THE STANDARDS

As well as by regulatory bodies and governmental departments, authorities and agencies, the standards are used by authorities and operating organizations in the nuclear industry; by organizations that design, manufacture for and apply nuclear and radiation related technologies, including operating organizations of facilities of various types; by users and others involved with radiation and radioactive material in medicine, industry, agriculture, research and education; and by engineers, scientists, technicians and other specialists. The standards are used by the IAEA itself in its safety reviews and for developing education and training courses.

DEVELOPMENT PROCESS FOR THE STANDARDS

The preparation and review of safety standards involves the IAEA Secretariat and four safety standards committees for safety in the areas of nuclear safety (NUSSC), radiation safety (RASSC), the safety of radioactive waste (WASSC) and the safe transport of radioactive material (TRANSSC), and a Commission on Safety Standards (CSS), which oversees the entire safety standards programme. All IAEA Member States may nominate experts for the safety standards committees and may provide comments on draft standards. The membership of the CSS is appointed by the Director General and includes senior government officials having responsibility for establishing national standards.

For Safety Fundamentals and Safety Requirements, the drafts endorsed by the Commission are submitted to the IAEA Board of Governors for approval for publication. Safety Guides are published on the approval of the Director General.

Through this process the standards come to represent a consensus view of the IAEA's Member States. The findings of the United Nations Scientific Committee on the Effects of Atomic Radiation (UNSCEAR) and the recommendations of international expert bodies, notably the International Commission on Radiological Protection (ICRP), are taken into account in developing the standards. Some standards are developed in cooperation with other bodies in the United Nations system or other specialized agencies, including the Food and Agriculture Organization of the United Nations, the International

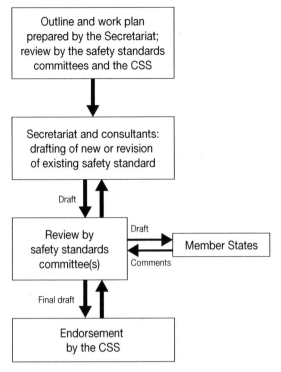

The process for developing a new safety standard or revising an existing one.

Labour Organization, the OECD Nuclear Energy Agency, the Pan American Health Organization and the World Health Organization.

The safety standards are kept up to date: five years after publication they are reviewed to determine whether revision is necessary.

APPLICATION AND SCOPE OF THE STANDARDS

The IAEA Statute makes the safety standards binding on the IAEA in relation to its own operations and on States in relation to operations assisted by the IAEA. Any State wishing to enter into an agreement with the IAEA concerning any form of Agency assistance is required to comply with the requirements of the safety standards that pertain to the activities covered by the agreement.

International conventions also contain similar requirements to those in the safety standards, and make them binding on contracting parties. The Safety Fundamentals were used as the basis for the development of the Convention on Nuclear Safety and the Joint Convention on the Safety of Spent Fuel Management and on the Safety of Radioactive Waste Management. The Safety

Requirements on Preparedness and Response for a Nuclear or Radiological Emergency reflect the obligations on States under the Convention on Early Notification of a Nuclear Accident and the Convention on Assistance in the Case of a Nuclear Accident or Radiological Emergency.

The safety standards, incorporated into national legislation and regulations and supplemented by international conventions and detailed national requirements, establish a basis for protecting people and the environment. However, there will also be special aspects of safety that need to be assessed case by case at the national level. For example, many of the safety standards, particularly those addressing planning or design aspects of safety, are intended to apply primarily to new facilities and activities. The requirements and recommendations specified in the IAEA safety standards might not be fully met at some facilities built to earlier standards. The way in which the safety standards are to be applied to such facilities is a decision for individual States.

INTERPRETATION OF THE TEXT

The safety standards use the form 'shall' in establishing international consensus requirements, responsibilities and obligations. Many requirements are not addressed to a specific party, the implication being that the appropriate party or parties should be responsible for fulfilling them. Recommendations are expressed as 'should' statements in the main text (body text and appendices), indicating an international consensus that it is necessary to take the measures recommended (or equivalent alternative measures) for complying with the requirements.

Safety related terms are to be interpreted as stated in the IAEA Safety Glossary (http://www-ns.iaea.org/standards/safety-glossary.htm). Otherwise, words are used with the spellings and meanings assigned to them in the latest edition of The Concise Oxford Dictionary. For Safety Guides, the English version of the text is the authoritative version.

The background and context of each standard within the Safety Standards Series and its objective, scope and structure are explained in Section 1, Introduction, of each publication.

Material for which there is no appropriate place in the body text (e.g. material that is subsidiary to or separate from the main text, is included in support of statements in the main text, or describes methods of calculation, experimental procedures or limits and conditions) may be presented in appendices or annexes.

An appendix, if included, is considered to form an integral part of the standard. Material in an appendix has the same status as the main text and the IAEA assumes authorship of it. Annexes and footnotes to the main text, if included, are used to provide practical examples or additional information or explanation. Annexes and footnotes are not integral parts of the main text. Annex material published by the IAEA is not necessarily issued under its authorship; material published in standards that is under other authorship may be presented in annexes. Extraneous material presented in annexes is excerpted and adapted as necessary to be generally useful.

CONTENTS

1. INTRODUCTION

BACKGROUND

1.1. This Safety Guide supports the Safety Requirements publication on The Management System for Facilities and Activities [1]. It provides generic guidance to aid in establishing, implementing, assessing and continually improving a management system that complies with the requirements established in Ref. [1]. In addition to this Safety Guide, there are a number of Safety Guides for specific technical areas. Together these provide all the guidance necessary for implementing the requirements of Ref. [1]. This publication supersedes Safety Series No. 50-SG-Q1–Q7 (1996) [2].

1.2. To meet the requirements established in Ref. [1], methods and solutions other than those set out in this Safety Guide may also be acceptable provided that they result in at least the same level of safety.

1.3. The guidance provided here may be used by organizations in the following ways:

— To assist in the development of the management systems of organizations directly responsible for operating facilities and activities and providing services, as described in para. 1.5;
— To assist in the development of the management systems of the relevant regulatory bodies [3];
— By the operator, to specify to a supplier, via contractual documentation, any guidance of this Safety Guide that should be included in the supplier's management system for the supply and delivery of products.

OBJECTIVE

1.4. The objective of this publication is to provide generic guidance for establishing, implementing, assessing and continually improving a management system that integrates safety, health, environmental, security[1], quality and

---

[1] This Safety Guide covers the security of facilities, nuclear material and sources of radiation only to the extent that security measures for physical protection are essential to safety and the failure of such measures has consequences for safety.

economic elements, in order to meet the requirements established in Ref. [1]. This Safety Guide also provides illustrative examples of the application of the management system requirements.

SCOPE

1.5. This publication is applicable to the establishment, implementation, assessment and continual improvement of management systems for:

— Nuclear facilities;
— Activities using sources of ionizing radiation;
— Radioactive waste management;
— The transport of radioactive material;
— Radiation protection activities;
— Any other practices or circumstances in which people may be exposed to radiation from naturally occurring or artificial sources;
— The regulation of such facilities and activities.

1.6. This Safety Guide is applicable throughout the lifetime of facilities and for the entire duration of activities in normal, transient and emergency situations. This includes any subsequent period of institutional control that may be necessary. For a facility, these phases usually include siting, design, construction, commissioning, operation and decommissioning (or close-out or closure).

STRUCTURE

1.7. This Safety Guide follows the structure of Ref. [1]. Section 2 provides guidance for implementing the management system, including guidance relating to safety culture, grading and documentation. Section 3 provides guidance on the responsibilities of senior management[2] for the development and implementation of a management system. Section 4 provides guidance on

_____

[2] 'Senior management' means the person who, or group of people which, directs, controls and assesses an organization at the highest level. Many different terms are used, including, for example: chief executive officer (CEO), director general, executive team, plant manager, top manager, chief regulator, site vice-president, managing director and laboratory director.

resource management, including guidance on human resources, infrastructure and the working environment. Section 5 provides guidance on how the processes of the organization can be identified and developed, including guidance on some generic processes of the management system. Section 6 provides guidance on measuring, assessing and improving the management system. The appendices and annexes provide illustrative examples to supplement the text.

2. MANAGEMENT SYSTEM

AN INTEGRATED MANAGEMENT SYSTEM

2.1.   An integrated management system should provide a single framework for the arrangements and processes necessary to address all the goals of the organization. These goals include safety, health, environmental, security, quality and economic elements and other considerations such as social responsibility.

2.2.   A management system, including organizational models, concepts and tools, should also cover human factor issues and other integrated management approaches that complement the traditional approach to achieving results, which was based on inspections and verification checks.

2.3.   Technological innovations have radically altered the interactions between systems and humans, and therefore the management of the entire organization. Complex activities and multiple objectives involve individuals operating at different levels in the organization, while operating processes are modified by the introduction of new management practices and new requirements. Daily practices and the results achieved by the organization, the organizational culture and the management processes are deeply interrelated. The management system should be able to evolve accordingly, to accommodate change and to ensure that individuals understand what has to be done to meet all the requirements applicable and relevant to them.

2.4.   Organizations should integrate all their components into an integrated management system. These components of the organization include the structure, resources and processes. Individuals, equipment and culture should therefore be as much a part of the integrated management system as the documented policies and processes.

2.5. In an integrated management system, all goals, strategies, plans and objectives of an organization should be considered in a coherent manner. This implies:

— Identifying their interdependences and their potential to impact on each other;
— Assigning priorities to the goals, strategies, plans and objectives;
— Establishing procedures to ensure that these priorities are respected in decision making.

2.6. Guidance on the transition to an integrated management system is provided in Appendix I.

GENERAL

2.7. A robust and effective management system should support the enhancement and improvement of safety culture and the achievement of high levels of safety performance. The management system should therefore be designed with these purposes in mind and should be implemented in such a way that it is known, understood and followed by all individuals.

2.8. The management system should be designed to enable the organization's objectives to be achieved in a safe, efficient and effective manner.

2.9. The management system should be binding on all individuals.

2.10. The management system should specify all work delegated to external organizations. The lines of communication and the interfaces between internal and external organizations should be specified in the management system, and the responsibility of each organization for work assigned to it should be described.

2.11. The management system should assign responsibility to achieve the organization's objectives and should empower the individuals in the organization to perform their assigned tasks. Managers should be responsible for achieving quality and safety in the final outputs of work under their responsibility within the organization. Individuals should take responsibility for quality and safety while carrying out the work that is assigned to them. In order to discharge this responsibility, individuals should be technically competent in using the appropriate hardware, equipment, tools and measuring devices and should have a clear understanding of the work processes.

2.12. The management system should ensure that a review of the controls that affect work, such as the training of individuals and the work package that accompanies it, is conducted prior to restarting work after interruptions.

2.13. The management system should provide a common vocabulary consistent with the work being performed. All key terms used in the management system should be defined and should become an integral part of the training programme to ensure that communications and understanding are consistent throughout the organization.

2.14. Senior management should set the goals of the organization and should assign the responsibilities and authorities, define the policies and requirements, and provide for the performance and assessment of work.

2.15. Responsibility and authority to stop unsatisfactory work should be assigned in such a manner that planning, scheduling and other considerations do not override safety requirements.

2.16. The actions of managers and supervisors or team leaders have a strong influence on the safety culture within the organization. These actions should promote good working practices and eliminate poor practices. Managers and supervisors or team leaders should maintain a presence in the workplace by carrying out tours, walk-downs of the facility and periodic observations of tasks with particular safety significance.

2.17. Managers and supervisors should talk to other individuals during workplace tours and should take these opportunities to reinforce awareness of management expectations.

2.18. Managers and supervisors should encourage and welcome the reporting by other individuals of potential safety concerns, incidents and near-misses, and accident precursors, and should respond to valid concerns promptly and in a positive manner. Where appropriate, contractors should give the same high priority to safety, especially when they are working at a facility.

2.19. Strategies to identify, disseminate information on and promote good practices should be adopted, and strategies to eliminate poor practices should be adopted. Such strategies should involve the balanced use of appropriate incentives and sanctions. To be effective, these strategies should be well understood and should be applied consistently and fairly throughout the organization.

2.20. The organization should develop a management system that is appropriate to the stage in the lifetime and the maturity of the nuclear facility or activity.

2.21. All work that is to be done should be planned and authorized before it is commenced. Work should be accomplished under suitably controlled conditions by technically competent individuals using technical standards, instructions, procedures or other appropriate documents.

See Ref. [1], paras 2.1–2.4.

Implementing the management system

2.22. To establish a management system, an organization:

— Should review applicable regulations and standards and the organization's management and technical practices to determine whether the processes adequately address all requirements;
— Should review the Safety Requirements publication [1], the Safety Guides on management systems and other relevant safety related publications to identify shortcomings in the organization and to assign priorities to those areas where improvement or development is necessary;
— Should establish time frames within which the necessary changes are to be implemented.

2.23. The individual in the most senior managerial position in the organization should be responsible for ensuring that the management system is implemented. Implementing the management system demands the collaborative efforts of managers, those performing the work and those assessing the work. For satisfactory implementation, planning and the deployment of adequate resources are necessary. All individuals should be trained to achieve proficiency. It should be ensured that all individuals understand the management processes that apply to the performance of their work. The effectiveness of the management system should be assessed and reviewed at all stages of implementation. The information gained from assessments should be used to achieve continuing improvements in work performance.

Implementation plan

2.24. Senior management should prepare a plan to achieve full implementation of the management system. The implementation plan should be subject to approval and monitoring by the most senior manager assigned the responsibility for development and implementation of the management system.[3]

2.25. The implementation plan should include provisions for recruiting, selecting, training, assigning and retraining adequate numbers of individuals, in a manner consistent with schedules for implementation and workloads. Consideration should be given to needs for special skills and training. Such provisions should take into account demographic and economic conditions.

2.26. Work plans, schedules, instructions, technical specifications and drawings that are necessary to define the specific actions to perform work should be developed, should be subject to approval, and should be used or referred to as necessary in the processes of the management system. Their preparation should be planned and scheduled so that individuals have clear instructions on how to sequence and perform their work correctly.

2.27. Plans should be prepared for assessing the effectiveness of instructions and their implementation in relation to the performance of work, and for assessing the results achieved in relation to quality and safety. Implementation of these plans should commence as soon as possible. Frequent early assessments may be necessary to ensure the adequacy of instructions and to prevent the endorsement of poor practices. The involvement of individuals in the development of these procedures and instructions should be considered to ensure the usefulness and ease of application of these documents.

---

[3] In some Member States the individual in the most senior position appoints a full time management system manager (see para. 3.18). This management system manager may be supported by a team composed of representatives of all organizational units that meets regularly to exchange experience and good practices and to resolve any problems or difficulties that arise during the development of the management system.

Interface arrangements

2.28. There should be a clear understanding of the division of responsibilities and the working relationships between all organizational units participating in or supporting the management system. Such units include centralized corporate and technical departments providing support, and company safety committees. They also include public services such as fire services and medical services.

2.29. Consistent methods of defining relative responsibilities and lines of communication between organizational units should be implemented.

2.30. Interface agreements, sometimes referred to as 'memoranda of understanding', or equivalent formal agreements that define interfaces between organizational units should be developed where appropriate. For example, such agreements may be appropriate where safety could be affected, where the working arrangements are complex or where the interfaces involve several organizations. Their acceptance by the managers of the interfacing organizations and units should be obtained in writing. The interface agreements should be distributed to all affected participants.

2.31. In the preparation of interface documents, the following points should be addressed:

— The participating units should be identified and included on the circulation list.
— The prime responsibilities, authority and accountability for the work should be stated clearly.
— The responsibilities for review and comment, approval of technical issues, implementation, reporting, verification and audit should be specified where appropriate.
— Key positions within each unit to act as focal points for communication should be specified.
— The contents of the documents necessary to carry out the activity or convey technical information across the interface (typically programmes, plans, specifications, procedures, instructions, drawings and records) should be defined.
— The flow of documents across organizational interfaces and the schedules for actions by interfacing units or groups should be specified.

See Ref. [1], paras 3.12–3.14.

SAFETY CULTURE

2.32. The management system should provide structure and direction to the organization in a way that permits and promotes the development of a strong safety culture together with the achievement of high levels of safety performance. The management system should establish a working environment in which staff can raise safety issues without fear of harassment, intimidation, retaliation or discrimination.

2.33. The management system will both influence and be influenced by the overall culture of the organization. The relationship between the management system and the culture of the organization should be understood by all individuals of the organization.

2.34. Senior management should have an understanding of the key characteristics and attributes that support a strong safety culture and should provide the means to ensure that this understanding is shared by all individuals. Senior management should provide guiding principles and should reinforce behavioural patterns that promote the continual development of a strong safety culture.

2.35. Management at all levels should promote the types of behaviour, values and basic beliefs that lead to the development of a strong safety culture. Managers should monitor and reinforce the attributes that have been identified as essential for achieving a strong safety culture and should pay attention to early signs of decline in these attributes and thus in the safety culture.

2.36. A strong safety culture has the following important attributes:

— Safety is a clearly recognized value:
  • The high priority given to safety is shown in documentation, communications and decision making.
  • Safety is a primary consideration in the allocation of resources.
  • The strategic business importance of safety is reflected in the business plan.
  • Individuals are convinced that safety and production go hand in hand.
  • A proactive and long term approach to safety issues is shown in decision making.
  • Safety conscious behaviour is socially accepted and supported (both formally and informally).

— Leadership for safety is clear:
- Senior management is clearly committed to safety.
- Commitment to safety is evident at all levels of management.
- There is visible leadership showing the involvement of management in safety related activities.
- Leadership skills are systematically developed.
- Management ensures that there are sufficient competent individuals.
- Management seeks the active involvement of individuals in improving safety.
- Safety implications are considered in change management processes.
- Management shows a continual effort to strive for openness and good communication throughout the organization.
- Management has the ability to resolve conflicts as necessary.
- Relationships between managers and individuals are built on trust.

— Accountability for safety is clear:
- An appropriate relationship with the regulatory body exists that ensures that the accountability for safety remains with the licensee.
- Roles and responsibilities are clearly defined and understood.
- There is a high level of compliance with regulations and procedures.
- Management delegates responsibility with appropriate authority to enable clear accountabilities to be established.
- 'Ownership' for safety is evident at all organizational levels and for all individuals.

— Safety is integrated into all activities:
- Trust permeates the organization.
- Consideration of all types of safety, including industrial safety and environmental safety, and of security is evident.
- The quality of documentation and procedures is good.
- The quality of processes, from planning to implementation and review, is good.
- Individuals have the necessary knowledge and understanding of the work processes.
- Factors affecting work motivation and job satisfaction are considered.
- Good working conditions exist with regard to time pressures, workload and stress.
- There is cross-functional and interdisciplinary cooperation and teamwork.
- Housekeeping and material conditions reflect commitment to excellence.

— Safety is learning driven:
- A questioning attitude prevails at all organizational levels.

- Open reporting of deviations and errors is encouraged.
- Internal and external assessments, including self-assessments, are used.
- Organizational experience and operating experience (both internal and external to the facility) are used.
- Learning is facilitated through the ability to recognize and diagnose deviations, to formulate and implement solutions and to monitor the effects of corrective actions.
- Safety performance indicators are tracked, trended, evaluated and acted upon.
- There is systematic development of individual competences.

See Ref. [1], para. 2.5.

GRADING THE APPLICATION OF MANAGEMENT SYSTEM REQUIREMENTS

Graded approach

2.37. A structured approach to determining how the management system requirements are to be applied to products and activities should be developed and implemented.

2.38. The degree to which the management system requirements are applied to a product or activity should reflect the importance of the product or activity to safety, health, environmental, security, quality and economic expectations, the complexity of the product or activity, and the possible consequences if the product fails or if the activity is carried out incorrectly.

2.39. Grading the application of the management system requirements should enable valuable resources and attention to be targeted at the products or activities of greater significance. This can result in minimizing total costs while improving safety.

2.40. For all products and activities within a process, all the requirements of and demands on the relevant process should first be considered. By using the grading methodology it may be possible to identify products and activities of lesser significance within a process. For products and activities of lesser significance, it is then possible to determine whether all the controls and checks of the process are necessary. Controls and checks that could be graded include, for example, aspects such as qualification and training for individuals, type and format of procedures, and requirements on verification, inspection, testing, material, records and the performance of suppliers.

Grading process

2.41. The grading process should determine the extent of the application of the requirements of the management system to the products and activities of the organization.

2.42. Applying controls demands resources. Resources should be applied and focused where they are necessary on the basis of aspects such as safety significance and risks. They should be applied to a lesser degree for less important products or activities. Errors in more significant products or activities could potentially lead to the diversion of large amounts of resources, could shut down a facility or production line, and could cause a threat to individuals and the environment. Introducing additional controls that may reduce or eliminate such errors is therefore highly beneficial.

2.43. It is common sense to apply tighter controls to more important products and activities. A methodology for grading should be developed that ensures that all individuals in the organization apply this common sense approach in a uniform manner.

2.44. Examples of the controls that could be graded are:

- For the document and records management process:
  - Preparation of documents and records;
  - Need for and extent of validation;
  - Degree of review and the individuals involved;
  - Level of approval to which documents are subjected;
  - Need for distribution lists;
  - Types of document that can be supplemented by temporary documents;
  - Need to archive superseded documents;
  - Need to categorize, register, index, retrieve and store document records;
  - Retention time of records;
  - Responsibilities for the disposal of records;
  - Types of storage medium, in accordance with the specified length of time of storage.
- For the procurement process:
  - Expectations of suppliers for assessment, evaluation and qualification;

- Scope and level of detail of the procurement specification;
- Need for and scope of supplier quality plans;
- Extent of inspection, surveillance and audit activities for suppliers;
- Scope of documents to be submitted by the supplier and approved by the organization;
- Records to be provided or stored and preserved.

The selected grading process should be consistent with the applicable codes and standards, local rules and regulatory requirements.

See Ref. [1], paras 2.6–2.7.

DOCUMENTATION OF THE MANAGEMENT SYSTEM

General

2.45. The management system should be described by a set of documents that establish the overall controls and measures to be developed and applied by an organization to achieve its goals. These controls and measures should apply to every unit and individual within the organization.

2.46. The documentation of the management system should be appropriate to the organization and to the work that it performs and should be readily understandable to users. The documentation should also be flexible enough to accommodate changes in policy; in strategic aims; in safety, health, environmental, security, quality and economic considerations; and in regulatory requirements and other statutes. It should also accommodate the feedback of experience from implementation and from internal and external lessons learned.

2.47. The management system should adopt a vocabulary that is coherent, makes sense, and is clear, unambiguous and readily understandable. To this end, each document should be written in a manner appropriate to the level of expertise of its users and in a manner that reflects the correct ways of working (i.e. 'user friendly').

2.48. The management system should include measures to ensure that documentation is available in a language appropriate to the user. Management should state the languages to be used for the work instructions and procedures and should specify measures to ensure that individuals understand what they are asked to do.

2.49. Documents that have been translated should be reviewed to ensure that the text reflects the intent of the original document and is not just a literal translation. Vocabulary that is internal to an organization should be made available to contractors and subcontractors who are engaged by the organization to carry out work or to provide services.

2.50. The content of documents should be determined with the participation of the individuals who will use them to do their work and of other individuals whose work will be affected by the documents. These individuals should also be consulted during subsequent revisions of the documents. For detailed working documents, there should be a period of trial use, and validation should be carried out and recorded to determine the accuracy of the documents. Changes should then be made, as necessary, to ensure the effective communication of expectations.

2.51. An organization may operate facilities at several sites, or it may operate a facility or activity using nuclear or radiation technology that is part of a large organization (e.g. a radiotherapy department may be part of a hospital or a research reactor may be part of a research centre). In such cases, the management system for the whole organization should be established to integrate the objectives common to both the facility and the whole organization, and the mission and work of the facility. To complement such management systems, specific local processes may be necessary and should be used to address work that is unique to one or more of the organization's facilities, sites or organizational units.

Information structure

2.52. A three level structure of information promotes clarity and avoids repetition by establishing the amount of information and the level of detail appropriate to each type of document and by using cross-references between specific documents at the different levels. A typical three level structure consists of:

— Level 1: An overview of how the organization and its management system are designed to meet its policies and objectives;

— Level 2: A description of the processes to be implemented to achieve the policies and objectives and the specification of which organizational unit is to carry them out;
— Level 3: Detailed instructions and guidance that enable the processes to be carried out and specification of the individual or unit that is to perform the work.

Level 1

2.53. Level one should provide an overview of the policies and objectives of the organization and should describe the management system that addresses the requirements that apply to the organization's work. The information at this level of the management system should be the most senior manager's primary means of communicating to individuals the expectations of management, their strategies for success and the methods for achieving the organization's objectives.

2.54. Information on the following should be provided at level 1:

— Vision, mission and goals of the organization;
— Policy statements of the organization;
— Organizational structure;
— Levels of authority and responsibilities and accountabilities of senior management and organizational units;
— Structure of the management system documentation;
— An overview of the organization's processes;
— Responsibilities of owners of the processes (see para. 5.14);
— Arrangements for measuring and assessing the effectiveness of the management system.

2.55. The most senior manager in the organization should ensure that level 1 information is distributed to individuals for the purposes of implementation and that its contents are effectively understood and implemented.

Level 2

2.56. This level of information describes the processes of the organization and provides specific detail on which activities should be performed and which organizational unit should carry them out. This information:

— Should define the process map of the management system, including the interactions between processes;
— Should define the responsibilities and lines of communication that are internal and external to the organization in each area of activity, for example in processes and interface arrangements;
— Should define measurable objectives and specify which activities are to be carried out and controlled and who is responsible and accountable, and, where appropriate, should refer to supporting information;
— Should identify and plan activities to ensure that work is dealt with in a safe, systematic and expeditious manner.

2.57. Information at this level should provide administrative direction to managers in all positions. It should outline the actions that managers should take to implement the organization's management system. It should not be used to provide the details of how technical tasks are to be performed. Technical tasks should be detailed in information at level 3.

2.58. The contents of sections typically contained in documents at level 2 are:

— Purpose: Why does the document exist? The specific objectives of the document should be stated clearly and concisely.
— Scope: What management actions are addressed by the document and who is supposed to use it? The type of work and situations to which the document applies should be defined. The boundaries of application of the document should be stated.
— Responsibilities: Who is responsible for the document and for the activities described within the document? The individuals should be identified by title and their responsibilities should be defined.
— Definitions and abbreviations: What words or acronyms are used in the document that may not be commonly understood? Such terms and any jargon that may cause confusion should be defined and clearly explained.
— References: Would other documents be of use to those who have to use the document? If so, the specifications, standards or other documents that are cited in the text and which may possibly provide additional information to users should be listed. If documents are referenced in part, the page and paragraph numbers should be stated.
— Details: How is the work that is the subject matter of the document conducted? This information may take the form of a flow chart or process map describing the sequence of actions necessary to accomplish the work. The text should be simple and direct. Approved numbering and nomenclature for job titles and documents should be used. The details

section of a document should describe what is to be done, typically by providing the following information:

- Planning and scheduling considerations, to ensure that work is dealt with safely, systematically and expeditiously;
- Administrative and technical information;
- Work steps and actions to be carried out;
- Responsibilities and authorities;
- Interfaces;
- Lines of communication both within and outside the organization;
- Any cross-references between the document and other documents, including working documents at level 3.

— Records: Which records are necessary to permit the work and which ones need to be retained after the work has been completed? The records that are necessary to demonstrate that the tasks specified in the document have been accomplished should be identified.

— Appendices (where applicable), if additional information is necessary.

2.59. To avoid unnecessary detail, cross-reference should be made to level 3 information such as supporting guidance or detailed working documents.

Level 3

Detailed working documents

2.60. Level 3 information consists of a wide range of documents to prescribe the specific details for the performance of tasks by individuals or by small functional groups or teams. The type and format of documents at this level can vary considerably, depending on the application involved. The primary consideration should be to ensure that the documents are suitable for use by the appropriate individuals and that the contents are clear, concise and unambiguous, whatever the format.

Job descriptions

2.61. Job descriptions should be developed for the different competences or types of work to define the total scope of each individual's job. Job descriptions should be used to establish baselines for identifying training and competence needs. While job descriptions are usually mandatory only at supervisory levels and above, they are an excellent way for senior management to communicate responsibilities, authority and interfaces to all individuals.

2.62. A typical job description should contain the following information:

— Job title;
— Purpose of the job;
— Name of the organization;
— Organizational structure;
— Position in the organization;
— Lines of reporting;
— Duties and authorities;
— Key tasks and responsibilities;
— Accountability;
— Necessary minimum training;
— Necessary qualifications;
— Necessary knowledge, skills and abilities;
— Necessary education;
— Necessary experience;
— Necessary medical fitness.

See Ref. [1], paras 2.8–2.10.

3. MANAGEMENT RESPONSIBILITY

MANAGEMENT COMMITMENT

3.1. The efficiency of a management system begins at the level of senior management. Responsibility for the effectiveness of the management system should not be delegated.

3.2. The senior management is responsible and accountable for the planning and implementation of a management system that is appropriate to the organization. It is the role of senior management to establish and cultivate principles that integrate all requirements into daily work. Senior managers should provide the individuals performing the work with the necessary information, tools, support and encouragement to perform their assigned work properly.

3.3. Visible and active support, strong leadership and the commitment of senior management are fundamental to the success of the management system. Senior managers should communicate the beliefs that underlie the organization's policies through their own behaviour and management practices. The whole organization should share the management's perception and beliefs about the importance of the management system and the need to achieve the policies and objectives of the organization.

3.4. Managers should be held responsible for ensuring that individuals working under their supervision have been provided with the necessary training, resources and direction. These elements should be provided before any work begins.

3.5. In assigning responsibilities and accountabilities, managers should ensure that the individuals concerned have the capabilities and the appropriate resources to discharge these responsibilities effectively. They should also ensure that individuals are aware of and accept their responsibilities, and that they know how their responsibilities relate to those of others in the organization.

3.6. Managers should examine samples of work practices and related information on a regular basis to identify areas needing improvement. They should also encourage each individual under their supervision to look for more efficient and effective ways of accomplishing assigned tasks.

3.7. The act of empowering individuals and making them accountable for their work should encourage individuals to take 'ownership' of their work and to seek improvement in their performance.

See Ref. [1], paras 3.1–3.5 and 3.12.

SATISFACTION OF INTERESTED PARTIES

General

3.8.   Every organization has interested parties (also known as 'stakeholders'[4]), all of whom have needs and expectations. In order to ensure that the formally agreed expectations of interested parties are determined and met and to enhance their satisfaction, senior management should identify all of the organization's interested parties and should understand their 'products' or interests and their requirements, needs and expectations.

See Ref. [1], para. 3.6.

Statutory and regulatory compliance

3.9.   Senior management should ensure that the organization has identified all applicable statutory and regulatory requirements that apply to its products, processes and activities, and it should include in the management system the methods of complying with these requirements.

ORGANIZATIONAL POLICIES

3.10. As part of the management system, senior management should develop and disseminate throughout the organization a documented set of policies that

---

[4] Stakeholder: interested party; concerned party. 'Stakeholder' means an interested party — whether a person or a company, etc. — with an interest or concern in ensuring the success of an organization, business, system, etc. To have a stake in something figuratively means to have something to gain or lose by, or to have an interest in, the turn of events. The term stakeholder is used in a broad sense to mean a person or group having an interest in the performance of an organization. Those who can influence events may effectively become interested parties — whether their 'interest' is regarded as 'genuine' or not — in the sense that their views need to be considered. Interested parties have typically included the following: customers, owners, operators, employees, suppliers, partners, trade unions, the regulated industry or professionals; scientific bodies; governmental agencies or regulators (local, regional and national) whose responsibilities may cover nuclear energy; the media; the public (individuals, community groups and interest groups); and other States, especially neighbouring States that have entered into agreements providing for an exchange of information concerning possible transboundary impacts, or States involved in the export or import of certain technologies or materials.

establish the management's plans, objectives and priorities with regard to safety, health, environmental, security, quality and economic considerations. The policies should reflect the commitment of senior management to attaining their goals and objectives; their priorities; and the means by which continual improvement will be implemented and measured.

3.11. The policies:

— Should be appropriate to the purpose and the activities of the organization and should contain statements on safety, health, environmental, security, quality and economic considerations;
— Should include a commitment to comply with management system requirements and to seek continual improvement;
— Should be aligned with and should support the development of a strong safety culture;
— Should reflect relevant statutory requirements;
— Should provide an appropriate framework for action and for establishing and reviewing goals and objectives;
— Should be reviewed periodically for their continuing suitability and applicability;
— Should be effectively communicated, understood and followed within the organization;
— Should commit management to providing adequate financial, material and human resources.

3.12. Senior management should demonstrate its commitment to all the policies through its actions and should provide firm and unambiguous support for the implementation of these policies. Its actions should foster a corresponding commitment to high levels of performance by all individuals. All individuals should be expected to demonstrate their commitment to the policies. Adequate resources should be made available to implement all the policies. This includes provision of the necessary:

— Tools, equipment and material;
— Sufficiently competent individuals;
— Knowledge resources;
— Financial resources.

See Ref. [1], paras 3.7–3.8.

PLANNING

3.13. The establishment of goals, strategies, plans and objectives is a primary role of senior management. Senior management should provide the leading direction for the organization and should ensure a high level of safety. All levels within the organization should understand the direction set by senior management and should feel personally accountable for meeting the objectives. As a minimum, the priorities and objectives of the organization should be such as to ensure that regulatory requirements continue to be met.

3.14. To achieve a more highly developed safety culture and a well established business planning process, management should identify objectives that incorporate and effect continual improvement.

3.15. The objectives described in the plans should be widely communicated inside the organization. The entire organization should know and be fully committed to the objectives.

3.16. The organization's plans and objectives should represent an ambitious picture of the future of the organization, especially with regard to safety. For other areas of performance (availability of products, costs, industrial safety and communication with interested parties), the objectives should also reflect a strong willingness to undertake continual improvement. If a need for a strategic change is identified, senior management should integrate the necessary change into the corporate vision.

See Ref. [1], paras 3.8–3.11.

RESPONSIBILITY AND AUTHORITY FOR THE MANAGEMENT SYSTEM

3.17. Senior management should be fully committed to the management system and should regard it as a tool for use in managing the organization. The commitment of senior management should foster long term commitment and engagement on the part of the management and of all individuals of the organization, through a process of participation and consultation.

3.18. The individual who has responsibility for the management system should have the authority to raise issues relating to the management system at senior management meetings and to report on the status of corrective actions and improvements. If necessary, the individual should become involved in resolving any conflicts.

3.19. In some cases, the organization may appoint external organizations or individuals to develop all or part of the management system. However, the disadvantage of doing this is that there is no 'ownership' of the management system within the organization.

3.20. If the management system is developed by an external organization, care should be taken to ensure that the management system is relevant to the objectives of the organization and that it addresses the actual processes of the organization, and is not only a 'model' management system as used in other industries.

See Ref. [1], paras 3.12–3.14.

4. RESOURCE MANAGEMENT

PROVISION OF RESOURCES

4.1. Senior management should ensure that the resources[5] that are essential to the implementation of the strategy for the management system and the achievement of the organization's objectives are identified and made available.

4.2. To improve the performance of the organization, consideration should be given to the way resources are managed. This should include:

— Effective, efficient and timely provision of resources in the context of the opportunities and constraints;
— Management of tangible resources such as support facilities;
— Management of intangible resources such as intellectual capital;
— Inclusion of resources and mechanisms to encourage continual innovative improvement;
— Consideration of organizational structures, including needs for project and matrix management;

---

[5] 'Resources' includes individuals, infrastructure, the working environment, information and knowledge, and suppliers, as well as material and financial resources.

— Use of information management, knowledge management and the corresponding technology;
— Enhancement of competence by means of focused training, education and learning;
— Development of leadership skills and profiles for future managers of the organization;
— Use of natural resources and consideration of the impact of the use of resources on the environment;
— Planning for future resource needs, for example by analysing completed projects and by using such tools as predictive models for workloads.

Involvement of individuals

4.3. Senior management should improve both the effectiveness and the efficiency of the organization and its management system by involving and supporting all individuals. As an aid to achieving its objectives for performance improvement, the organization should encourage the involvement and development of its individuals by:

— Providing ongoing training and career succession planning;
— Defining individuals' responsibilities and authorities;
— Establishing individual and team objectives, and managing the performance of processes and the evaluation of results;
— Facilitating involvement in the setting of objectives and decision making;
— Recognizing and rewarding good performance;
— Facilitating the open, effective communication of information;
— Continually reviewing the needs of individuals;
— Creating conditions to encourage innovation;
— Ensuring effective teamwork;
— Communicating suggestions and opinions;
— Measuring individuals' satisfaction;
— Investigating the reasons why individuals join and leave the organization;
— Understanding and accommodating individual work styles and competences to gain the highest level of performance from each individual;
— Articulating instructions for achieving the expected quality of work;
— Obtaining feedback from individuals on a regular basis.

See Ref. [1], para. 4.1.

Managing information and knowledge

4.4. Data should be converted to information for the continual development of an organization's knowledge, and senior management should treat information as a fundamental resource that is essential for making factually based decisions and stimulating innovation. To manage information and knowledge, senior management:

- Should identify the organization's information needs;
- Should identify and access internal and external sources of information;
- Should convert information to knowledge of use to the organization;
- Should use the data, information and knowledge to set and meet the organization's strategies and objectives;
- Should ensure appropriate security and confidentiality;
- Should evaluate the benefits derived from the use of the information in order to improve the management of information and knowledge;
- Should ensure the preservation of organizational knowledge and capture tacit knowledge for appropriate conversion to explicit knowledge.

See Ref. [1], para. 4.2.

Financial resources

4.5. Resource management should include activities for determining the needs for, and sources of, financial resources. The control of financial resources should include activities for comparing actual usage against plans and for taking necessary action. Senior management should plan for, make available and control the financial resources necessary for: meeting safety standards; maintaining the safety culture; implementing and maintaining an effective and efficient management system; and achieving the organization's goals.

HUMAN RESOURCES

Competence, awareness and training

Competence

4.6. Senior management should ensure that the necessary individual competences are available for the effective and efficient operation of the organization. Senior management should evaluate both present and expected needs for competences against the competences already available in the organization.

4.7. In the identification of the future needs for competence of the organization, the following should be taken into account:

— Future demands in relation to strategic and operational plans and objectives;
— Anticipated needs for succession for the management and the workforce;
— Demographic and economic conditions;
— Planned changes to the organization's processes, tools and equipment;
— The present competence of individuals to perform defined activities;
— Known changes to statutory and regulatory requirements and standards that may affect the organization and its interested parties;
— International experience in relevant businesses and industries.

Awareness and training

4.8. In planning for education and training needs, account should be taken of changes caused by the nature of the organization's processes, the competence levels of individuals and the culture of the organization. The objective should be to provide individuals with knowledge and skills that, together with attitudes and experience, will enhance their competence. In education and training, emphasis should be placed on the importance of safety, of meeting requirements and of the needs and expectations of interested parties. Training should also cover awareness of the consequences for the organization and individuals of failing to meet the requirements.

4.9. The organization's training plan[6] should include:

— The objectives of the organization's training plan;
— An analysis of any areas not covered and a needs assessment for the training;
— A description of the training programmes and methods to be employed;
— The resources necessary and responsibilities;
— Measurement of the transfer of knowledge (questionnaire, diploma, qualification, accreditation, assessment);

---

[6] In some Member States an annual training plan is prepared that reflects the schedule of planned training courses.

— Identification of the necessary internal support;
— An evaluation of the effectiveness of the training, including individual performance, the performance results of the organization carrying out the training, and the training process.

4.10. To support the achievement of the organization's objectives and the development of individuals, the following should be considered in planning for education and training:

— Safety and regulatory requirements;
— The experience of individuals;
— Tacit knowledge and explicit knowledge;
— Leadership and management skills;
— Planning and improvement tools;
— Team building;
— Adult learning styles and techniques;
— Decision making techniques;
— Problem solving techniques;
— Communication skills;
— Cultural diversity;
— The organizational culture;
— The needs and expectations of interested parties;
— Creativity and innovation.

4.11. To facilitate the involvement of individuals, education and training should address:

— The vision for the future of the organization;
— The organization's policies and objectives;
— How the actions of individuals affect the integration of safety, health, environmental, security, quality and economic objectives;
— Organizational change and development;
— The initiation and implementation of improvement processes;
— Individual benefits from creativity and innovation;
— The organization's impact on society;
— Introductory programmes for new individuals;
— Professional development programmes;
— Periodic refresher programmes for individuals who have already been trained;
— Programmes and results from other relevant businesses and industries.

4.12. To achieve quality and to maintain safety, individuals should be capable of performing their assigned tasks. Training should emphasize the correct performance of work and should provide an understanding of:

— The principles of the management system and the relevant management processes and procedures;
— Accountabilities and responsibilities in the organization;
— Individual and organizational values and behavioural standards;
— The relationship between the management system and the development of a strong safety culture;
— Key characteristics and attributes of safety culture;
— The importance of involving interested parties and how to best involve them.

4.13. Training should address the knowledge of concepts, including safety culture. It should also address the enhancement of skills and the reinforcement of good practices by applying lessons learned from experience.

4.14. Training should ensure that individuals understand the processes and tools that they are using and understand what constitutes acceptable quality for the products they produce and the processes they control. Training should focus attention on 'doing things right the first time' and on the safety consequences of inadequate or incorrect work.

4.15. Individual training plans for senior management should address and stimulate professional development and should include professional, managerial, communication and interpersonal skills. A process for the selection, training, assessment and development of all managers should be established.

4.16. Individual training plans should not be limited to initial qualification but should provide for maintaining proficiency and for progressive improvement. This should ensure that individuals are always aware of the state of the art in technology and best practices in relation to the work they perform.

4.17. Specific requirements for qualification should be established for critical or unique jobs if highly technical, specialized skills are necessary or if the job has a potential impact on safety and quality, and if it is necessary to ensure that the individual is competent prior to performing the task. Such jobs should be identified by the organization and the qualification requirements that are established should be satisfied.

4.18. Consideration should be given to the qualification and training of individuals performing work that needs special competence. In some cases this should involve individuals taking a practical and a written examination to demonstrate proficiency before they begin work.

4.19. Periodic requalification should be required, to demonstrate that individuals continue to be capable of performing their assigned tasks.

4.20. Training should be designed to ensure that the training content addresses the specific needs of individuals and the overall organization. This means that training should be planned and carried out using a systematic approach, with established measurable objectives and with a means of evaluating its effectiveness. Qualified instructors who are competent in the area of expertise and in the necessary instructional techniques should be involved in the analysis, design, development, implementation and evaluation of training. Training is crucial to the continuing development of personnel. Senior management should therefore also allocate technically competent experts in the subject matter to develop the training curricula necessary for the achievement of the organization's objectives and to enhance the development of personnel. Line managers should participate personally in the analysis of training needs, in the review and approval of training programmes and plans (as well as in the delivery of some parts of the training), and in the evaluation of the effectiveness of the training.

4.21. The training plans of the organization should be subject to ongoing review to determine their effectiveness. The training plans should be revised whenever necessary improvements or enhancements are identified on the basis of the results of the reviews.

4.22. The organization's overall objectives and their direct relation to the policies and the management system should be explained in the initial and continuing training of all individuals who are managing, performing and assessing work.

4.23. The success of the management system in bringing about continual improvement depends on acceptance of and confidence in the management system within the organization. All individuals, including those at the various management levels, should be informed about the importance of their respective roles.

4.24. Training in the application of procedures and instructions should be given to those individuals who have to apply the procedures to do their work. Additional training should be given when procedures or instructions undergo major revision. This training is an opportunity for senior management to explain the importance of complying with the requirements of the management system. Feedback of information on the application of the requirements should be sought and revisions should be made to correct any difficulties identified.

4.25. As a means of improving future training plans, all the education and training provided should be evaluated in terms of management expectations and the impact of the education and training on safety and on the effectiveness and efficiency of the organization. To improve processes and the quality of the products and training programmes and to enhance the organization's learning culture, competence in core subjects should be built up by means of engagement with academia and industry.

See Ref. [1], paras 4.3–4.4.

INFRASTRUCTURE AND THE WORKING ENVIRONMENT

Infrastructure

4.26. Senior management should define the infrastructure necessary for safety and for achieving the organization's objectives. The infrastructure includes resources such as workspace, equipment, support services, information and communication technology, and transport facilities.

4.27. The process for defining the infrastructure necessary for achieving the organization's objectives effectively and efficiently should include the following:

— Consideration of the organization's plans and objectives; safety, health, environmental, security and quality policies; performance requirements; cost restrictions; and renewal needs;
— Evaluation of the infrastructure against the needs and expectations of interested parties;
— Consideration of environmental issues associated with the infrastructure, such as issues relating to conservation, pollution, waste and recycling.

4.28. Natural phenomena that cannot be controlled may affect the infrastructure. The plan for the infrastructure should address the identification and mitigation of the associated risks and should include strategies for protection to meet the needs and expectations of interested parties.

Working environment

4.29. Senior management should ensure that the working environment has a positive influence on the motivation, satisfaction and performance of individuals so as to enhance the performance of the organization. A suitable working environment depends on a combination of human and physical factors, and its creation should include the consideration of:

— Creative working methods and opportunities for greater involvement to realize the potential of individuals in the organization;
— Safety rules and guidance, including the use of protective equipment;
— Ergonomics;
— Location of the workplace;
— Diversity of skill in the workforce;
— Long term contracts;
— Possibilities to move from one site to another site of the same organization, from one unit to another unit, or from one department to another department;
— Career planning;
— The promotion system;
— Possibilities of access to knowledge or education programmes (i.e. external training);
— Social interaction;
— Facilities for individuals in the organization;
— Heat, humidity, light and airflow;
— Hygiene, housekeeping, noise, vibration and pollution.

See Ref. [1], para. 4.5.

5. PROCESS IMPLEMENTATION

DEVELOPING PROCESSES

5.1. There are always processes in place in an organization and the initial approach should be to identify, develop and manage them in the most appropriate way. No single 'process catalogue' — listing of processes that should be documented – can apply to every organization. Instead, each organization should determine which processes are to be documented, on the basis of applicable regulatory and statutory safety requirements, the nature of the organization's activities and its overall strategy. A common understanding should be developed of what a process is, how many processes are in place in the organization and how they interrelate.

5.2. A specific management process should, on an ongoing basis, provide a vehicle for establishing priorities, including priorities for new work, and excluding lower priority activities. This process should also integrate all review and oversight activities by management, to ensure that there is a structured approach to decision making that meets the needs of the business plan.

5.3. In determining to what extent a process should be documented, the organization should consider factors including the following:

— The effects of the process on safety, health, environmental, security, quality and economic elements;
— Statutory and regulatory requirements;
— The satisfaction of interested parties;
— Economic risk;
— Effectiveness and efficiency within the organization;
— The competence levels of individuals;
— The need to retain process knowledge;
— The complexity of processes.

5.4. Where it is necessary to document processes, appropriate methods should be used, such as graphical representations, written instructions, checklists, flow charts, methods using visual media and electronic methods.

5.5. Processes developed using a top-down approach should be hierarchically linked and should be more detailed the closer they are to the technical or task level. At the technical level the process may be better described in a procedure or instruction. The operational framework within an organization is typically made up of a number of processes, most of which have interfaces across the organization. Some organizations have found it beneficial to structure their processes as follows:

— Core processes, the output of which is critical to the success of the facility or activity;
— Supporting processes, which provide the infrastructure necessary for the core processes (e.g. procurement training);
— Management processes, which ensure the operation of the entire management system.

5.6. To develop the processes necessary for the effective implementation of the management system (see para. 5.13), the organization should consider the following:

— The satisfaction of interested parties;
— Planning;
— Grading of the application of management system requirements;
— Process management;
— The approach to decision making;
— Communication;
— Knowledge management;
— Human resources;
— Infrastructure and the working environment;
— Control of products;
— Purchasing;
— Management of organizational change and resolution of conflicts;
— Documentation of the management system;
— Control of records;
— Measurement, assessment and improvement;
— Interactions between the processes;
— Documentation of the processes.

5.7. Analysis of the processes should be the driving force for defining the amount of documentation necessary for the management system; the documentation should not determine the processes.

5.8. The following approach should be used to develop the processes of an organization:

— Identifying the processes necessary for the management system and for its application throughout the organization:
  • What are the processes needed for the management system?
  • Who are the interested parties for each process (internal and/or external interested parties)?
  • What are the statutory and mandatory requirements?
  • What are the expectations of the interested parties?
  • What are the safety, health, environmental, security, quality and economic requirements affecting each process?
  • Who is the owner of the process (see para. 5.14)?
  • Are any of the processes outsourced?
  • What are the inputs and outputs for each process?
— Determining the sequence of and the interactions between these processes:
  • What is the overall flow of the processes?
  • How can the flow be described?
  • What are the interfaces between the processes?
  • What documentation is necessary?
— Determining the criteria and methods necessary to ensure that the operation and control of these processes are effective:
  • What are the characteristics of the intended and unintended results of each process?
  • What are the criteria for monitoring, measurement and analysis?
  • How can these criteria be incorporated into the planning of the management system and the product realization processes?
  • What are the economic issues (cost, time, waste, etc.)?
  • What methods are appropriate for data gathering?
— Ensuring the availability of the resources and information necessary to support the operation and monitoring of these processes:
  • What are the resources necessary for each process?
  • What are the communication channels?
  • How can external and internal information about each process be provided?
  • How is feedback of information to be obtained?
  • What data need to be collected?
  • What records need to be kept?
— Measuring, monitoring and analysing the processes:
  • How can process performance (process capability, satisfaction of interested parties) be monitored?
  • What measurements are necessary?
  • How can the data gathered best be analysed (statistical techniques)?

- What information do the results of this analysis provide?
— Implementing the actions necessary to achieve the planned results and the continual improvement of these processes:
- How can each process be improved?
- What corrective and/or preventive actions are necessary?
- Have these corrective/preventive actions been implemented?
- Are they effective?

5.9. For each process, the following activities should be performed:

— Selecting a process team, made up of the team leader (normally the process owner (see para. 5.14)), the team itself (representatives from the departments that are affected) and a facilitator;
— Developing a description of the process;
— Identifying the major inputs and outputs and the interested parties;
— Determining the risks and hazards of the proposed process so as to identify its acceptability and the appropriate control measures necessary to ensure that risks and hazards are managed;
— Identifying additional expectations from the process so as to be able to control performance;
— Developing a flow chart for the process that incorporates the relevant expectations and identifies related documentation;
— Developing a process description that identifies:
- Governing documents, definitions and key requirements;
- Key process responsibilities and descriptions of activities;
- Supporting documentation and requirements for records;
- How the process is or has been validated where necessary;
- Procedures for the approval and distribution of the process documents.

See Ref. [1], paras 5.1–5.5.

PROCESS MANAGEMENT

General

5.10. To manage the processes of the organization, an organization should determine the following:

— The processes that implement the vision, goals, strategy, policies and objectives of the organization;

— The requirements for the input to the processes and the output from the processes;
— How the processes interact to enable the organization's objectives to be achieved.

5.11. Managing the processes of the organization efficiently is critical to its success. Process management should incorporate mapping, planning, designing, building, operating, maintaining and improving the processes. Incorporating these elements into process management should lay the groundwork for achieving an organization's objectives for its long term success through effective process solutions that integrate individuals, processes and technology.

5.12. Process management should use information from the processes to evaluate them with the aim of optimizing performance. Where appropriate, statistical process control should be established and should be used to reduce product and process variability and to improve quality.

Identifying the organizational processes

5.13. The processes of the organization should be identified on the basis of a review of the working practices involved in achieving the objectives, satisfying the requirements and delivering the products and services. The key elements of this review should be:

— Identifying what work is done, who carries it out and how it is performed;
— Identifying the resource needs (in terms of individuals, financing and equipment);
— Clarifying the constraints or requirements that affect how a process operates;
— Creating a logical hierarchy of the processes.

Process responsibilities

5.14. The designated individual who has the authority and responsibility for each process is often referred to as the process owner. When designating the process owner for each process, the following considerations should be taken into account. A process owner:

— Should have the authority to assess the impact of the process on safety and on the plans and objectives of the organization;
— Should have the authority to monitor the effectiveness of the process;

— Should have a good understanding of the process;
— Should be concerned when the process does not work well;
— Should have the authority to propose and initiate changes in the process;
— Should have the authority to monitor and control the major resources used in the process;
— Should have the authority to effect changes to instructions.

5.15. Process ownership should not be regarded as a status issue. Process owners should not be selected on the basis of their position in the management structure. Ownership of processes should extend down to lower levels of management of the organization.

5.16. Senior managers should not feel they have to 'own' all the processes personally. However, they should use information about the processes from the process owners to help them direct and manage the organization.

5.17. The process owner:

— Should track indicators so that performance of the process is clear and any necessary immediate adjustment of the process is possible;
— Should use additional indicators to show the improvement of the process and to show whether the specified targets have been reached;
— Should conduct reviews of processes to identify preventive actions and improvements.

See Ref. [1], paras 5.6–5.9.

Processes contracted to other organizations

5.18. Processes contracted to other organizations (i.e. outsourced), such as processes in relation to security, safety assessment or the calibration of equipment, should be controlled to ensure that the process is performed according to the relevant requirements of the organization's management system. The nature of this control should depend on the importance of the outsourced process and the risks involved in outsourcing it.

5.19. Control may include a contractual agreement with the provider of the outsourced process that includes, for example, the following topics:

— Specification and validation requirements for the process;
— Any statutory or regulatory requirements to be met;

— Management system requirements, including requirements on process monitoring and methods of measurement, performance targets for processes and the reporting of results;
— Audits to be performed by the organization.

5.20. Where an organization has the competence to carry out a process but chooses to outsource that process for commercial or other reasons, the process control criteria should be defined within the organization and transferred into requirements for the provider of the outsourced process.

5.21. Where the organization chooses to outsource a process because it does not have the competence or resources to carry out the process in-house, the organization should ensure that the controls proposed by the provider of the outsourced process are adequate.

5.22. Outsourced processes sometimes interact with other processes within the organization's management system. These interactions should also be managed as part of the management system. These other processes may be carried out by the organization itself or may themselves be outsourced processes. Management of the interactions should include:

— Discussion of and agreement on the outputs from the organization that will serve as inputs to the outsourced process and the outputs from the outsourced process that will serve as inputs to the organization;
— Arrangements for the transfer of information between the organization and the provider of the outsourced process;
— Arrangements for monitoring and measurement of the outsourced process to be carried out by the organization;
— Possible interactions and communication channels between the provider of the outsourced process and the organization's interested parties.

5.23. In some situations, it may not be possible to verify the output from the outsourced process by means of subsequent monitoring or measurement. In such cases, the organization should ensure that the control over the outsourced process includes process validation.

See Ref. [1], para. 5.10.

GENERIC MANAGEMENT SYSTEM PROCESSES

Document control

5.24. A document control process should be established to provide for the preparation, review, approval, issuing, distribution, revision and validation (where appropriate) of documents essential to the management, performance and assessment of work. An electronic document management system can be used to aid in document control and management (see Annex I).

5.25. The responsibilities of each participating organization or individual should be defined in the document control process.

5.26. The types of document to be controlled should include, but should not be limited to: documents that define the management system; safety requirements; work instructions; assessment reports; drawings; data files; specifications; computer codes; purchase orders and related documents; and supplier documents.

5.27. Senior management (or an appointed individual, e.g. the process owner) should identify the need for documents and should provide guidance to the organizations and individuals preparing them so that they are prepared in a consistent manner. The guidance should cover the status, scope and content of the documents, and the policies, standards and codes that apply to them. It should also explain the need for the feedback of experience. Documents, and changes to documents, should be distributed to and should be made available at the location where the activities described in the documents are conducted.

5.28. The process for document control should explain the following:

— How to prepare documents;
— How to review documents and confirm their acceptability;
— How documents at different levels are to be subject to approval;
— How to issue and distribute documents;
— How to control any temporary documents;
— How documents are to be modified or changed;
— How to suspend or cancel documents;
— How to control documents from sources outside the organization;
— How to archive documents.

Appendix II provides more detailed guidance on these process activities. See Ref. [1], paras 5.12–5.13.

Control of products

5.29. Senior management (or an appointed individual, e.g. the process owner) should specify the types of work for which formal inspection, testing, verification and validation activities are needed and should state the acceptance criteria and the responsibilities for carrying out the work. A process should be established to specify what types of inspection, testing, verification and validation are to be performed, and when, for the types of work being carried out.

5.30. Each process should be subject to review, inspection, testing, self-assessment, verification and validation by either the organizational unit responsible for the work, another department or an independent outside agency.

5.31. Administrative controls and indicators should be incorporated into each process. These controls and indicators should be used to preclude inadvertent bypassing of the necessary inspection, testing, verification and validation requirements and to prevent inadvertent use of the product or operation of the process.

5.32. Performance indicators should be developed for each process to measure whether or not performance is satisfactory. Performance indicators should have particular emphasis on safety and should be monitored so that changes can be recorded and trends can be determined.

5.33. Trends in performance indicators should be analysed to identify both beneficial and adverse factors. Beneficial factors should be used to encourage improvement. The causes of adverse factors should be determined and eliminated.

See Ref. [1], paras 5.14–5.20.

Measuring and testing equipment

5.34. The selection, identification and means of use, calibration requirements and calibration intervals of all measuring and testing equipment used for determining the quality of the product or its operational status should be specified. Responsibilities for controls for measuring and testing equipment should be defined. See Ref. [1], para. 5.15.

Control of records

Establishment of a records process

5.35. Records provide objective evidence of activities performed or results achieved. The processes or procedures of an organization generate an entire range of information, such as:

— Specifications;
— Assessment reports;
— Safety reports;
— Procurement documents;
— Non-conformance reports;
— Receipt and storage inspection reports;
— Test results;
— Calibration data of measuring and testing equipment.

5.36. The requirements for the management of records, such as statutory obligations, codes and standards, and customer expectations, should be identified and understood to ensure that they are addressed by the organization's management processes.

5.37. Responsibilities for maintaining and operating the records process and the facilities for the storage of records should be clearly defined and documented.

5.38. It should be ensured in the records process that records are specified, prepared, authenticated and maintained as required by the applicable codes, standards and specifications.

5.39. It should be ensured in the records process that records:

— Are categorized;
— Are registered upon receipt;
— Are readily retrievable;
— Are indexed and placed in their proper locations in the files of the record facility with the retention times clearly specified;
— Are stored in a controlled and safe environment;

— Are stored in appropriate storage media (see Annex I);
— Remain unchanged under normal circumstances.

If it becomes necessary to correct errors, any revisions of records should be adequately controlled and tracked.

5.40. Storage facilities for records should be maintained to prevent damage from causes such as fire, water, air, rodents, insects, earthquakes and the actions of visitors without admission rights.

5.41. Records that need special processing and control, such as computer codes and software and information stored on high density media or optical disks, should be maintained and controlled to ensure that they are readily retrievable and usable.

Categorization of records

5.42. Records should be categorized according to the needs of the organization and the necessary retention period of the records. Annex II provides guidance on retention periods for records.

Administration of records

5.43. All records should be readable, complete and identifiable with the product or process involved. They should be preserved to resist deterioration for the necessary retention times.

5.44. To prevent the deterioration of records during the retention period, it may be necessary to transfer records to a different medium. The transfer process should include control and verification that the information has been transferred accurately. If any copying is necessary to maintain image quality during the retention period, this should also be controlled and verified.

5.45. Records should be logged and listed in an index. The methods of logging and indexing to be used should be established before the receipt of records. The index should provide sufficient information to identify both the products and the relevant records.

Retrieval and accessibility

5.46. The senior management (or an appointed individual, e.g. the process owner) should ensure that records are indexed, filed, stored and maintained in facilities that allow their retrieval when necessary. The records should be accessible at all times during the specified retention periods. Access to locations where records are retained should be controlled. Consideration should be given to storing documents that may be necessary in emergency conditions at a location away from the facility.

Storage requirements

5.47. Senior management should establish expectations for the storage and the location for the maintenance, preservation and protection of records and associated test materials and specimens from the time of their receipt until the time of their disposal. Annex III provides supplementary guidance.

5.48. If the necessary storage conditions are unattainable, consideration should be given to the provision of a duplicate set of records to be stored in a separate facility. In such cases, the location and the construction features of both facilities should be such that the probability of the simultaneous destruction, loss or deterioration of both sites for records is sufficiently low.

Disposal

5.49. Senior management should identify who is responsible for the transfer or disposal of records. Records should be categorized and retained for the retention period specified by the organization. After the retention period specified for a record has elapsed, the record can be disposed of. This should be done by, or with the agreement of, the organization.

See Ref. [1], paras 5.21–5.22.

Purchasing

5.50. Individuals carrying out procurement activities:

— Should ensure that the information provided to suppliers is clear, concise and unambiguous, fully describes the products and services necessary, and includes technical and quality requirements;

— Should ensure, as a basis for selection, that the supplier is capable of supplying the products and services as specified;
— Should monitor suppliers to confirm that they continue to perform satisfactorily;
— Should ensure that the products and services conform to the requirements of procurement documents and perform as expected;
— Should specify the contact individual for all communications on procurement with the supplier;
— Should define, where necessary, the interfaces between the organization and suppliers and between different suppliers to ensure that key dates for supply are met.

Appendix III provides an example of a typical procurement process and includes additional guidance.

5.51. Senior management should establish relationships with suppliers so as to promote and facilitate communication, with the aim of improving the effectiveness and efficiency of processes on both sides. There are various opportunities for organizations to increase the quality of their products through working with their suppliers, such as:

— Optimizing the number of suppliers;
— Establishing two way communication at appropriate levels in both organizations to facilitate the rapid solution of problems and to avoid costly delays or disputes;
— Cooperating with suppliers in carrying out validation of the capabilities of their processes;
— Monitoring the abilities of suppliers to deliver conforming products with the aim of eliminating redundant verifications;
— Encouraging suppliers to implement programmes for continual improvement of performance and to participate in other joint initiatives for improvements;
— Involving suppliers in the organization's development activities to share knowledge and to improve the realization and delivery processes for conforming products effectively and efficiently;
— Involving suppliers in the identification of purchasing needs and the development of joint strategies;
— Evaluating, recognizing and rewarding the efforts and achievements of suppliers.

See Ref. [1], paras 5.23–5.25.

Communication

5.52. Communication in any organization should be recognized as very important when a specific process is being developed. The development of the process should involve individuals at all levels of the organization and, where appropriate, external interested parties, to ensure that the process addresses their needs.

5.53. Communication should be simple and to the point and should be designed to reach the widest audience. Communication should have the following purposes:

— To share relevant information;
— To involve all relevant organizations;
— To raise issues and resolve them.

5.54. Communication should be recognized as especially important when implementing changes. In such situations, the communication strategy:

— Should explain what is happening and why;
— Should address the effects on interested parties;
— Should describe what impact the activity or change will have on safety and on the organization's processes;
— Should include training for those who are involved in the communication of changes.

5.55. The communication process:

— Should be managed in such a way as to improve performance;
— Should make use of appropriate communication channels, such as letters, email and personal meetings;
— Should engage external interested parties to ensure that they understand the messages, especially when it is necessary to gain their acceptance;
— Should engage internal interested parties to improve their performance by making sure that they:
  • Know how their everyday actions relate to the organization's objectives and policies;
  • Know how they can influence business decisions;
  • Have the information they need to guide their actions;
  • Know they will share in success on the basis of their individual and team contributions;

— Should ensure that all external interested parties are kept up to date with relevant information;
— Should evaluate the effectiveness of the processes and the messages being communicated.

See Ref. [1], paras 5.26–5.27.

Managing organizational change

5.56. When organizational change is necessary, no reduction in the level of safety achieved should be acceptable, even for short periods of time, without appropriate justification and approval.

5.57. The drive to improve efficiency and reduce costs can result in organizational changes that can have significant safety implications. Examples of such changes are:

— Mergers of organizations, leading to a drive for harmonized standards and procedures;
— Changes in the arrangements for providing central support services;
— Reassignment of work activities, thereby increasing the likelihood that expertise in critical areas will be lost;
— Changes in the policies for recruitment, selection, induction and training of individuals;
— Reductions in the number of management levels and in the grades of individuals carrying out activities in the organization.

5.58. When major organizational changes are planned, they should be rigorously and independently scrutinized. Senior management should remain aware that it has the ultimate responsibility for safety and should ensure that safety considerations are given a priority commensurate with their significance during any process of major change.

5.59. Individuals should be made aware of how their responsibilities will change both during and after organizational changes. Consideration should be given to the possible need for temporary additional resources and for compensatory measures to manage the impacts during any transitional phase.

5.60. For changes for which it is judged that potentially significant effects on safety could arise, assessments should be carried out to ensure that the following factors are considered:

— The final organizational structure should be fully adequate in terms of safety. In particular, it should be ensured that adequate provision has been made to maintain a sufficient number of trained, competent individuals in all areas critical to safety. It should also be ensured that any new processes introduced are documented with clear and well understood roles, responsibilities and interfaces. All retraining needs should be identified by carrying out a training needs analysis of each of the new roles. The retraining of key individuals should be planned. These issues are especially important if individuals from outside the organization are to be used for work that was previously carried out internally, or if their roles are to be otherwise substantially extended.
— The transitional arrangements should be fully adequate in terms of safety. Sufficient personnel with knowledge and expertise that are critical to safety should be maintained until training programmes are complete. Organizational changes should be made in such a way as to maintain clarity about roles, responsibilities and interfaces. Any significant departures from preplanned transitional arrangements should be subject to further review.

5.61. Senior management should develop a specific process to manage and review organizational changes. The process should ensure that there is no degradation in the safety culture of the organization.

5.62. A safety assessment should be developed for any changes that have the potential to affect safety. For more significant changes, advice should be sought from internal and external experts.

5.63. Criteria for assessing the implications and controlling the impacts of organizational changes should include the following considerations:

— Changes should be classified against agreed criteria and in accordance with their safety significance.
— Changes may necessitate different levels of approval on the basis of their significance.
— The organization should explain how the planned changes will help in continuing to maintain acceptable levels of safety. This applies to both the final state of the organization and the arrangements during the transitional period from the old organizational arrangement to the new one.
— A review mechanism should be agreed on to ensure that the cumulative effects of small changes do not reduce safety.

— A method of monitoring progress in the planned introduction of significant changes should be developed and any shortfalls should be rapidly identified so that remedial action can be taken.

5.64. Communication with interested parties, including individuals, should be carried out honestly and openly, addressing the safety implications and other implications of the changes and explaining the steps being taken. The appropriate mechanisms for the feedback of information to monitor the effects of the changes that are implemented should be set up.

5.65. For each change, the project leader should apply a systematic and transparent project management process, the rigour of which should be commensurate with the significance of the change. In parallel, senior management should consider the overall integration of all changes, and should oversee very significant changes that are imposed and the cumulative effects of smaller changes that may interact with each other. Effects on ongoing activities during the implementation of changes should be studied well and given careful consideration.

5.66. For each project for change proposed, the risks to the objectives of the organization, including safety, health, environmental, security, quality and economic risks, should be identified and evaluated.

5.67. The interactions between different changes should be given careful consideration. Changes that on their own may have only a limited effect on safety may combine and interact to produce much more significant effects. Where possible, different initiatives for changes that are pursued at any one time and that may affect safety should be minimized. In addition, the total workload imposed on the organization to implement the changes in parallel with continued operational activities should be given careful consideration.

5.68. The individual who has the authority to approve changes to be implemented should be clearly designated. For each change, and on the basis of the significance of the change, controls should be applied to ensure that it is possible to identify the individual in the organization who is authorized to approve the change.

5.69. Preferably, one individual should approve each change, and the change should be endorsed by those individuals whose areas of responsibility are most affected. This should be given particular importance when the activities that will permit the change to be made are the responsibility of different parts of the organization. Evidence that the change satisfies safety requirements should be made available and an endorsement should be sought from the organization's safety unit. The approval should indicate whether an independent review has been carried out and how the recommendations from the review, if any, have been addressed.

5.70. If changes may affect any third party approvals, licences, accreditations or certifications, then these parties should be consulted.

5.71. Adequate monitoring should be carried out to provide early warning of any effects on performance, thereby ensuring that there is sufficient time to take remedial action before acceptable safety levels are challenged. Wherever possible, such remedial action should be planned in advance. Care should be taken in choosing the measures to be monitored and in assessing their effectiveness in providing early warning of any trend towards deterioration. Changes with the potential for major effects on safety levels should be subject to more extensive monitoring to detect adverse trends earlier. The likely effectiveness of changes should also be considered and the speed with which a situation that may be critical to safety can be rectified should be assessed.

See Ref. [1], paras 5.28–5.29.

6. MEASUREMENT, ASSESSMENT AND IMPROVEMENT

GENERAL

6.1. Measurement, assessment and improvement should be part of the establishment of a learning culture in the organization. Individuals at all levels should review their work critically on a routine basis to identify areas needing improvement and the means of achieving it.

6.2. To avoid any decline in safety performance, senior management should remain vigilant and objectively self-critical. As a key to this, objective assessment activities should be established. The nature and types of assessment activity should be adjusted to suit the size and product of the organization, should reduce the dangers of complacency and should act as a counter to any tendency towards denial. In addition to the early detection of any deterioration, an assessment of weaknesses in the management system could also be used to identify potential enhancements of performance and safety and to learn from both internal and external experience.

6.3.   The relationships between the activities of measurement, assessment and improvement are shown graphically in Fig. 1. Independent assessment includes internal audits, external audits, surveillance and reviews, checks, inspections and tests. Self-assessment should be conducted at all levels in the organization to assess performance and safety culture. At the organizational level it can be carried out by senior management. At the unit or work group level other managers and individuals can carry it out. The management system review is carried out for senior management to determine the suitability, adequacy, effectiveness and efficiency of the management system in achieving objectives and improving performance. Senior management should use the information yielded by all these activities to improve safety and performance; small improvements can always be implemented as they are found.

MONITORING AND MEASUREMENT

6.4.   The management system should ensure that standards of performance are established. These standards should be directly related to the product provided by the organization and based on the objectives set by senior management. Once the standards have been established, performance should

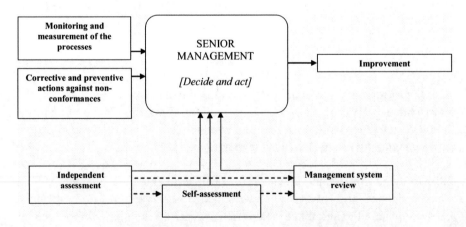

FIG. 1.   *Relationships between the activities of measurement, assessment and improvement. The broken lines show where one activity is used as an input to focus the activities of another assessment.*

be measured against them. These measurements should be monitored at regular intervals to ascertain whether or not improvements in the quality of the product or process are necessary. Performance indicators should be used and other appropriate methods of measurement should be developed.

6.5.   Senior management should bear in mind that problems often have their origins in the management system and that individuals have little or no control over eliminating these problems or improving performance. When the need to change management processes is identified, such changes should be formally proposed, agreed and introduced. It may be necessary to refer recommendations for change to senior management.

See Ref. [1], para. 6.1.

SELF-ASSESSMENT

Self-assessment by senior management

6.6.   The purpose of self-assessment by senior management should be to identify, correct and prevent management problems that hinder the achievement of the organization's objectives. Self-assessment by senior management should go beyond such matters as conformance to regulations, product standards or established procedures. Self-assessment by senior management should evaluate issues such as:

— Are the plans and goals of the organization still appropriate and valid?
— Are managers regularly monitoring the plans and goals and the achievement of these goals?
— Do individuals understand the plans, goals and objectives?
— Is the overall performance focused effectively on meeting objectives?
— What is expected of the organization?
— What is expected of individuals in the organization?
— Are the expectations being met?
— What opportunities are there for enhancing safety and improving quality?
— Are there any declining trends in effective and safe performance?
— How could the organization make better use of its human resources?

6.7.   Effective self-assessment by senior management should evaluate such conditions as: the state of the knowledge, motivation and morale of individuals;

safety culture; the amount of mutual trust and communication among individuals; the existence of an atmosphere of creativity and improvement; and the adequacy of human and material resources.

6.8. The results and decisions of the self-assessment by senior management should be recorded and related actions resulting from the recommendations should be taken promptly. Senior management should evaluate the effectiveness of these actions.

6.9. Reports from managers, summary results of self-assessment, and independent assessment and feedback are useful sources of information on the overall performance of the organization and should all be used to assist senior management in targeting improvement actions.

6.10. Senior management should retain overall responsibility for carrying out self-assessment for management. Direct participation by senior management is essential to the success of the process since it is in a position to have an overview of the organization as a whole.

6.11. The results of self-assessment by senior management should be used as input to the organization's continual improvement process. The improvement process should lead to enhanced levels of safety and performance.

Self-assessment by managers and individuals

6.12. Individuals and management (other than senior management) at all levels in the organization should periodically compare present performance with management expectations, worldwide industry standards of excellence and regulatory requirements to identify areas needing improvement.

6.13. Each unit within the organization should routinely conduct its own self-assessments of processes and performance.

6.14. Managers and individuals should seek continual improvement by identifying areas needing improvement and then taking corrective actions. The need for improvement should be recognized as a normal part of routine work.

6.15. Senior management should reinforce a questioning attitude in individuals and should encourage the discovery and reporting of all areas needing improvement. Managers should avoid punishing or intimidating individuals for unintentional errors and should not react defensively to suggestions for improvement.

6.16. Managers at every level should periodically assess the performance of their respective units to determine the quality of the leadership being provided, to enable the organization to meet requirements and expectations. This self-assessment should place emphasis on the use of human and material resources to achieve the organization's objectives.

6.17. Self-assessment should actively identify opportunities for improvement. To prevent significant performance problems, self-assessment should seek to identify weaknesses that could cause more serious errors or events.

6.18. Self-assessment should rely on certain organizational characteristics that provide support and enhance the effectiveness of self-assessment. These characteristics, which are common in highly effective organizations, are as follows:

— The organization has an environment or organizational culture that encourages individuals (and workers temporarily assigned to the facility) to participate actively in the self-assessment processes.
— Senior management encourages this environment by communicating to individuals the importance of self-assessment and the teamwork necessary for it to be successful in improving performance.
— Self-critical behaviour occurs in this environment.
— Senior management demonstrates ownership of the self-assessment process by directing, prioritizing and providing sufficient resources.
— Individuals recognize that minor problems may often lead to more significant events, and they identify undesirable work practices and behaviour and weaknesses in processes from these minor problems.

6.19. Various methods of self-assessment may be used. Examples of self-assessment techniques include the following:

— Workspace inspections or observations and routine communications with individuals, including informal interviews, to determine whether expectations are understood;
— Coaching or observation programmes in which weaknesses in performance are documented for further action;
— Review, analysis and trending of important performance and safety data;
— Reviews of new corrective action reports by senior management;

— Reviews of important data on process performance;
— Benchmarking to identify opportunities for improvements in performance;
— Periodic reviews of performance by senior management, such as management review meetings in which managers provide a summary of key performance weaknesses or strengths in areas for which they are responsible.

6.20. Self-assessments should be initiated in response to situations that indicate a need for a closer review of performance, such as:

— Adverse trends in performance data or problems tracked in the corrective action programme;
— Indications of process inefficiencies;
— Input from ongoing self-assessment activities or information provided by independent or external assessment groups;
— Significant changes for which an early progress check is necessary;
— Implementation of new programmes or revisions to existing programmes or processes;
— New or recent issues or problems.

6.21. Information used in preparing for and conducting self-assessments typically includes:

— Historical information, such as open actions (actions not yet completed) and completed actions from the corrective action programme, performance trends, lessons learned, critiques, operating experience and regulatory or other commitments;
— Current performance information, such as the results of observation programmes or measurements of performance;
— Information that may indicate that more significant problems could result if the error is not corrected, such as problems identified from the results of observation programmes;
— Reports from previous self-assessments or inspections.

See Ref. [1], para. 6.2.

INDEPENDENT ASSESSMENT

Types of independent assessment

6.22. Independent assessment may include reviewing, checking, inspecting, testing, internal audits, audits performed by external organizations and surveillance. Independent assessment should be focused on safety aspects and areas where problems have been found. Assessment plans should be reviewed and adjusted to reflect new or emergent management concerns and performance problems. Appropriate combinations of various types of assessment should be used to provide a balanced evaluation of performance. Results should be verified in accordance with written criteria and, where possible, evaluated objectively against specified standards and/or requirements. Appendix IV provides detailed guidance on how to perform independent assessments.

Internal audits

6.23. A schedule of internal audits should be established by the assessment unit and endorsed by the senior management of the organization.

6.24. Internal audits should not be conducted for the sole purpose of determining compliance with requirements. They should be conducted to evaluate the need for corrective actions, with the emphasis on seeking opportunities for improvement and enhancing performance.

6.25. Internal audits should also be prompted by significant changes in the management system or the associated processes, or by weaknesses in performance or in safety.

Surveillance

6.26. Surveillance of work performance is considered to be the best technique for assessing and reporting on a specific area or an ongoing activity. It is flexible and less formal than audits and can be performed in a relatively short period of time with limited preparation. However, advance notice should usually be given.

6.27. Surveillance should be carried out:

— To provide information and data in a specific performance area;

— To provide information and data on an individual activity;
— To provide immediate feedback of results;
— To follow up on observations in previous assessments.

6.28. Surveillance should be applied where:

— Flexibility in timing, methods, individuals and reporting is desirable.
— Additional information is necessary to develop conclusions regarding previous assessments.
— There is a need to respond to opportunities that arise at short notice.

6.29. For work or tasks that occur frequently, several surveillance visits should be carried out over a period of time to determine whether any adverse trends exist.

6.30. A single instance of surveillance should not be considered sufficient to assess fully the overall effectiveness of the management system. In addition to monitoring and observing work that is being done, reviews of documentation and interviews should also be carried out.

Responsibilities of the assessment unit

6.31. The assessment unit should be responsible for assessing, as a minimum, whether activities are being performed in accordance with specified requirements. The unit should, where possible, identify opportunities for improvement. In some organizations, an outside agency is assigned the task of conducting independent assessments on behalf of management. The following material is also relevant to such an outside agency, particularly if the agency uses individuals from the organization as part of the assessment team.

6.32. The assessment unit, in conjunction with senior management:

— Should define the assessment techniques;
— Should identify the resources necessary to achieve an effective assessment;
— Should obtain access by assessment teams to levels of senior management having the responsibility and authority to ensure corrective actions;
— Should make arrangements for the temporary assignment of specialists to assessment teams;
— Should define the scope, methods and schedules for initiating, conducting and reporting assessments;

— Should determine the distribution lists for assessment reports;
— Should make provisions for follow-up activities.

6.33. The assessment unit should operate as an arm of and an advisor to senior management. The assessments should focus on evaluating the performance of work and actions and should include the review and evaluation of management system documents.

6.34. Individuals carrying out assessments should view the organization being assessed as if they were interested parties of the organization, so as to produce meaningful feedback on the organization's performance.

6.35. Peers who are technically competent to review and evaluate the work and processes being assessed could also conduct assessments. These peers should not be individuals who have direct responsibilities in the areas being assessed.

6.36. Independent assessments do not necessarily always need to be carried out by the assessment unit. Independent assessments could also be carried out by other individuals who have been brought together for a specific assessment or by a joint team that includes members of the assessment unit and other individuals in the organization.

6.37. Individuals from other departments on short term secondments could supplement the assessment unit or could participate in assessments conducted by any external organizations for the duration of the independent assessment. Such individuals should have an understanding of the work area being assessed and should be conversant with the type of assessment being used.

6.38. Individuals within the organization that is conducting independent assessments should not have responsibility for the work performance being assessed. Individuals carrying out assessments should exercise objectivity in examining evidence and in forming conclusions.

6.39. A team leader should be appointed to manage all phases of each assessment. The team leader should be responsible for:

— Selecting the team members;
— Planning;
— Representing the team;
— Managing the team during the assessment;
— Interacting with the managers of work that is being assessed;

— Preparing and submitting the report;
— Checking the effectiveness of any corrective actions.

6.40. Team members should abide by the leadership, direction and guidance of the team leader.

6.41. Inexperienced members of the team should be adequately monitored and supervised until they are considered proficient in the type of assessment being carried out.

6.42. Assessors should be capable of looking for opportunities for improvement and providing recommendations to senior management. Problems and good practices should be reported in a way that will help senior management to understand what actions are necessary.

6.43. Individuals performing assessment activities should be trained in and familiar with:

— The principles of the management system;
— Methods of assessment;
— Observation and interview techniques;
— Evaluation and objective reporting;
— Communication and leadership skills.

6.44. Individuals could be assigned to the assessment unit teams on a rotational basis as part of career development.

See Ref. [1], paras 6.3–6.6.

MANAGEMENT SYSTEM REVIEW

6.45. Senior management should develop activities for management system review into a process that extends to the whole organization. Management system reviews should be platforms for the exchange of new ideas, with open discussion and evaluation of the inputs, and should be stimulated by the leadership of senior management.

6.46. The frequency of review should be determined by the needs of the organization. Inputs to the review process should result in outputs that provide data for use in planning for improvements in the performance of the organization.

Review inputs

6.47. Inputs that will allow the evaluation of the efficiency and effectiveness of the management system in the review should cover:

— The status and the organization's objectives and the results of improvement activities;
— The status of actions from past management system reviews;
— The performance of the organization in achieving its objectives, plans and goals;
— The results of assessments of all types;
— Feedback on the satisfaction of interested parties;
— Advances in technology, research and development;
— Results from benchmarking activities;
— The performance of suppliers;
— New opportunities for improvement;
— The control of process and product non-conformances;
— The status of activities in strategic partnerships;
— Other factors that may impact the organization, such as financial, social or environmental conditions;
— Relevant statutory and regulatory changes.

Review outputs

6.48. Senior management should use the outputs from the management system review as inputs to the improvement process. Senior management should use this review as a powerful tool in the identification of opportunities for improvement in the performance of the organization. The schedule of reviews should facilitate the timely provision of data for strategic planning for the organization. Selected outputs should be communicated to the individuals in the organization to demonstrate how the process of management system review conducted by senior management leads to new objectives that will benefit the organization.

6.49. Additional outputs to enhance efficiency should include:

— Performance objectives for safety, products and processes;

— Objectives of improvements in performance and safety for the organization;
— Appraisals of the suitability of the organization's structure and resources;
— Strategies and initiatives for satisfying interested parties;
— Loss prevention and mitigation plans for identified risks;
— Information for strategic planning for meeting the future needs of the organization.

See Ref. [1], paras 6.7–6.10.

NON-CONFORMANCES AND CORRECTIVE AND PREVENTIVE ACTIONS

6.50. In many organizations there are several processes to control non-conforming products or processes, for example product inspections. The process or processes should include provisions to prevent the inadvertent use or installation of products or processes that do not conform and to ensure that effective corrective action is taken.

6.51. Non-conformances should be regarded as opportunities for improvement and as such should be used as an input to the management system improvement process.

6.52. Senior management should foster a 'no blame' culture to encourage individuals to identify non-conforming products and processes. Senior management should also be involved in the resolution of difficult issues and should provide a process for resolving professional differences of opinion.

6.53. Senior management should ensure that those performing work are aware of and use the process for prompt notification and reporting of non-conformances.

6.54. All individuals should have the opportunity to identify, and should be encouraged to identify, non-conforming products and processes, and should have the opportunity to identify improvements and suggest them via the management system.

6.55. Senior management should allocate responsibilities so that non-conformances are monitored and followed up until it has been verified that the agreed corrective actions have been completed, including the provision of feedback to the individuals who identified the non-conformances.

6.56. Individuals responsible for classifying and analysing non-conformances should have an adequate understanding of the area in which they are working and should have access to pertinent background information concerning the non-conformances. Safety considerations should have priority over cost and schedule considerations in the classification and analysis of non-conformances.

6.57. Determination of the cause of a non-conformance may require a thorough investigation by technically qualified and experienced individuals. The investigation may need to include the participation of the individuals involved and those who identified the non-conformance, to gain a complete understanding of the problem. The managers responsible for the determination of the cause of the non-conformance should assign sufficient resources to the task.

6.58. Non-conforming products should be properly identified, segregated, controlled, recorded and reported The impact of the non-conformance should then be evaluated and reviewed and the non-conforming product should be (a) accepted; or (b) reworked or corrected within a specified time period; or (c) rejected and discarded or destroyed to prevent its inadvertent use.

Non-conformance control

Identification of non-conformances

6.59. Any individual who finds products or processes that do not meet specified requirements, or who observes abnormal behaviour, should be obliged to report the matter formally using the appropriate process.

6.60. Conditions and events to be handled by the non-conformance control process should include:

— Deviations from approved process parameters or procedures;
— Delivery or procurement of items or services that do not meet requirements;
— Failures of individuals to implement work instructions;
— Inadequate documentation containing incorrect or incomplete information;

— Inadequate training of individuals to perform the safety related tasks for which they have been given responsibility.

Reporting

6.61. A formal report of a non-conformance:

— Should identify who is reporting the non-conformance, when it was found and to whom it was initially reported;
— Should identify the non-conforming product or process and state its location and the method used to physically mark, label, segregate or otherwise control the product or process to prevent its inadvertent use;
— Should include a description of the non-conformance;
— Should describe the immediate action taken by the individual reporting the non-conformance, or by others, to minimize the adverse effects of the non-conformance.

6.62. Non-conformances should be reported in sufficient detail to allow proper review. Unique identification should be given to each report to allow effective tracking of the non-conforming product or process.

Initial actions

6.63. Promptly on being advised of a non-conformance, managers:

— Should ensure that a report has been drawn up, verify the details contained in it and acknowledge notification;
— Should initiate any necessary immediate action to minimize the effect of the non-conformance;
— Should confirm that the product or process has been identified (i.e. physically marked, labelled, segregated or otherwise controlled) as non-conforming;
— Should determine what restrictions on further use of the product, service or process should be put in place;
— Should arrange for a more detailed review of the non-conformance;
— Should review other related non-conformances.

6.64. Non-conformances should be reviewed as soon as practicable by appropriate individuals. The review should determine:

— The cause of the identified non-conformance;

— Any safety implications of the non-conformance;
— The actions to correct the non-conformance and to prevent the repetition of similar non-conformances; these corrective actions should be agreed upon and should be subject to approval.

6.65. Information about the non-conformance and its implications for safety should then be used to determine the impact on affected activities until the agreed and approved corrective action is verified as having been satisfactorily completed.

Corrective actions

6.66. The objective of a corrective action process should be to identify, document, evaluate and trend non-conformances and to take actions to correct non-conformances.

6.67. Senior management should support the corrective action process by encouraging the effective identification and correction of non-conformances.

6.68. The degree of evaluation used for non-conformances that have been reported and are subject to the corrective action process can vary widely. Because of the time and effort involved in the evaluation of non-conformances, a graded approach should be applied to ensure that the most intensive evaluation is reserved for the problems of highest significance.

6.69. The following criteria should typically be considered for a successful corrective action process:

— Senior management encourages individuals at all levels in the organization to identify and report all types of problem.
— Problems include issues needing more evaluation before corrective action, as well as those that are easily corrected and are documented for trending purposes only.
— Individuals have a thorough understanding of the problem reporting process.
— Individuals have easy access to methods of reporting problems.
— An individual discovering a problem takes immediate actions that include:
  • Reporting the problem to supervisors as necessary;
  • Ensuring that a document reporting the problem is initiated;

- If immediate actions are considered sufficient to correct a problem, closing the document that drew attention to the problem without further evaluation. In this instance, the problem report remains in the corrective action database for trending purposes. Minor problems may be symptoms or indicators of more significant issues, and trending can provide early indications of such issues.

6.70. New non-conformances that are reported in the corrective action process should be reviewed promptly for their effect on safety.

6.71. Senior management should ensure that corrective actions are subject to approval, prioritized and completed in a timely manner, on the basis of their significance. Managers should be held accountable for meeting due dates for corrective actions. Extensions or exceptions to due dates for completing corrective actions should be controlled and should be made only in response to new issues of higher priority.

6.72. Non-conformances and associated causes should be trended to identify repeat occurrences, generic (common) issues and weaknesses while the weaknesses are still at a level at which they do not pose a significant hazard.

6.73. Trend analysis data should be reviewed and summarized periodically. Senior management should review a report of the results.

6.74. Corrective actions designed to prevent any recurrence of significant non-conformances should be reviewed for effectiveness. These reviews help to determine whether corrective actions are also effective in preventing recurrence.

6.75. Senior management should monitor the status of corrective actions frequently and should consider:

— Whether the time delay is reasonable for corrective actions that are still open (not completed);
— Whether the necessary resources are available to complete open corrective actions;
— Whether managers are being held accountable for completing corrective actions.

Preventive actions

6.76. The purpose of preventive actions is to prevent the potential causes of non-conformances from occurring and to maintain safety and performance. A process for preventive actions:

— Should take proactive steps to ensure that a potential non-conformance does not occur;
— Should use process analysis to determine how to build in process changes.

6.77. Preventive actions should include, but should not be limited to, the following:

— Changing processes or the organizational structure;
— Retraining and requalifying individuals;
— Improving safety culture;
— Changing or modifying documents;
— Improving the management system;
— Enforcing requirements for documents;
— Issuing new documents.

See Ref. [1], paras 6.11–6.16.

IMPROVEMENT

6.78. A strategic objective of an organization should be the continual improvement of processes in order to enhance the organization's performance. Opportunities for improvement should be identified from the following:

— The performance of the management system in meeting goals and plans;
— Feedback from use;
— Experience from outside organizations;
— Technological developments in the field;
— Improvements identified by individuals;
— Improvements identified from reviews of the characteristics of products and processes, such as their reliability;
— The results of assessments, corrective and preventive actions, and management system reviews.

6.79. Continual improvement can be achieved:

— At the working level, by introducing small incremental improvement activities conducted within existing processes by those directly involved from day to day;
— At the process level, where each individual process owner is in charge of improvement;
— At the organizational level, through significant improvement projects throughout the organization (at the level of the management system) which lead either to the revision and improvement of existing processes or to the implementation of new processes. These projects are usually carried out by cross-functional teams and are distinct from routine operations.

6.80. Significant improvement projects often involve a major redesign of existing processes and should include:

— Definition of the objectives and an outline of the improvement project;
— Analysis of the existing process (the 'as is' process) and investigation of opportunities for change;
— Specification and planning of the improvement to the process;
— Implementation of the improvement;
— Verification and validation of the process improvement;
— Evaluation of the improvement achieved, including lessons learned.

6.81. Significant improvements should be made in an effective and efficient way using project management methods.

6.82. Individuals in the organization should be considered the best source of ideas for improvements. Even small improvements should be controlled in order to understand their cumulative effects.

6.83. Those individuals in the organization who are involved in implementing an improvement should be provided with the authority, technical support and resources necessary for the changes associated with the improvement.

6.84. Continual improvement should be made by means of a process that contains the following elements:

— Reason for improvement: A process problem should be identified and an area for improvement selected, noting the reason for working on it.
— Current situation: The effectiveness and efficiency of the existing process should be evaluated. Data should be collected and analysed to determine

what types of problem occur most often. A specific problem should be selected and an objective for the improvement process should be set.

— Analysis: The causes of the problem should be identified and verified.
— Identification of possible solutions: Alternative solutions should be explored. The process with the best solution should be selected and implemented. The best solution is one that will eliminate the causes of the problem and prevent the problem from recurring.
— Evaluation of effects: It should then be confirmed that the problem and its causes have been eliminated or their effects reduced, that the solution has been effective and that the objective for the improvement process has been met.
— Implementation and standardization of the new solution: The old process should be replaced with the improved process, thereby preventing the problem and its causes from recurring.
— Evaluation of the effectiveness and efficiency of the new process: The effectiveness and efficiency of the improvement project should be evaluated and consideration should be given to using its solution elsewhere in the organization.

See Ref. [1], paras 6.17–6.18.

Appendix I

TRANSITION TO AN INTEGRATED MANAGEMENT SYSTEM

I.1.   Having an integrated management system that is focused on satisfying all requirements is essential to an organization if it is to compete and survive in the global environment, while also maintaining and enhancing safety. An integrated management system can provide a number of benefits, together with enhanced safety and business performance. An integrated management system can lead to considerable savings in developing and maintaining organizational activities such as individual training, and reviews and approvals by interested parties, particularly when the costs and efforts of maintaining a number of separate activities and their review and upkeep are considered. Senior management should evaluate its needs and existing management systems, including its quality assurance systems, against the guidance provided in this Safety Guide and should take steps to develop and implement an effective transition plan to move to an integrated management system.

I.2.   The following key steps will assist organizations with different types of management system in any stage of development and will aid in achieving an integrated management system:

— Organizations with existing management systems that are not integrated:

Those organizations that have separate management systems for the safety, health, environmental, security, quality and economic areas should examine the commonalities between various programmes such as documentation control, records and assessments. They should then address the generic approaches and processes to manage their activities on the basis of the requirements and guidance provided in their national requirements and in IAEA publications. A detailed transition plan and a team of experts from the different areas should be established to develop the overall framework and processes for the integrated system.

Organizations that at present have a quality assurance programme that meets the requirements of Ref. [2] should already have defined most of their activities in its processes. Many of the concepts in this Safety Guide may already have been introduced. The objective of the new guidance on management systems is to bring together all the requirements in an integrated way rather than having separate systems for safety management, health management, environmental management, security management, quality management and business management.

— Organizations with a management system that does not use processes to manage activities:

If the organization has a quality assurance system that does not use a process approach, it should consider the benefits of an integrated approach, should identify all requirements and define its processes and their sequences and interactions, and should develop an integrated management system following the guidance in this Safety Guide.

— Organizations with no management system:

Those organizations that are just starting to establish their management system should seriously consider the advantages and benefits of taking a holistic view of their business and should consider investing the efforts and resources necessary to move in the direction of an integrated management system. This Safety Guide and the related Safety Guides provide the relevant guidance for establishing, implementing, assessing and continually improving a management system.

Appendix II

ACTIVITIES IN THE DOCUMENT CONTROL PROCESS

PREPARATION OF DOCUMENTS

II.1. Individuals preparing, revising, reviewing or approving documents should have access to the appropriate information.

II.2. When documents are in their preparatory phase, they should be marked and controlled so that their draft status clearly distinguishes them from documents that have already been issued.

II.3. An appropriate document identification system should be established. Each document should be uniquely identified.

II.4. Standard forms should be identified and controlled, whether the document is to be taken alone or as part of another document.

II.5. The need for traceability of a document to related hardware or software should be determined.

II.6. During preparation, the activities described by the documents should be assessed using the grading process, so that the appropriate controls are chosen and included.

REVIEW OF DOCUMENTS AND CONFIRMATION OF ACCEPTABILITY

II.7. Documents should be reviewed before issue. The review should comprise a critical examination of the need for and the adequacy of the document, with respect to prescribed requirements, guidelines and relevant modifications. Account should be taken of the safety significance of the document.

II.8. The document review process should identify the organizations and individuals involved in the review process and the levels of independence necessary for reviewing the documents.

II.9. The reviewing organization or individuals should have access to the relevant information upon which to base an effective review, to ensure that safety considerations are adequately addressed.

II.10. The reviewing organization or individuals should be competent in the specific topic that they are being asked to review.

II.11. A record of the review should be prepared showing the date of the review and the name of the reviewer and including the reviewer's comments and their resolution.

II.12. One aspect of review can involve validating the implementation of the document through simulation, a mock-up of the proposed product, a walk-through of the proposed procedure or a similar activity. This validating process is usually applied to significant working level instructions and procedures.

APPROVAL OF DOCUMENTS

II.13. Documents should be approved according to a prescribed method before they are issued for use. The responsibilities for approval should be clearly defined by senior management. Acceptance by, or the approval of, the regulatory body should be obtained where this is required.

ISSUE AND DISTRIBUTION OF DOCUMENTS

II.14. An issue and distribution process for documents that uses up to date distribution lists should be established. Those individuals who participate in an activity should be aware of, should have access to and should use the documents that have been approved for performing the activity. The process should ensure that changes to documents are relayed to all affected individuals and organizations. Copies subject to revision updating (controlled copies) should be identifiable.

II.15. The documents issued should be marked so that the nature of their use is made clear, especially if their use is restricted to a certain purpose. Examples of marking include 'approved for use' or 'for test purposes only'.

II.16. Controlled documents should be distributed to and used by the individual performing the activity. Obsolete documents should be removed from circulation to prevent their inadvertent use.

II.17. To preclude the use of inapplicable documents and to ensure the control of current documents, the distributor should employ a written acknowledgement system. The recipient should indicate receipt of the document and should return or dispose of the previous issue.

II.18. Master copies of documents should be retained until they are superseded or withdrawn. The need for archiving master copies of documents should be considered.

II.19. Uncontrolled copies of documents may be supplied, provided that they clearly indicate that they will not be automatically updated and are valid on the day of issue only. In these circumstances it is the responsibility of those using the information contained in the documents to check before use that the documents are still current.

TEMPORARY DOCUMENTS

II.20. Under certain circumstances, a temporary document may be necessary to cover an activity for a limited period. This will be necessary when an immediate amendment to an existing document cannot be justified. Temporary documents should be subject to the same controls as permanent documents.

II.21. Temporary documents should have a defined period of validity. When this period expires, the document should be withdrawn or its contents should be integrated into an appropriate document, or the temporary period of validity should be renewed.

CONTROL OF MODIFICATIONS TO DOCUMENTS

II.22. Modifications to documents should be subject to the same level of review and approval as the original documents. A modification to one document may affect other documents and affected documents should be revised accordingly. Where practicable, modifications to documents should be highlighted in the documents by the use of sidelining (marking clearly in the margin any text that should be modified or deleted) or other suitable means.

SUSPENSION OR CANCELLATION OF A DOCUMENT

II.23.   When a document is to be suspended or cancelled, it should be removed from use. Suspension and cancellation notices should identify uniquely the reference and issue numbers of the document to which they apply and should give the document's effective date of application and the reasons for its suspension or cancellation. In the case of suspension notices, the duration of suspension should also be provided.

II.24.   Suspension and cancellation notices should be subject to approval at the same level as the original document, and should be distributed to all controlled copy holders, to preclude the use of suspended or cancelled documents.

DOCUMENTS EXTERNAL TO THE ORGANIZATION

II.25.   A registration system should be established and maintained to record and control the receipt and amendment of documents that are generated and controlled externally. The registration system should, as a minimum, register the receipt date of the document, its reference number, title, date of issue and/ or issue status, and the individual or individuals to whom it was passed for distribution or, if appropriate, review.

II.26.   Documents from external sources should be reviewed to ensure their suitability before acceptance and use.

DOCUMENT ARCHIVES

II.27.   When documents such as procedures and drawings that were subjected to the formal issue process are withdrawn from use, the master copies should be archived as records, following the guidance in this Safety Guide.

Appendix III

ACTIVITIES IN THE PROCUREMENT PROCESS

III.1. The following flow chart depicts a typical procurement process. The text that follows provides guidance on some of the steps in the process.

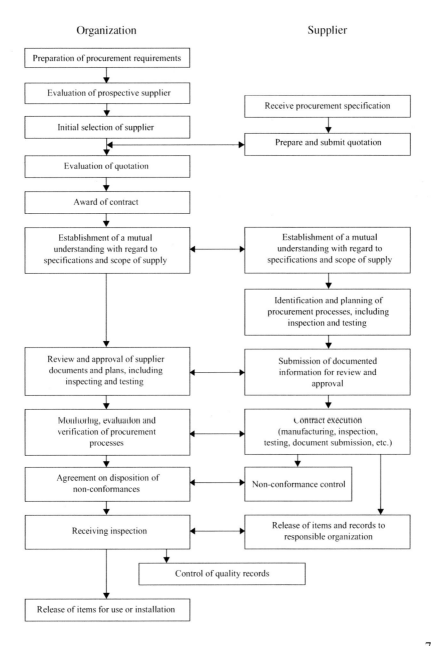

PREPARATION OF PROCUREMENT DOCUMENTS

III.2.   Procurement documents should generally cover the points below. The associated responsibilities should also be identified.

— Scope of the work: A full description of the work to be undertaken by a supplier, including interfaces with other work, so that the intent is clearly understood and prospective suppliers can deliver the products or services as specified.
— Technical requirements: The technical requirements for products or services should be specified with reference to technical documents such as: codes, specifications, regulatory requirements, standards, design basis documents and drawings, process requirements and requirements for the approval or qualification of the products, procedures or processes. Each specified requirement should be achievable and its achievement should be verifiable. It should be ensured that, when the requirement is met, the product or service is rendered fit for its intended purpose.
— Training requirements: Needs and requirements should be identified and the necessary resources should be provided, for example the need for nuclear facility induction training to enable individuals to work on the site and move around the site unescorted.
— Inspection and testing requirements: When inspection or testing of products is necessary, this should be specified. Acceptance criteria for the requirements should also be specified.
— Access to the supplier's facilities: Conditions of access to the supplier's premises to carry out activities such as inspections, audits and surveillance should be defined. These activities may be performed by the organization or by other authorized parties acting on its behalf.
— Identification of the standards applicable to the management system: The management system standards to be complied with must be clearly defined. If the organization wishes to quote national or international management system standards, an evaluation should be performed to determine whether additional requirements other than those established in Ref. [1] are necessary. When international standards other than those of the IAEA are quoted, care should be taken to ensure that the additional requirements are adequately addressed by the management system.
— Document requirements: The documents that the supplier is required to submit to the organization for approval or comment should be clearly identified in the procurement documents.

— Record requirements: Requirements on records and on material samples should be made clear to the supplier prior to concluding the contract. This could best be achieved by providing or requiring a record schedule that details all record requirements to be submitted by the supplier. Instructions for the retention by or transfer of records from the supplier and/or subsidiary suppliers should be specified. These should include the records that are requested by the organization to ensure that the products or services have met or will meet the requirements. Retention periods and responsibilities for the maintenance of records by the supplier should also be specified.
— Timing of submissions: Clear instructions should be given to suppliers regarding the times when the necessary documents and records should be submitted.
— Non-conformance reporting: The supplier should have a clear understanding of the non-conformance control process. It should be made clear which party may sanction which type of non-conformance.
— Subsidiary supplier controls: Unless otherwise specified by the organization, the supplier should be responsible for the control of subsidiary suppliers. Therefore, if a subcontract is placed, the supplier should be requested to secure from the subsidiary supplier all rights of access as a contractual requirement. The supplier should be required to impose management system requirements on the subsidiary supplier consistent with the importance of the subcontracted product. This would include, for example, the responsibility to monitor and evaluate the performance of the subsidiary supplier.

REVIEW AND APPROVAL OF PROCUREMENT DOCUMENTS AND CHANGES TO THEM

III.3. The responsibilities for review and approval of procurement documents within the organization should be defined.

III.4. Procurement documents should be reviewed and approved before issue to ensure that all requirements have been included and are in accordance with the specified procedures of the purchasing organization and regulatory requirements. Changes to procurement documents should be undertaken in a controlled manner. Changes to procurement documents should be subject to the same level of control as the original documents.

SELECTION OF SUPPLIERS

III.5. The selection of suppliers should be based on an evaluation of their capability to provide products or services in accordance with the requirements of the procurement documents.

III.6. Senior management should use specified criteria to evaluate and select suppliers. Responsibilities for determining suppliers' capabilities should be identified.

III.7. Methods to be used in evaluating prospective suppliers should include, for example:

— Evaluating the prospective supplier's history of providing a product that performs satisfactorily in actual use, such as:
  • The experience of users of identical or similar products and services provided by the prospective supplier;
  • Review of records that have been accumulated in connection with previous procurement actions and operating experience with the product;
  • Review of historical data relevant to the products or services being procured that are representative of the prospective supplier's current capability. If there has been no recent experience, the prospective supplier should be requested to submit information on an equivalent product or service for evidence of current capabilities.
— Evaluating the prospective supplier's management system:
  • Assessing the capability of the prospective supplier by evaluating the supplier's facilities and evaluating individuals and the implementation by the supplier of the management system;
  • Objectively evaluating the prospective supplier's current records supported by documented qualitative or quantitative information such as statistical records or other records attesting to the prospective supplier's performance.
— Evaluating the capability of the prospective supplier by investigating samples of current production.

III.8. After the initial selection of prospective suppliers, procurement documents should be forwarded to them indicating the date for submitting tenders (quotations), and the procedures for resolving questions and seeking clarification (for example by meetings, presentations and/or assessments).

EVALUATION OF QUOTATIONS AND AWARD OF CONTRACT

III.9. Submitted quotations (bids or tenders) from prospective suppliers should be evaluated in a logical manner to ensure that they conform to the requirements of the procurement documents.

III.10. The evaluation of quotations carried out by the organization should be a team effort involving the organizational units responsible for the technical and procurement activities. The size of the team undertaking the evaluation should be determined by the size and complexity of the product to be purchased.

III.11. The award of the contract should be based on the capability of the supplier to meet the requirements of the procurement documents. All actions arising from the evaluation of quotations should be fully documented and resolved, including the grounds for awarding the contract.

EVALUATION OF SUPPLIER PERFORMANCE

III.12. Senior management should monitor, evaluate and verify how the supplier performs against the procurement requirements. The organization, its designated representative or other parties authorized by the organization may do this. These activities should provide for:

— Establishing a mutual understanding, between the organization and the supplier, of the specifications and intent of the procurement documents;
— Requiring the supplier to identify planning techniques and processes to be used in fulfilling procurement requirements;
— Reviewing documents that are generated or processed in activities that fulfil procurement requirements;
— Coordinating feedback of experience between the organization and suppliers;
— Identifying and processing changes to information;
— Establishing a method for the exchange of documents between the organization and the supplier.

III.13. Depending on the complexity and scope of the products, senior management should initiate activities prior to and following the award of a contract. These activities may take the form of meetings, or other means of communication, to establish a mutual understanding between the organization and the supplier regarding:

— Procurement document requirements;
— The intent of the organization in monitoring and evaluating the supplier's performance;
— Financial arrangements, schedules, safety impacts and regulatory impacts;
— Training of individuals, if necessary, by the organization or suppliers to ensure the proper usage of supplied products;
— The planning and processes to be employed by the supplier to meet procurement requirements.

III.14. Senior management should identify notification points for evaluation as early as practicable in the procurement process. These should be documented and agreed between the organization and the supplier.

III.15. The necessity and extent of communication prior to and following the award of a contract depend on the uniqueness of the product, its complexity, the frequency of procurement from the supplier in the past and the supplier's past performance in supplying similar products.

NON-CONFORMANCES IN PROCUREMENT

III.16. Non-conformances identified during the procurement process should be handled in accordance with the guidance in Section 6 of this Safety Guide. The identity of the individual responsible for sanctioning each level of non-conformance should be made clear to the supplier. Non-conformances identified by the organization should be reported to the supplier immediately for processing through the supplier's non-conformance control process.

ACCEPTANCE OF PRODUCTS

III.17. Products and associated documents should be inspected immediately upon receipt in order to verify that they meet specified requirements.

RELEASE OF PRODUCTS

III.18. Products should not be released for use or installation until all inspections have been satisfactorily concluded and all specified documents have been received and checked.

SUPPLIER ASSESSMENTS

III.19. The assessment unit of the organization should develop a schedule of supplier assessments. The frequency of assessments should be determined by factors such as the importance of products and the performance of the supplier.

III.20. Supplier assessments should be carried out when:

— It is necessary to determine the capability of a supplier and the adequacy of its management system before awarding a contract or placing a purchase order;
— After the award of a contract, it is necessary to determine whether the supplier is appropriately performing the functions as defined in the management system, applicable codes and standards, and other contract documents;
— Significant changes are made in the supplier's management system, such as significant reorganization or significant revisions of procedures;
— It is suspected that the quality of a product or service is in jeopardy owing to a deficiency either in the regulatory requirements or in the management system.

Appendix IV

PERFORMANCE OF INDEPENDENT ASSESSMENTS

PLANNING AND SCHEDULING

IV.1.   A schedule of independent assessments should be established, with account taken of those activities of the organization that affect safety. The schedule should include assessments of all major processes over a defined period.

IV.2.   The schedule should be flexible and should allow for changes on the basis of:

— The frequency and results of previous assessments;
— Any significant changes to requirements resulting from new regulations;
— Changes in the organization or boundaries of responsibility for organizational units;
— Any significant findings from external or third party assessments;
— Feedback from non-conformances and from processes for preventive and corrective actions;
— External events that may potentially affect assessment results;
— The possibility of placing contracts with organizations that have previously not been used by the organization.

The schedule should also be updated after agreeing any new contracts.

IV.3.   The assessment schedule should allow adequate time for preparation, the conduct of the assessment, the evaluation of identified concerns and the reporting of results.

IV.4.   For each assessment, a plan should be established to select areas, processes or activities and requirements to be assessed.

CONDUCT

IV.5.   Assessments should concentrate on the observation of how activities are actually being performed. Assessors should also interview individuals and examine completed work activities.

IV.6. Information on the qualification and training of individuals should be examined. The assessor may need to ask individuals specific questions to determine, for example, their experience or knowledge of procedures. The assessor may also check the conformance with, and the adequacy of, the procedures.

IV.7. The planning and conduct of an assessment should follow an organized plan. Nonetheless, circumstances may arise that require flexibility. The assessor should pursue any questionable area after consultation with the team leader. This consultation should ensure that the investigation is necessary.

IV.8. When suspected non-conformances are encountered, the assessor should check to determine whether senior management has already identified them and whether actions are being implemented to correct them. Conditions found during the assessment that need prompt attention should immediately be brought to the attention of senior management.

IV.9. Assessors should be alert for conditions that reflect good practices from which the organization might transfer lessons learned. This could include areas where objectives are consistently achieved or exceeded.

IV.10. When suspected non-conformances are detected, they should be discussed with the responsible individuals to avoid misunderstandings.

EVALUATION

IV.11. The assessor should analyse and consider the cause of non-conformances in order to evaluate and identify the proposed corrective actions. The findings should describe the non-conformance and identify any areas where improvement could be made. Similarly, when good practices are recognized, they too should be analysed to determine those factors that contributed to their success.

REPORTING

IV.12. Assessment results should be reported clearly and promptly. The assessment report should communicate the findings in a way that makes their significance readily apparent. For reports to be effective, they should be submitted in their final form as quickly as possible, emphasizing particular products if necessary. The report should include:

- A list of positive and negative findings;
- A list of individuals contacted, procedures reviewed and areas visited;
- A description of assessment methods adopted by the assessors;
- References to the assessment plan that indicate which areas were assessed and why they are important;
- A summary statement on whether the activities assessed were satisfactory or not;
- Opportunities for improvement and good practices.

FOLLOW-UP ACTIVITIES

IV.13. Senior management should evaluate and investigate the assessment findings and should ensure that managers determine, schedule and approve corrective actions. For corrective actions, the implementation time frame should be such that the impact on safety is taken into account.

IV.14. The organization that has been assessed should report to the assessment unit and senior management the progress achieved in completing corrective actions.

IV.15. The implementation of the corrective actions should be subject to verification by the assessment unit.

REFERENCES

[1] INTERNATIONAL ATOMIC ENERGY AGENCY, The Management System for Facilities and Activities, IAEA Safety Standards Series No. GS-R-3, IAEA, Vienna (2006).

[2] INTERNATIONAL ATOMIC ENERGY AGENCY, Quality Assurance for Safety in Nuclear Power Plants and other Nuclear Installations, Code and Safety Guides Q1–Q14, Safety Series No. 50-C/SG-Q, IAEA, Vienna (1996).

[3] INTERNATIONAL ATOMIC ENERGY AGENCY, Legal and Governmental Infrastructure for Nuclear, Radiation, Radioactive Waste and Transport Safety, IAEA Safety Standards Series No. GS-R-1, IAEA, Vienna (2000).

Annex I

ELECTRONIC DOCUMENT MANAGEMENT SYSTEM

I–1. An effective electronic document management system (EDMS) will build on and utilize the controls applied for and the experience gained with the paper document management system.

I–2. An EDMS consists of the computer hardware, software and databases that allow for the integrated preparation, input, distribution, storage, location and retrieval of electronic documents, whether initially created electronically or produced from paper documents.

I–3. An EDMS employs a number of technologies that were developed specifically to manage document based information. These include:

— Document capture tools such as scanning, optical character recognition, electronic data interchange, electronic forms and bar coding;
— Work flow management and electronic forms that support an orderly flow of documents through an organized production system and flexible collaboration across teams and departments;
— Archival and document management tools that support organized electronic storage, indexing, version control, archiving, search, retrieval and distribution of documents.

I–4. An EDMS permits the rapid retrieval and distribution of documents. Documents can be used without regard to their actual storage location. Documents received from any source (scanning, fax, electronic data interchange or the Internet) can be routed to individuals according to content, priority or workload. Various offices can share documents and data across networks in a manner that is transparent to the user.

I–5. The incorporation of EDMS related technology into day to day operations enables several users to have access to a single document simultaneously. In addition, documents do not need to be physically in one place to be processed as a whole. Storing documents in the EDMS permits them to be viewed by any user with the proper security clearance.

I–6. In organizations where an EDMS is used to aid in managing work flow, the status of all work can be known at any time, as managers and supervisors can electronically view any work queues and move or reallocate work as appropriate.

I–7. Documents stored in the EDMS will need to be protected by online security.

I–8. The master copies of documents stored electronically will need to be archived so that the organization is able to restore even the oldest of documents.

I–9. The EDMS will need to support version and revision control of documents such as contracts, guides, documentation or publications.

I–10. Modifications and comments will need to be stored electronically with the original and used to produce revisions to the document on-line. Modifications of documents carried out under the EDMS will need to be done under specific authorization.

I–11. An EDMS will need to manage the whole document lifetime. This includes:

— Identifying the originator of the document;
— Identifying the owner or manager of the document;
— Keeping track of when the document was created and last modified, for each version of the document;
— Distinguishing whether the document is present in a draft version or its final version;
— Keeping track of any form template that is associated with the document;
— Identifying the elements of the document that are saved and managed as separate documents and the relationship between those elements.

I–12. An EDMS will further need to be able to do the following:

— Manage document security with access provisions for documents of various types to ensure that documents are stored correctly and can be exchanged (sent, processed and distributed) using acceptable standards and formats appropriate to the documents.
— Secure documents, especially valuable documents, by maintaining their availability and confidentiality. The confidentiality of the intellectual content of documents may be compromised by unauthorized access. Documents can also be lost owing to unauthorized access or deliberate

interference causing corruption. The proposed software will need to have extensive security features built into it.

— Provide appropriate access to documents. Documents will need to be available to all individuals who need access to the information they contain and who are able to gain the appropriate level of authorization for access. Individuals will need to be able to identify readily what documents are available. Appropriate standards will need to be in place to ensure that access is possible across different technological environments and that documents are accessible over time as technology develops.

EDMS DOCUMENT CAPTURE

I–13.   Some organizations capture digitally their paper based document vaults. Many benefits accrue to users who expend the resources necessary to capture documents digitally. In simple terms, digitally capturing paper documents is accomplished by scanning the paper documents (imaging) and indexing the scanned files in an EDMS. Records stored electronically will need to be stored in such a way that they are compliant with applicable standards for legally admissible evidence.

I–14.   Although some organizations adopt a 'from this day forward' approach, using the EDMS to manage newly created documents, many organizations stress the ability to convert existing data warehouses into electronic repositories. Organizations that need to convert hard copy information to electronic files quickly will need to analyse the demands on the entire imaging subsystem carefully. In a paper based environment, significant amounts of time are spent in simply managing the paper files rather than actually using the information stored on the paper. Once the digital image is created, it will need to be indexed in order to be accessible to the user community.

I–15.   The methods used to capture document specific information will need to facilitate future document retrieval.

EDMS DOCUMENT RETRIEVAL

I–16.   Viewer software is used to allow users to have 'read only' access to documents. Document users will need to be given access to read documents only, without the capability to modify them.

I–17.   The EDMS stores documents in the proper locations on the appropriate devices. Proper logical storage allows the retrieval of documents for other activities. Storage and subsequent retrieval will need to be accomplished automatically. For example, when a user makes a request to modify an engineering design document, it will not be necessary for the user to know where the original document resides within the EDMS. Rather, the EDMS will need to retrieve the document transparently and to execute automatically the appropriate application, focusing on the retrieved document.

I–18.   The EDMS will need to be able to manage archived documents as well as documents under preparation, amendment or approval. The EDMS will need to control access to the archived documents so that they cannot be modified.

I–19.   Documents can also be lost owing to unauthorized access or deliberate interference causing corruption. Most breaches come from within an organization. Standard system security packages will need to be designed to counteract this threat with several means of security built into them, such as:

— Enforcing sign-on disciplines (e.g. unique sign-on identifiers for each authorized user, no group accounts, suspending unused identifiers, lockouts after three unsuccessful attempts to sign on, password protected screen savers and timeouts for inactive sessions on critical systems);
— Enforcing password disciplines (e.g. passwords to be mandatory, changed frequently and stored in encrypted format, and their immediate reuse prevented);
— Establishing formalized procedures for granting access to information systems, including a declaration that the user will comply with the organization's policy on information technology security;
— Limiting access to sensitive information to those who need it and preventing access for others. Saving sensitive information on a personal computer that has no access restrictions is a breach of security. In such a case, either access restrictions on the computer are necessary or, alternatively, the storage of sensitive material on the computer needs to be forbidden;
— Classifying documents according to their content. Electronic access can be granted on a need to know basis and by the use of classification levels;
— Making all authorized users aware of their responsibility to maintain the confidentiality of documents, to protect their passwords, to abide by the organization's security policy and to report any breaches of which they become aware;

— Employing encryption for both the storage and the transmission of confidential information;
— Educating individuals about the vulnerability of non-encrypted information held on networked computers.

Annex II

MEDIA FOR RECORD STORAGE

II–1. Examples of media that may be used to store records are:

— Paper with a pH (acidity level) of between 6 and 9;
— Film, 35 mm roll;
— Silver–gelatine type microfilm or X ray film;
— Microfiche;
— Magnetic tape or disk;
— Optical laser disk;
— Hardware such as graphite samples, weld samples or other materials that have been or are able to be subjected to qualification testing;
— Electronic firmware (computer or component) such as thermal luminescent dosimeters (for short term use only);
— Media for records that need special processing and control, such as computer codes and software, and information stored on high density media or optical disks, which will need to be maintained and controlled to ensure that the records are readily retrievable and usable.

II–2. The following media are considered to be acceptable for records with retention periods of up to 30 years:

— Paper copy retained in a controlled environment with an indexing system to allow retrieval within a reasonable time (e.g. one working day).
— Microfilm or other microforms prepared appropriately and stored in adequate conditions.
— Punched paper tape or cards where the information is stored as physical artefacts on a paper/card medium. Such media will need to be stored in equivalent environmental conditions to hard paper copy.
— Magnetic media stored and maintained appropriately, such as disk packs, storage modules or disk cartridges.

II–3. The following media are considered to be acceptable for records with retention times of up to five years:

— Any of those media considered acceptable for retention periods of up to 30 years, plus optical disks. Records using optical disk media may be held for periods beyond five years provided that periodic checks are made for any deterioration in image quality. The record will need to be copied onto a new optical disk if any deterioration in image quality is found. This may be before the manufacturer's certified lifetime of the original disk is exceeded.

II–4. The following media are considered to be acceptable for records with retention times of up to three years:

— Any of those media with retention times of five years or 30 years, plus flexible disk cartridges (floppy disks) and magnetic tape cartridges stored and maintained appropriately.

II–5. The preparation and storage requirements for the different media should reflect the manufacturer's guidance for the media.

Annex III

RECORD RETENTION AND STORAGE

III–1. Records that might be considered for long term storage include:

— Approved specifications of products;
— Records of the condition of products;
— Records demonstrating that individuals are competent to perform their work;
— Records demonstrating compliance with statutory and regulatory requirements;
— Configuration management records;
— Records of the investigation of an accident, malfunction or non-conformance.

III–2. Records such as management system documentation, procedures and assessment reports might also be considered for long term storage.

III–3. It is recognized that the nomenclature and type of records may vary from organization to organization, and alternative categories may be chosen at the discretion of the organization. Retention times could be standardized to the following:

— Greater than 30 years;
— 30 years;
— Five years;
— Three years.

III–4. Senior management will need to establish storage and location requirements for the maintenance, preservation and protection of records and associated test materials and specimens from the time of their receipt until their disposal. A record storage process will need to include the following:

— A description of the document or record storage facility;
— A description of the filing system to be used;
— A method for verifying that the records received are in agreement with the transmittal document and that the records are in good condition;
— A method for verifying that the records agree with the records index;
— Rules governing access to and control of the files;

— A method for maintaining control of and accountability for records removed from the storage facility;
— A method for filing corrected or supplemental information and disposing of records that have been superseded;
— Periodic checking to ensure that the records are not damaged, deteriorating or missing.

III–5. Continued ability to read the data will need to be ensured, with account taken of any technological changes that occur. Any changes in reading equipment and technology should only be made after consideration of how the capability to access and read existing recorded data will be maintained. This may necessitate transferring data to new media. In such cases checks will need to be carried out to ensure that the data are readable and accessible and that they are an exact copy of the original.

III–6. Paper records will need to be firmly attached in binders or placed in folders or envelopes for storage on shelves or in containers. Steel file cabinets or safes are preferred.

III–7. Records that are processed by special methods will need to be packaged and stored as recommended in the manufacturer's instructions, in line with applicable standards. Examples are: radiographs, photographs, microfilm, magnetic tapes, microdiskettes, laser disks and those records that might be sensitive to light, pressure, humidity, magnetic fields, dust and temperature.

III–8. Record storage facilities will need to protect the contents from possible damage or destruction by such causes as fire, flooding, insects and rodents, and from possible deterioration under adverse environmental conditions of light, temperature and humidity.

III–9. The following factors among others will need to be considered in the construction of a storage facility:

— Location and security;
— Type of construction, including structural features and internal surface treatment;
— Pipework layout and drainage;
— Control of ventilation, temperature and humidity;
— Prevention, detection and fighting of fires;
— Protection against electromagnetic radiation.

GLOSSARY

facilities and activities. A general term encompassing nuclear facilities, uses of all sources of ionizing radiation, all radioactive waste management activities, transport of radioactive material and any other practice or circumstances in which people may be exposed to radiation from naturally occurring or artificial sources.

independent assessment. Assessments such as audits or surveillances carried out to determine the extent to which the requirements for the management system are fulfilled, to evaluate the effectiveness of the management system and to identify opportunities for improvement. They can be conducted by or on behalf of the organization itself for internal purposes, by interested parties such as customers and regulators (or by other persons on their behalf), or by external independent organizations.

management system. A set of interrelated or interacting elements (system) for establishing policies and objectives and enabling the objectives to be achieved in an efficient and effective way.

The management system integrates all elements of an organization into one coherent system to enable all of the organization's objectives to be achieved. These elements include the structure, resources and processes. Personnel, equipment and organizational culture as well as the documented policies and processes are parts of the management system. The organization's processes have to address the totality of the requirements on the organization as established in, for example, IAEA safety standards and other international codes and standards.

management system review. A regular and systematic evaluation by senior management of an organization of the suitability, adequacy, effectiveness and efficiency of its management system in executing the policies and achieving the goals and objectives of the organization.

operator. Any organization or person applying for authorization or authorized and/or responsible for nuclear, radiation, radioactive waste or transport safety when undertaking activities or in relation to any facilities or sources of ionizing radiation. This includes, inter alia, private individuals, governmental bodies, consignors or carriers, licensees, hospitals, self-employed persons, etc.

regulatory body. An authority or a system of authorities designated by the government of a State as having legal authority for conducting the regulatory process, including issuing authorizations, and thereby regulating nuclear, radiation, radioactive waste and transport safety. The national competent authority for the regulation of radioactive material transport safety is included in this description, as is the Regulatory Authority for radiation protection and safety.

(nuclear) safety. The achievement of proper operating conditions, prevention of accidents or mitigation of accident consequences, resulting in protection of workers, the public and the environment from undue radiation hazards.

safety culture. The assembly of characteristics and attitudes in organizations and individuals which establishes that, as an overriding priority, protection and safety issues receive the attention warranted by their significance.

self-assessment. A routine and continuing process conducted by senior management and management at other levels to evaluate the effectiveness of performance in all areas of their responsibility.

CONTRIBUTORS TO DRAFTING AND REVIEW

Aeberli, W.	Beznau nuclear power plant, Switzerland
Alikhan, S.	Atomic Energy of Canada Ltd, Canada
Aoki, M.	Nuclear and Industrial Safety Agency, Ministry of Economy, Trade and Industry, Japan
Arrieta, L.A.	Comissão Nacional de Energia Nuclear, Brazil
Astrand, K.	Radiation and Nuclear Safety Authority, Finland
Balakrishnan, S.	Bhabha Atomic Research Centre, India
Bannai, T.	International Atomic Energy Agency
Bezdegumeli, U.	Turkish Atomic Energy Authority, Turkey
Boal, T.	International Atomic Energy Agency
Bruno, N.	International Atomic Energy Agency
Bull, P.	British Energy, United Kingdom
Caubit Da Silva, A.	Comissão Nacional de Energia Nuclear, Brazil
Chen, X.	Suzhou Nuclear Power Research Institute, China
Clark, C.R.	International Atomic Energy Agency
Dahlgren Persson, K.	International Atomic Energy Agency
Danielson, G.E.	Department of Energy, United States of America
Delattre, D.	DGSNR, France
Diaz, F.	Electronuclear, Brazil
Dua, S.S.	Atomic Energy of Canada Ltd, Canada
Durham, L.	International Atomic Energy Agency
Florescu, N.	CNE-PROD Cernavoda, Romania

Frischknecht, A.	Swiss Federal Nuclear Safety Inspectorate, Switzerland
Garcin, R.	Eskom, South Africa
Hille, M.	Framatome-ANP, Germany
Hughes, P.	Health and Safety Executive, United Kingdom
Ichimura, T.	International Atomic Energy Agency
Ingemarsson, K.-F.	Vattenfall AB, Sweden
Jaarvinen, M.-L.	Radiation and Nuclear Safety Authority, Finland
Karbassioun, A.	International Atomic Energy Agency
Kazennov, A.	International Atomic Energy Agency
Koskinen, K.	Radiation and Nuclear Safety Authority, Finland
Kossilov, A.	International Atomic Energy Agency
Kotthoff, K.	Gesellschaft für Anlagen- und Reaktorensicherheit mbH, Germany
Lazo, E.	OECD Nuclear Energy Agency
Lekberg, A.	Nuclear Power Inspectorate, Sweden
Meyers, S.	British Nuclear Group, United Kingdom
Mononen, J.	Radiation and Nuclear Safety Authority, Finland
Munakata, Y.	Nuclear and Industrial Safety Agency, Ministry of Economy, Trade and Industry, Japan
Nichols, R.	International Atomic Energy Agency
Perramon, F.	International Atomic Energy Agency
Peyrouty, P.	Institut de radioprotection et de sûreté nucléaire, France
Pieroni, N.	International Atomic Energy Agency

Redman, N.	Amethyst Management Ltd, United Kingdom
Reiman, L.	Radiation and Nuclear Safety Authority, Finland
Robinson, I.	Health and Safety Executive, United Kingdom
Ruuska, V.	Radiation and Nuclear Safety Authority, Finland
Saint Raymond, P.	Autorité de sûreté nucléaire, France
Sajaroff, P.	Nuclear Regulatory Authority, Argentina
Schmocker, U.	Swiss Federal Nuclear Safety Inspectorate, Switzerland
Sharma, D.N.	Bhabha Atomic Research Centre, India
Sharma, S.	Atomic Energy Regulatory Board, India
Stephens, M.	Atomic Energy of Canada Ltd, Canada
Szabo, Z.	Atomic Energy Research, Hungary
Taylor, T.	International Atomic Energy Agency
Versteeg, J.	International Atomic Energy Agency
Vincent, D.	Canadian Nuclear Safety Commission, Canada
Vincze, P.	International Atomic Energy Agency
Watanabe, K.	Tokyo Electric Power Company, Japan
Watson, A.G.	International Organization for Standardization
Wickstrom, G.	Vattenfall AB, Sweden
Yang Sung Ho	Korea Institute of Nuclear Safety, Republic of Korea
Yuki, N.	Nuclear and Industrial Safety Agency, Ministry of Economy, Trade and Industry, Japan
Zeger, J.	International Atomic Energy Agency

BODIES FOR THE ENDORSEMENT
OF IAEA SAFETY STANDARDS

An asterisk denotes a corresponding member. Corresponding members receive drafts for comment and other documentation but they do not generally participate in meetings.

Commission on Safety Standards

Argentina: Oliveira, A.; *Australia*: Loy, J.; *Brazil*: Souza de Assis, A.; *Canada*: Pereira, J.K.; *China*: Li, G.; *Czech Republic*: Drábová, D.; *Denmark*: Ulbak, K.; *Egypt*: Abdel-Hamid, S.B.; *France*: Lacoste, A.-C. (Chairperson); *Germany*: Majer, D.; *India*: Sharma, S.K.; *Israel*: Levanon, I.; *Japan*: Abe, K.; *Korea, Republic of*: Eun, Y.-S.; *Pakistan*: Hashmi, J.; *Russian Federation*: Malyshev, A.B.; *South Africa*: Magugumela, M.T.; *Spain*: Azuara, J.A.; *Sweden*: Holm, L.-E.; *Switzerland*: Schmocker, U.; *United Kingdom*: Weightman, M.; *United States of America*: Virgilio, M.; *European Commission*: Waeterloos, C.; *IAEA*: Karbassioun, A. (Coordinator); *International Commission on Radiological Protection*: Holm, L.-E.; *OECD Nuclear Energy Agency*: Tanaka, T.

Nuclear Safety Standards Committee

Argentina: Sajaroff, P.; *Australia*: MacNab, D.; *Austria*: Sholly, S.; *Belgium*: Govaerts, P.; *Brazil*: de Queiroz Bogado Leite, S.; **Bulgaria*: Gantchev, Y.; *Canada*: Newland, D.; *China*: Wang, J.; *Croatia*: Valcic, I.; **Cyprus*: Demetriades, P.; *Czech Republic*: Böhm, K.; *Egypt*: Aly, A.I.M.; *Finland*: Reiman, L. (Chairperson); *France*: Saint Raymond, P.; *Germany*: Herttrich, M., **Greece*: Camarinopoulos, L.; *Hungary*: Vöröss, L.; *India*: Kushwaha, H.S.; *Iran, Islamic Republic of*: Alidousti, A.; **Iraq*: Khalil Al-Kamil, A.-M.; *Ireland*: Hone, C.; *Israel*: Hirshfeld, H.; *Italy*: Bava, G.; *Japan*: Nakamura, K.; *Korea, Republic of*: Kim, H.-K.; *Lithuania*: Demcenko, M.; *Mexico*: González Mercado, V.; *Netherlands*: Jansen, R.; *Pakistan*: Habib, M.A.; *Paraguay*: Troche Figueredo, G.D.; **Peru*: Ramírez Quijada, R.; *Portugal*: Marques, J.J.G.; *Romania*: Biro, L.; *Russian Federation*: Shvetsov, Y.E.; *Slovakia*: Uhrik, P.; *Slovenia*: Levstek, M.F.; *South Africa*: Bester, P.J.; *Spain*: Zarzuela, J.; *Sweden*: Hallman, A.; *Switzerland*: Aeberli, W.; **Thailand*: Tanipanichskul, P.; *Turkey*: Bezdegumeli, U.; *Ukraine*: Bezsalyi, V.; *United Kingdom*: Vaughan, G.J.; *United*

States of America: Mayfield, M.E.; *European Commission*: Vigne, S.; *IAEA*: Feige, G. (Coordinator); *International Organization for Standardization*: Nigon, J.L.; *OECD Nuclear Energy Agency*: Reig, J.; *World Nuclear Association*: Saint-Pierre, S.

Radiation Safety Standards Committee

Belgium: Smeesters, P.; *Brazil*: Rodriguez Rochedo, E.R.; *Bulgaria*: Katzarska, L.; *Canada*: Clement, C.; *China*: Yang, H.; *Costa Rica*: Pacheco Jimenez, R.; *Cuba*: Betancourt Hernandez, L.; *Cyprus*: Demetriades, P.; *Czech Republic*: Petrova, K.; *Denmark*: Ohlenschlager, M.; *Egypt*: Hassib, G.M; *Finland*: Markkanen, M.; *France*: Godet, J.; *Germany*: Landfermann, H.; *Greece*: Kamenopoulou, V.; *Hungary*: Koblinger, L.; *Iceland*: Magnusson, S. (Chairperson); *India*: Sharma, D.N.; *Indonesia*: Akhadi, M.; *Iran, Islamic Republic of*: Rastkhah, N.; *Iraq*: Khalil Al-Kamil, A.-M.; *Ireland*: Colgan, T.; *Israel*: Laichter, Y.; *Italy*: Bologna, L.; *Japan*: Yoda, N.; *Korea, Republic of*: Lee, B.; *Latvia*: Salmins, A.; *Malaysia*: Rehir, D.; *Mexico*: Maldonado Mercado, H.; *Morocco*: Tazi, S.; *Netherlands*: Zuur, C.; *Norway*: Saxebol, G.; *Pakistan*: Mehboob, A.E.; *Paraguay*: Idoyago Navarro, M.; *Philippines*: Valdezco, E.; *Portugal*: Dias de Oliviera, A.; *Romania*: Rodna, A.; *Russian Federation*: Savkin, M.; *Slovakia*: Jurina, V.; *Slovenia*: Sutej, T.; *South Africa*: Olivier, J.H.I.; *Spain*: Amor, I.; *Sweden*: Hofvander, P.; *Switzerland*: Pfeiffer, H.J.; *Thailand*: Wanitsuksombut, W.; *Turkey*: Okyar, H.; *Ukraine*: Holubiev, V.; *United Kingdom*: Robinson, I.; *United States of America*: Miller, C.; *European Commission*: Janssens, A.; *Food and Agriculture Organization of the United Nations*: Byron, D.; *IAEA*: Boal, T. (Coordinator); *International Commission on Radiological Protection*: Valentin, J.; *International Labour Office*: Niu, S.; *International Organization for Standardization*: Perrin, M.; *OECD Nuclear Energy Agency*: Lazo, T.; *Pan American Health Organization*: Jimenez, P.; *United Nations Scientific Committee on the Effects of Atomic Radiation*: Crick, M.; *World Health Organization*: Carr, Z.; *World Nuclear Association*: Saint-Pierre, S.

Transport Safety Standards Committee

Argentina: López Vietri, J.; *Australia*: Sarkar, S.; *Austria*: Kirchnawy, F.; *Belgium*: Cottens, E.; *Brazil*: Mezrahi, A.; *Bulgaria*: Bakalova, A.; *Canada*: Faille, S.; *China*: Qu, Z.; *Croatia*: Kubelka, D.; *Cuba*: Quevedo Garcia, J.R.; *Cyprus*: Demetriades, P.; *Czech Republic*: Ducháček, V.; *Denmark*:

Breddan, K.; *Egypt*: El-Shinawy, R.M.K.; *Finland*: Tikkinen, J.; *France*: Aguilar, J.; *Germany*: Rein, H.; *Greece*: Vogiatzi, S.; *Hungary*: Sáfár, J.; *India*: Agarwal, S.P.; *Iran, Islamic Republic of*: Kardan, M.R.; *Iraq*: Khalil Al-Kamil, A.-M.; *Ireland*: Duffy, J. (Chairperson); *Israel*: Koch, J.; *Italy*: Trivelloni, S.; *Japan*: Amano, M.; *Korea, Republic of*: Kim, Y.-J.; *Malaysia*: Sobari, M.P.M.; *Netherlands*: Van Halem, H.; *New Zealand*: Ardouin, C.; *Norway*: Hornkjøl, S.; *Pakistan*: Rashid, M.; *Paraguay*: More Torres, L.E.; *Philippines*: Kinilitan-Parami, V.; *Portugal*: Buxo da Trindade, R.; *Romania*: Vieru, G.; *Russian Federation*: Ershov, V.N.; *South Africa*: Jutle, K.; *Spain*: Zamora Martin, F.; *Sweden*: Dahlin, G.; *Switzerland*: Knecht, B.; *Thailand*: Wanitsuksombut, W.; *Turkey*: Ertürk, K.; *Ukraine*: Sakalo, V.; *United Kingdom*: Young, C.N.; *United States of America*: Brach, W.E.; Boyle, R.; *European Commission*: Venchiarutti, J.-C.; *International Air Transport Association*: Abouchaar, J.; *IAEA*: Wangler, M.E. (Coordinator); *International Civil Aviation Organization*: Rooney, K.; *International Federation of Air Line Pilots' Associations*: Tisdall, A.; *International Maritime Organization*: Rahim, I.; *International Organization for Standardization*: Malesys, P.; *United Nations Economic Commission for Europe*: Kervella, O.; *Universal Postal Union*: Giroux, P.; *World Nuclear Transport Institute*: Green, L.

Waste Safety Standards Committee

Argentina: Siraky, G.; *Australia*: Williams, G.; *Austria*: Hohenberg, J.; *Belgium*: Baekelandt, L.; *Brazil*: Heilbron, P.; *Bulgaria*: Simeonov, G.; *Canada*: Lojk, R.; *China*: Fan, Z.; *Croatia*: Subasic, D.; *Cuba*: Salgado Mojena, M.; *Cyprus*: Demetriades, P.; *Czech Republic*: Lieteva, P.; *Denmark*: Nielsen, C.; *Egypt*: El-Adham, K.E.A.; *Finland*: Ruokola, E.; *France*: Cailleton, R.; *Hungary*: Czoch, I.; *India*: Raj, K.; *Indonesia*: Yatim, S.; *Iran, Islamic Republic of*: Ettehadian, M.; *Iraq*: Abass, H.; *Israel*: Dody, A.; *Italy*: Dionisi, M.; *Japan*: Ito, Y.; *Korea, Republic of*: Park, W.; *Latvia*: Salmins, A.; *Lithuania*: Paulikas, V.; *Mexico*: Aguirre Gómez, J.; *Morocco*: Soufi, I.; *Netherlands*: Selling, H.; *Norway*: Sorlie, A.; *Pakistan*: Rehman, R.; *Paraguay*: Facetti Fernandez, J.; *Portugal*: Flausino de Paiva, M.; *Romania*: Tuturici, I.; *Russian Federation*: Poluektov, P.P.; *Slovakia*: Konečný, L.; *Slovenia*: Mele, I.; *South Africa*: Pather, T. (Chairperson); *Spain*: Sanz, M.; *Sweden*: Wingefors, S.; *Switzerland*: Zurkinden, A.; *Turkey*: Özdemir, T.; *Ukraine*: Iievlev, S.; *United Kingdom*: Wilson, C.; *United States of America*: Camper, L.; *European Commission*: Hilden, W.; *IAEA*: Hioki, K. (Coordinator); *International Organization for Standardization*: Hutson, G.; *OECD Nuclear Energy Agency*: Riotte, H.; *World Nuclear Association*: Saint-Pierre, S.

IAEA SAFETY STANDARDS SERIES No. GS-R-3

THE MANAGEMENT SYSTEM
FOR FACILITIES AND ACTIVITIES

SAFETY REQUIREMENTS

INTERNATIONAL ATOMIC ENERGY AGENCY
VIENNA, 2006

COPYRIGHT NOTICE

All IAEA scientific and technical publications are protected by the terms of the Universal Copyright Convention as adopted in 1952 (Berne) and as revised in 1972 (Paris). The copyright has since been extended by the World Intellectual Property Organization (Geneva) to include electronic and virtual intellectual property. Permission to use whole or parts of texts contained in IAEA publications in printed or electronic form must be obtained and is usually subject to royalty agreements. Proposals for non-commercial reproductions and translations are welcomed and will be considered on a case by case basis. Enquiries should be addressed by email to the Publishing Section, IAEA, at sales.publications@iaea.org or by post to:

Sales and Promotion Unit, Publishing Section
International Atomic Energy Agency
Wagramer Strasse 5
P.O. Box 100
A-1400 Vienna
Austria
fax: +43 1 2600 29302
tel.: +43 1 2600 22417
http://www.iaea.org/books

IAEA Library Cataloguing in Publication Data

The management system for facilities and activities : safety requirements.
 — Vienna : International Atomic Energy Agency, 2006.
    p. ; 24 cm. (IAEA safety standards series, ISSN 1020–525X ; no. GS-R-3)
    STI/PUB/1252
    ISBN 92–0–106506–X
    Includes bibliographical references.

    1. Nuclear facilities — Management. 2. Radiation — Safety measures. I. International Atomic Energy Agency. II. Series: Safety standards series ; GS-R-3.

IAEAL   06–00444

CONTENTS

1. INTRODUCTION

BACKGROUND

1.1. This Safety Requirements publication defines the requirements for establishing, implementing, assessing and continually improving a management system. A management system designed to fulfil these requirements integrates safety, health, environmental, security[1], quality[2] and economic[3] elements. Safety is the fundamental principle upon which the management system is based. These requirements must be met to ensure the protection of people and the environment and they are governed by the objectives, concepts and principles of the IAEA Safety Fundamentals publication [1].

1.2. The standards of the International Organization for Standardization on environmental management systems [2] and on quality management systems [3] were considered in developing this publication. The experience of Member States in developing, implementing and improving management systems was also taken into account.

1.3. The content of this publication supports the achievement of the two general aims of the management system, as stated by the International Nuclear Safety Group (INSAG) [4]:

— "To improve the safety performance of the organization through the planning, control and supervision of safety related activities in normal, transient and emergency situations;
— "To foster and support a strong safety culture through the development and reinforcement of good safety attitudes and behaviour in individuals and teams so as to allow them to carry out their tasks safely."

---

[1] This Safety Requirements publication covers the security of facilities, nuclear material and sources of radiation only to the extent that security measures for physical protection are essential to safety and the failure of such measures has consequences for safety.

[2] Quality refers to the degree to which a product, process or service satisfies specified requirements.

[3] Economic objectives are included in the list of elements that have to be integrated, as it is recognized that economic decisions and actions may introduce or may mitigate potential risks.

1.4. This Safety Requirements publication supersedes the Code on Quality Assurance for Safety in Nuclear Power Plants and other Nuclear Installations [5]. It uses the term 'management system' rather than 'quality assurance'. The term management system reflects and includes the initial concept of 'quality control' (controlling the quality of products) and its evolution through quality assurance (the system to ensure the quality of products) and 'quality management' (the system to manage quality). The management system is a set of interrelated or interacting elements that establishes policies and objectives and which enables those objectives to be achieved in a safe, efficient and effective manner.

1.5. The content of this publication is based on two key concepts: that work may be structured and interpreted as a set of interacting processes; and that all individuals involved contribute to achieving safety and quality objectives.

1.6. The requirements established in this publication may be used by organizations in the following ways:

— As the basis for the management systems of organizations directly responsible for operating facilities and activities and providing services, as described in para. 1.8;
— As the basis for the regulation of these facilities and activities by the regulatory body;
— As the basis for the management systems of the relevant regulatory bodies [6];
— By the operator, to specify to a supplier, via contractual documentation, any specific requirements of this Safety Requirements publication that must be included in the supplier's management system for the supply and delivery of products[4].

1.7. A Safety Guide in support of this publication provides generic guidance on the application of the management system for all facilities and activities and for their regulation [7]. In addition to the generic guidance, there are several specific Safety Guides that provide additional guidance on implementing these requirements in specific areas.

---

[4] A product is the result or output of a process. Examples include a radionuclide, a waste package and electricity.

2

OBJECTIVE

1.8. The objective of this publication is to define requirements for establishing, implementing, assessing and continually improving a management system that integrates safety, health, environmental, security, quality and economic elements to ensure that safety is properly taken into account in all the activities of an organization.

1.9. The main objective of the requirements for the management system is to ensure, by considering the implications of all actions not within separate management systems but with regard to safety as a whole, that safety is not compromised.[5]

SCOPE

1.10. This publication is applicable to the establishment, implementation, assessment and continual improvement of management systems for:

— Nuclear facilities;
— Activities using sources of ionizing radiation;
— Radioactive waste management;
— The transport of radioactive material;
— Radiation protection activities;
— Any other practices or circumstances in which people may be exposed to radiation from naturally occurring or artificial sources;
— The regulation of such facilities and activities.

1.11. This Safety Requirements publication is applicable throughout the lifetime of facilities and for the entire duration of activities in normal, transient and emergency situations. This includes any subsequent period of institutional control that may be necessary. For a facility, these phases usually include siting, design, construction, commissioning, operation and decommissioning (or close-out or closure).

1.12. This publication does not attempt to define all those specific health, environmental, security, quality and economic requirements to be addressed

---

[5] There have been many instances in which decisions have been taken without considering the impact on safety (e.g. economic decisions such as reducing costs by cutting staff), which has led to safety related problems.

that have already been established elsewhere (in other IAEA publications and in international codes and standards). Furthermore, this publication does not set out to duplicate any of those specific requirements; rather, it defines the requirements for managing their fulfilment in an integrated manner.

1.13. The integrated management system requirements defined in this publication cover topics that either relate directly to safety or are part of the managerial framework without which safety cannot be ensured and maintained. Thus topics such as management commitment, communications and other aspects are included from the perspective of seeking to enhance safety as well as performance.

STRUCTURE

1.14. This Safety Requirements publication consists of six sections. Section 2 establishes the general requirements for the management system, including those relating to safety culture, grading and documentation. Section 3 establishes the requirements for and responsibilities of senior management[6] for the development and implementation of a management system. Section 4 establishes the requirements for resource management. Section 5 establishes the requirements for the processes of the organization — their specification, development and management — and for the generic processes of the management system. Section 6 establishes the requirements for measuring, assessing and improving the management system.

2. MANAGEMENT SYSTEM

GENERAL REQUIREMENTS

2.1. A management system shall be established, implemented, assessed and continually improved. It shall be aligned with the goals of the organization and

---

[6] 'Senior management' means the person who, or group of people which, directs, controls and assesses an organization at the highest level. Many different terms are used, including, for example: chief executive officer (CEO), director general, executive team, plant manager, top manager, chief regulator, site vice-president, managing director and laboratory director.

shall contribute to their achievement. The main aim of the management system shall be to achieve and enhance safety by:

— Bringing together in a coherent manner all the requirements for managing the organization;
— Describing the planned and systematic actions necessary to provide adequate confidence that all these requirements are satisfied;
— Ensuring that health, environmental, security, quality and economic requirements are not considered separately from safety requirements, to help preclude their possible negative impact on safety.

2.2. Safety shall be paramount within the management system, overriding all other demands.

2.3. The management system shall identify and integrate with the requirements contained within this publication:

— The statutory and regulatory requirements of the Member State;
— Any requirements formally agreed with interested parties (also known as 'stakeholders'[7]);
— All other relevant IAEA Safety Requirements publications, such as those on emergency preparedness and response [8] and safety assessment [9];

---

[7] Stakeholder: interested party; concerned party. 'Stakeholder' means an interested party — whether a person or a company, etc. — with an interest or concern in ensuring the success of an organization, business, system, etc. To 'have a stake in' something figuratively means to have something to gain or lose by, or to have an interest in, the turn of events. The term stakeholder is used in a broad sense to mean a person or group having an interest in the performance of an organization. Those who can influence events may effectively become interested parties — whether their 'interest' is regarded as 'genuine' or not — in the sense that their views need to be considered. Interested parties have typically included the following: customers, owners, operators, employees, suppliers, partners, trade unions, the regulated industry or professionals; scientific bodies; governmental agencies or regulators (local, regional and national) whose responsibilities may cover nuclear energy; the media; the public (individuals, community groups and interest groups); and other States, especially neighbouring States that have entered into agreements providing for an exchange of information concerning possible transboundary impacts, or States involved in the export or import of certain technologies or materials.

— Requirements from other relevant codes and standards adopted for use by the organization.

2.4. The organization shall be able to demonstrate the effective fulfilment of its management system requirements.

SAFETY CULTURE

2.5. The management system shall be used to promote and support a strong safety culture by:

— Ensuring a common understanding of the key aspects of safety culture within the organization;
— Providing the means by which the organization supports individuals and teams in carrying out their tasks safely and successfully, taking into account the interaction between individuals, technology and the organization;
— Reinforcing a learning and questioning attitude at all levels of the organization;
— Providing the means by which the organization continually seeks to develop and improve its safety culture.

GRADING THE APPLICATION OF MANAGEMENT SYSTEM REQUIREMENTS

2.6. The application of management system requirements shall be graded so as to deploy appropriate resources, on the basis of the consideration of:

— The significance and complexity of each product or activity;
— The hazards and the magnitude of the potential impact (risks) associated with the safety, health, environmental, security, quality and economic elements of each product or activity;
— The possible consequences if a product fails or an activity is carried out incorrectly.

2.7. Grading of the application of management system requirements shall be applied to the products and activities of each process.

DOCUMENTATION OF THE MANAGEMENT SYSTEM

2.8. The documentation of the management system shall include the following:

— The policy statements of the organization;
— A description of the management system;
— A description of the structure of the organization;
— A description of the functional responsibilities, accountabilities, levels of authority and interactions of those managing, performing and assessing work;
— A description of the processes and supporting information that explain how work is to be prepared, reviewed, carried out, recorded, assessed and improved.

2.9. The documentation of the management system shall be developed to be understandable to those who use it. Documents shall be readable, readily identifiable and available at the point of use.

2.10. The documentation of the management system shall reflect:

— The characteristics of the organization and its activities;
— The complexities of processes and their interactions.

3. MANAGEMENT RESPONSIBILITY

MANAGEMENT COMMITMENT

3.1. Management at all levels shall demonstrate its commitment to the establishment, implementation, assessment and continual improvement of the management system and shall allocate adequate resources to carry out these activities.

3.2. Senior management shall develop individual values, institutional values and behavioural expectations for the organization to support the implementation of the management system and shall act as role models in the promulgation of these values and expectations.

3.3. Management at all levels shall communicate to individuals the need to adopt these individual values, institutional values and behavioural expectations as well as to comply with the requirements of the management system.

3.4. Management at all levels shall foster the involvement of all individuals in the implementation and continual improvement of the management system.

3.5. Senior management shall ensure that it is clear when, how and by whom decisions are to be made within the management system.

SATISFACTION OF INTERESTED PARTIES

3.6. The expectations of interested parties shall be considered by senior management in the activities and interactions in the processes of the management system, with the aim of enhancing the satisfaction of interested parties while at the same time ensuring that safety is not compromised.

ORGANIZATIONAL POLICIES

3.7. Senior management shall develop the policies of the organization. The policies shall be appropriate to the activities and facilities of the organization.

PLANNING

3.8. Senior management shall establish goals, strategies, plans and objectives[8] that are consistent with the policies of the organization.

3.9. Senior management shall develop the goals, strategies, plans and objectives of the organization in an integrated manner so that their collective impact on safety is understood and managed.

3.10. Senior management shall ensure that measurable objectives for implementing the goals, strategies and plans are established through appropriate processes at various levels in the organization.

---

[8] These goals, strategies, plans and objectives are sometimes collectively referred to as a 'business plan'.

3.11. Senior management shall ensure that the implementation of the plans is regularly reviewed against these objectives and that actions are taken to address deviations from the plans where necessary.

RESPONSIBILITY AND AUTHORITY FOR THE MANAGEMENT SYSTEM

3.12. Senior management shall be ultimately responsible for the management system and shall ensure that it is established, implemented, assessed and continually improved.

3.13. An individual reporting directly to senior management shall have specific responsibility and authority for:

— Coordinating the development and implementation of the management system, and its assessment and continual improvement;
— Reporting on the performance of the management system, including its influence on safety and safety culture, and any need for improvement;
— Resolving any potential conflicts between requirements and within the processes of the management system.

3.14. The organization shall retain overall responsibility for the management system when an external organization is involved in the work of developing all or part of the management system.

4. RESOURCE MANAGEMENT

PROVISION OF RESOURCES

4.1. Senior management shall determine the amount of resources necessary and shall provide the resources[9] to carry out the activities of the organization

---

[9] 'Resources' includes individuals, infrastructure, the working environment, information and knowledge, and suppliers, as well as material and financial resources.

and to establish, implement, assess and continually improve the management system.

4.2.   The information and knowledge of the organization shall be managed as a resource.

HUMAN RESOURCES

4.3.   Senior management shall determine the competence requirements for individuals at all levels and shall provide training or take other actions to achieve the required level of competence. An evaluation of the effectiveness of the actions taken shall be conducted. Suitable proficiency shall be achieved and maintained.

4.4.   Senior management shall ensure that individuals are competent to perform their assigned work and that they understand the consequences for safety of their activities. Individuals shall have received appropriate education and training, and shall have acquired suitable skills, knowledge and experience to ensure their competence. Training shall ensure that individuals are aware of the relevance and importance of their activities and of how their activities contribute to safety in the achievement of the organization's objectives.

INFRASTRUCTURE AND THE WORKING ENVIRONMENT

4.5.   Senior management shall determine, provide, maintain and re-evaluate the infrastructure and the working environment necessary for work to be carried out in a safe manner and for requirements to be met.

5. PROCESS IMPLEMENTATION

DEVELOPING PROCESSES

5.1.   The processes of the management system that are needed to achieve the goals, provide the means to meet all requirements and deliver the products of the organization shall be identified, and their development shall be planned, implemented, assessed and continually improved.

5.2. The sequence and interactions of the processes shall be determined.

5.3. The methods necessary to ensure the effectiveness of both the implementation and the control of the processes shall be determined and implemented.

5.4. The development of each process shall ensure that the following are achieved:

— Process requirements, such as applicable regulatory, statutory, legal, safety, health, environmental, security, quality and economic requirements, are specified and addressed.
— Hazards and risks are identified, together with any necessary mitigatory actions.
— Interactions with interfacing processes are identified.
— Process inputs are identified.
— The process flow is described.
— Process outputs (products) are identified.
— Process measurement criteria are established.

5.5. The activities of and interfaces between different individuals or groups involved in a single process shall be planned, controlled and managed in a manner that ensures effective communication and the clear assignment of responsibilities.

PROCESS MANAGEMENT

5.6. For each process a designated individual shall be given the authority and responsibility for:

— Developing and documenting the process and maintaining the necessary supporting documentation;
— Ensuring that there is effective interaction between interfacing processes;
— Ensuring that process documentation is consistent with any existing documents;
— Ensuring that the records required to demonstrate that the process results have been achieved are specified in the process documentation;

— Monitoring and reporting on the performance of the process;

— Promoting improvement in the process;

— Ensuring that the process, including any subsequent changes to it, is aligned with the goals, strategies, plans and objectives of the organization.

5.7. For each process, any activities for inspection, testing, verification and validation, their acceptance criteria and the responsibilities for carrying out these activities shall be specified. For each process, it shall be specified if and when these activities are to be performed by designated individuals or groups other than those who originally performed the work.

5.8. Each process shall be evaluated to ensure that it remains effective.

5.9. The work performed in each process shall be carried out under controlled conditions, by using approved current procedures, instructions, drawings or other appropriate means that are periodically reviewed to ensure their adequacy and effectiveness. Results shall be compared with expected values.

5.10. The control of processes contracted to external organizations shall be identified within the management system. The organization shall retain overall responsibility when contracting any processes.

GENERIC MANAGEMENT SYSTEM PROCESSES

5.11. The following generic processes shall be developed in the management system.

Control of documents

5.12. Documents[10] shall be controlled. All individuals involved in preparing, revising, reviewing or approving documents shall be specifically assigned this work, shall be competent to carry it out and shall be given access to appropriate information on which to base their input or decisions. It shall be ensured that document users are aware of and use appropriate and correct documents.

---

[10] Documents may include: policies; procedures; instructions; specifications and drawings (or representations in other media); training materials; and any other texts that describe processes, specify requirements or establish product specifications.

5.13. Changes to documents shall be reviewed and recorded and shall be subject to the same level of approval as the documents themselves.

Control of products

5.14. Specifications and requirements for products, including any subsequent changes, shall be in accordance with established standards and shall incorporate applicable requirements. Products that interface or interact with each other shall be identified and controlled.

5.15. Activities for inspection, testing, verification and validation shall be completed before the acceptance, implementation or operational use of products. The tools and equipment used for these activities shall be of the proper range, type, accuracy and precision.

5.16. The organization shall confirm that products meet the specified requirements and shall ensure that products perform satisfactorily in service.

5.17. Products shall be provided in such a form that it can be verified that they satisfy the requirements.

5.18. Controls shall be used to ensure that products do not bypass the required verification activities.

5.19. Products shall be identified to ensure their proper use. Where traceability is a requirement, the organization shall control and record the unique identification of the product.

5.20. Products shall be handled, transported, stored, maintained and operated as specified, to prevent their damage, loss, deterioration or inadvertent use.

Control of records

5.21. Records shall be specified in the process documentation and shall be controlled. All records shall be readable, complete, identifiable and easily retrievable.

5.22. Retention times of records and associated test materials and specimens shall be established to be consistent with the statutory requirements and knowledge management obligations of the organization. The media used for records shall be such as to ensure that the records are readable for the duration of the retention times specified for each record.

Purchasing

5.23. Suppliers of products shall be selected on the basis of specified criteria and their performance shall be evaluated.

5.24. Purchasing requirements shall be developed and specified in procurement documents. Evidence that products meet these requirements shall be available to the organization before the product is used.

5.25. Requirements for the reporting and resolution of non-conformances shall be specified in procurement documents.

Communication

5.26. Information relevant to safety, health, environmental, security, quality and economic goals shall be communicated to individuals in the organization and, where necessary, to other interested parties.

5.27. Internal communication concerning the implementation and effectiveness of the management system shall take place between the various levels and functions of the organization.

Managing organizational change

5.28. Organizational changes shall be evaluated and classified according to their importance to safety and each change shall be justified.

5.29. The implementation of such changes shall be planned, controlled, communicated, monitored, tracked and recorded to ensure that safety is not compromised.

6. MEASUREMENT, ASSESSMENT AND IMPROVEMENT

MONITORING AND MEASUREMENT

6.1. The effectiveness of the management system shall be monitored and measured to confirm the ability of the processes to achieve the intended results and to identify opportunities for improvement.

SELF-ASSESSMENT

6.2. Senior management and management at all other levels in the organization shall carry out self-assessment to evaluate the performance of work and the improvement of the safety culture.

INDEPENDENT ASSESSMENT

6.3. Independent assessments shall be conducted regularly on behalf of senior management:

— To evaluate the effectiveness of processes in meeting and fulfilling goals, strategies, plans and objectives;
— To determine the adequacy of work performance and leadership;
— To evaluate the organization's safety culture;
— To monitor product quality;
— To identify opportunities for improvement.

6.4. An organizational unit shall be established with the responsibility for conducting independent assessments.[11] This unit shall have sufficient authority to discharge its responsibilities.

6.5. Individuals conducting independent assessments shall not assess their own work.

---

[11] The size of the assessment unit differs from organization to organization. In some organizations, the assessment function may even be a responsibility assigned to a single individual or to an external organization.

6.6. Senior management shall evaluate the results of the independent assessments, shall take any necessary actions, and shall record and communicate their decisions and the reasons for them.

MANAGEMENT SYSTEM REVIEW

6.7. A management system review shall be conducted at planned intervals to ensure the continuing suitability and effectiveness of the management system and its ability to enable the objectives set for the organization to be accomplished.

6.8. The review shall cover but shall not be limited to:

— Outputs from all forms of assessment;
— Results delivered and objectives achieved by the organization and its processes;
— Non-conformances and corrective and preventive actions;
— Lessons learned from other organizations;
— Opportunities for improvement.

6.9. Weaknesses and obstacles shall be identified, evaluated and remedied in a timely manner.

6.10. The review shall identify whether there is a need to make changes to or improvements in policies, goals, strategies, plans, objectives and processes.

NON-CONFORMANCES AND CORRECTIVE AND PREVENTIVE ACTIONS

6.11. The causes of non-conformances shall be determined and remedial actions shall be taken to prevent their recurrence.

6.12. Products and processes that do not conform to the specified requirements shall be identified, segregated, controlled, recorded and reported to an appropriate level of management within the organization. The impact of non-conformances shall be evaluated and non-conforming products or processes shall be either:

— Accepted;
— Reworked or corrected within a specified time period; or
— Rejected and discarded or destroyed to prevent their inadvertent use.

6.13. Concessions granted to allow acceptance of a non-conforming product or process shall be subject to authorization. When non-conforming products or processes are reworked or corrected, they shall be subject to inspection to demonstrate their conformity with requirements or expected results.

6.14. Corrective actions for eliminating non-conformances shall be determined and implemented. Preventive actions to eliminate the causes of potential non-conformances shall be determined and taken.

6.15. The status and effectiveness of all corrective and preventive actions shall be monitored and reported to management at an appropriate level in the organization.

6.16. Potential non-conformances that could detract from the organization's performance shall be identified. This shall be done: by using feedback from other organizations, both internal and external; through the use of technical advances and research; through the sharing of knowledge and experience; and through the use of techniques that identify best practices.

IMPROVEMENT

6.17. Opportunities for the improvement of the management system shall be identified and actions to improve the processes shall be selected, planned and recorded.

6.18. Improvement plans shall include plans for the provision of adequate resources. Actions for improvement shall be monitored through to their completion and the effectiveness of the improvement shall be checked.

REFERENCES

[1] INTERNATIONAL ATOMIC ENERGY AGENCY, Fundamental Safety Principles, IAEA Safety Standards Series No. SF, IAEA, Vienna (2006).

[2] INTERNATIONAL ORGANIZATION FOR STANDARDIZATION, Environmental Management Systems: Specification with Guidance for Use, ISO 14001:1996, ISO, Geneva (1996).

[3] INTERNATIONAL ORGANIZATION FOR STANDARDIZATION, Quality Management Systems: Requirements, ISO 9001:2000, ISO, Geneva (2000).

[4] INTERNATIONAL NUCLEAR SAFETY ADVISORY GROUP, Management of Operational Safety in Nuclear Power Plants, INSAG-13, IAEA, Vienna (1999).

[5] INTERNATIONAL ATOMIC ENERGY AGENCY, Quality Assurance for Safety in Nuclear Power Plants and other Nuclear Installations, Code and Safety Guides Q1–Q14, Safety Series No. 50-C/SG-Q, IAEA, Vienna (1996).

[6] INTERNATIONAL ATOMIC ENERGY AGENCY, Legal and Governmental Infrastructure for Nuclear, Radiation, Radioactive Waste and Transport Safety, IAEA Safety Standards Series No. GS-R-1, IAEA, Vienna (2000).

[7] INTERNATIONAL ATOMIC ENERGY AGENCY, Application of the Management System for Facilities and Activities, IAEA Safety Standards Series No. GS-G-3.1, IAEA, Vienna (2006).

[8] FOOD AND AGRICULTURE ORGANIZATION OF THE UNITED NATIONS, INTERNATIONAL ATOMIC ENERGY AGENCY, INTERNATIONAL LABOUR ORGANIZATION, OECD NUCLEAR ENERGY AGENCY, PAN AMERICAN HEALTH ORGANIZATION, UNITED NATIONS OFFICE FOR THE CO-ORDINATION OF HUMANITARIAN AFFAIRS, WORLD HEALTH ORGANIZATION, Preparedness and Response for a Nuclear or Radiological Emergency, IAEA Safety Standards Series No. GS-R-2, IAEA, Vienna (2002).

[9] INTERNATIONAL ATOMIC ENERGY AGENCY, Safety Assessment and Verification, IAEA Safety Standards Series No. GS-R-4, IAEA, Vienna (in preparation).

IAEA
International Atomic Energy Agency

Where to order IAEA publications

In the following countries IAEA publications may be purchased from the sources listed below, or from major local booksellers. Payment may be made in local currency or with UNESCO coupons.

Australia
DA Information Services, 648 Whitehorse Road, Mitcham Victoria 3132
Telephone: +61 3 9210 7777 • Fax: +61 3 9210 7788
Email: service@dadirect.com.au • Web site: http://www.dadirect.com.au

Belgium
Jean de Lannoy, avenue du Roi 202, B-1190 Brussels
Telephone: +32 2 538 43 08 • Fax: +32 2 538 08 41
Email: jean.de.lannoy@infoboard.be • Web site: http://www.jean-de-lannoy.be

Canada
Bernan Associates, 4611-F Assembly Drive, Lanham, MD 20706-4391, USA
Telephone: 1-800-865-3457 • Fax: 1-800-865-3450
Email: order@bernan.com • Web site: http://www.bernan.com

Renouf Publishing Company Ltd., 1-5369 Canotek Rd., Ottawa, Ontario, K1J 9J3
Telephone: +613 745 2665 • Fax: +613 745 7660
Email: order.dept@renoufbooks.com • Web site: http://www.renoufbooks.com

China
IAEA Publications in Chinese: China Nuclear Energy Industry Corporation, Translation Section, P.O. Box 2103, Beijing

Czech Republic
Suweco CZ, S.R.O. Klecakova 347, 180 21 Praha 9
Telephone: +420 26603 5364 • Fax: +420 28482 1646
Email: nakup@suweco.cz • Web site: http://www.suweco.cz

Finland
Akateeminen Kirjakauppa, PL 128 (Keskuskatu 1), FIN-00101 Helsinki
Telephone: +358 9 121 41 • Fax: +358 9 121 4450
Email: akatilaus@akateeminen.com • Web site: http://www.akateeminen.com

France
Form-Edit, 5, rue Janssen, P.O. Box 25, F-75921 Paris Cedex 19
Telephone: +33 1 42 01 49 49 • Fax: +33 1 42 01 90 90 • Email: formedit@formedit.fr

Lavoisier SAS, 145 rue de Provigny, 94236 Cachan Cedex
Telephone: + 33 1 47 40 67 02 • Fax +33 1 47 40 67 02
Email: romuald.verrier@lavoisier.fr • Web site: http://www.lavoisier.fr

Germany
UNO-Verlag, Vertriebs- und Verlags GmbH, Am Hofgarten 10, D-53113 Bonn
Telephone: + 49 228 94 90 20 • Fax: +49 228 94 90 20 or +49 228 94 90 222
Email: bestellung@uno-verlag.de • Web site: http://www.uno-verlag.de

Hungary
Librotrade Ltd., Book Import, P.O. Box 126, H-1656 Budapest
Telephone: +36 1 257 7777 • Fax: +36 1 257 7472 • Email: books@librotrade.hu

India
Allied Publishers Group, 1st Floor, Dubash House, 15, J. N. Heredia Marg, Ballard Estate, Mumbai 400 001,
Telephone: +91 22 22617926/27 • Fax: +91 22 22617928
Email: alliedpl@vsnl.com • Web site: http://www.alliedpublishers.com

Bookwell, 2/72, Nirankari Colony, Delhi 110009
Telephone: +91 11 23268786, +91 11 23257264 • Fax: +91 11 23281315
Email: bookwell@vsnl.net

Italy
Libreria Scientifica Dott. Lucio di Biasio "AEIOU", Via Coronelli 6, I-20146 Milan
Telephone: +39 02 48 95 45 52 or 48 95 45 62 • Fax: +39 02 48 95 45 48

Japan
Maruzen Company, Ltd., 13-6 Nihonbashi, 3 chome, Chuo-ku, Tokyo 103-0027
Telephone: +81 3 3275 8582 • Fax: +81 3 3275 9072
Email: journal@maruzen.co.jp • Web site: http://www.maruzen.co.jp

Korea, Republic of
KINS Inc., Information Business Dept. Samho Bldg. 2nd Floor, 275-1 Yang Jae-dong SeoCho-G, Seoul 137-130
Telephone: +02 589 1740 • Fax: +02 589 1746
Email: sj8142@kins.co.kr • Web site: http://www.kins.co.kr

Netherlands
De Lindeboom Internationale Publicaties B.V., M.A. de Ruyterstraat 20A, NL-7482 BZ Haaksbergen
Telephone: +31 (0) 53 5740004 • Fax: +31 (0) 53 5729296
Email: books@delindeboom.com • Web site: http://www.delindeboom.com

Martinus Nijhoff International, Koraalrood 50, P.O. Box 1853, 2700 CZ Zoetermeer
Telephone: +31 793 684 400 • Fax: +31 793 615 698 • Email: info@nijhoff.nl • Web site: http://www.nijhoff.nl

Swets and Zeitlinger b.v., P.O. Box 830, 2160 SZ Lisse
Telephone: +31 252 435 111 • Fax: +31 252 415 888 • Email: infoho@swets.nl • Web site: http://www.swets.nl

New Zealand
DA Information Services, 648 Whitehorse Road, MITCHAM 3132, Australia
Telephone: +61 3 9210 7777 • Fax: +61 3 9210 7788
Email: service@dadirect.com.au • Web site: http://www.dadirect.com.au

Slovenia
Cankarjeva Zalozba d.d., Kopitarjeva 2, SI-1512 Ljubljana
Telephone: +386 1 432 31 44 • Fax: +386 1 230 14 35
Email: import.books@cankarjeva-z.si • Web site: http://www.cankarjeva-z.si/uvoz

Spain
Díaz de Santos, S.A., c/ Juan Bravo, 3A, E-28006 Madrid
Telephone: +34 91 781 94 80 • Fax: +34 91 575 55 63 • Email: compras@diazdesantos.es
carmela@diazdesantos.es • barcelona@diazdesantos.es • julio@diazdesantos.es
Web site: http://www.diazdesantos.es

United Kingdom
The Stationery Office Ltd, International Sales Agency, PO Box 29, Norwich, NR3 1 GN
Telephone (orders): +44 870 600 5552 • (enquiries): +44 207 873 8372 • Fax: +44 207 873 8203
Email (orders): book.orders@tso.co.uk • (enquiries): book.enquiries@tso.co.uk • Web site: http://www.tso.co.uk

On-line orders:
DELTA Int. Book Wholesalers Ltd., 39 Alexandra Road, Addlestone, Surrey, KT15 2PQ
Email: info@profbooks.com • Web site: http://www.profbooks.com

Books on the Environment:
Earthprint Ltd., P.O. Box 119, Stevenage SG1 4TP
Telephone: +44 1438748111 • Fax: +44 1438748844
Email: orders@earthprint.com • Web site: http://www.earthprint.com

United Nations (UN)
Dept. 1004, Room DC2-0853, First Avenue at 46th Street, New York, N.Y. 10017, USA
Telephone: +800 253-9646 or +212 963-8302 • Fax: +212 963-3489
Email: publications@un.org • Web site: http://www.un.org

United States of America
Bernan Associates, 4611-F Assembly Drive, Lanham, MD 20706-4391
Telephone: 1-800-865-3457 • Fax: 1-800-865-3450
Email: order@bernan.com • Web site: http://www.bernan.com

Renouf Publishing Company Ltd., 812 Proctor Ave., Ogdensburg, NY, 13669
Telephone: +888 551 7470 (toll-free) • Fax: +888 568 8546 (toll-free)
Email: order.dept@renoufbooks.com • Web site: http://www.renoufbooks.com

Orders and requests for information may also be addressed directly to:

Sales and Promotion Unit, International Atomic Energy Agency
Wagramer Strasse 5, P.O. Box 100, A-1400 Vienna, Austria
Telephone: +43 1 2600 22529 (or 22530) • Fax: +43 1 2600 29302
Email: sales.publications@iaea.org • Web site: http://www.iaea.org/books

ISBN 978-1-332-05355-1
PIBN 10276911

1 MONTH OF
FREE
READING

at
www.ForgottenBooks.com

By purchasing this book you are eligible for one month membership to ForgottenBooks.com, giving you unlimited access to our entire collection of over 700,000 titles via our web site and mobile apps.

To claim your free month visit:

www.forgottenbooks.com/free276911

Similar Books Are Available from
www.forgottenbooks.com

THE DESIGN OF
AEROPLANES

BY

ARTHUR W. JUDGE, A.R.C.S.

Whitworth Scholar; Diploma of Imperial College of Science and Technology;
Associate Member of the Institute of Automobile Engineers

. WITH NUMEROUS ILLUSTRATIONS
AND TABLES

WHITTAKER & CO.

WHITE HART STREET, LONDON, E.C.

And 64, FIFTH AVENUE, NEW YORK

1916

PREFACE

THE present volume is the outcome of an endeavour to fulfil an aeronautical need, which must have been experienced by most designers, draughtsmen, and students, in entering the field of aeronautics—namely, the absence of collected data and design methods. In other branches of engineering one finds numerous design and pocket books containing a compendium of useful information, and fulfilling most of the ordinary requirements. In aeronautical engineering, however, although there are numerous works of a more or less popular and romantic nature, yet the absence of similar design and pocket books is marked, no doubt on account of the more recent development of this branch.

The chief object of the present work is to present in a simple yet brief form the principles underlying the design of aeroplanes from the standpoint of the mechanical engineer, and to collect and tabulate some of the data which experience has shown to be useful in design work.

A chapter has been included dealing with the more important mechanical principles involved in aeronautical design, with an indication as to their utility and application.

Obviously, the subject of aeroplane design is now so wide that it is impossible either to treat each branch of the subject in full, or to embrace every branch, but it is hoped in the complete series of aeronautical manuals to cover most of the ground; the author, for these reasons, seeks the indulgence of the reader for any apparent incompleteness in the present work.

In conclusion, the author would like to record his thanks to the proprietors of " Flight " for their kind permission to employ the diagrams indicated.

A. W. J.

LONDON,
1916.

CONTENTS

THE DESIGN OF AEROPLANES

CHAPTER I

GENERAL DESIGN PRINCIPLES

GENERAL PRINCIPLES.

There are four forces acting upon an aeroplane in flight—

1. The weight of the machine (W), acting vertically downwards through its Centre of Gravity (C.G.).
2. The aerodynamic lift (L) of the wings (and other supporting surfaces), acting through the Centre of of Pressure (C.P.).
3. The total head resistance (R) of the whole machine, which acts in a direction parallel to the direction of motion of the machine through the Centre of Resistance (C.R.)
4. The propeller thrust (T), acting through the Centre of Thrust (C.T.).

Case I.—In order that the aeroplane may be in equilibrium, these four forces must balance each other.

The ideal conditions of equilibrium are—

$$W = L \text{ and } T = R,$$

and that all four forces act through the same point, as shown in Fig. 1. In this case, if the engine ceases to work, $T = 0$; then for equilibrium to occur the machine will glide downwards at its "natural gliding angle," as shown in Fig. 2, in which the gliding angle is denoted by θ.

The forces required to balance the lift force (L) and head resistance (R) being obtained at the expense of the components of the weight, then—

$$L = W \cos \theta, \text{ and } D = W \sin \theta.$$

The gliding angle $\theta = \tan^{-1} \dfrac{D}{L}$.

Incidentally, this result suggests a method, made use of in

practice, for obtaining from the gliding angle of a machine (or glider) the lift to drift ratio.

Case II. Acentric Types. Line of Propeller Thrust above Centre of Resistance (Fig. 3).—For equilibrium in this case, the weight-lift couple must balance the thrust-resistance couple—that is,

$$W \times x = T \times y.$$

If the engine stops, T will be zero, and the machine will be

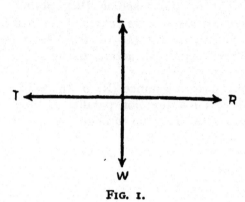

FIG. 1.

unbalanced. The weight-lift couple will then cause the nose of the machine to rise; the thrust being lost, the machine loses its flying speed, and the planes cease to support the weight, consequently a tail-dive occurs.

Case III. Line of Propeller Thrust below Centre of Resistance

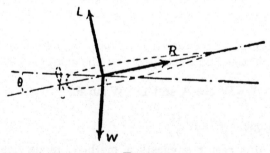

FIG. 2.

(Fig. 4).—As in Case II., the weight-lift couple must equal the thrust-resistance couple, and so

$$W \times x = T \times y.$$

An engine stoppage will, in this case, result in a nose dive, as the weight-lift couple acts so as to pull the nose of the machine down.

If the lines of thrust and resistance be not far apart—that is, do not exceed 2 feet in ordinary machines—the effects of engine stoppage may be counteracted by use of the rear elevator, moving same downwards in Case I. and upwards in Case II.

In many present-day machines the C.G. is below the C.R. by about 1 foot to 1 foot 6 inches.

Where the C.G. is very low, as in the " parasol " types of

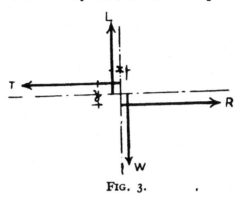

FIG. 3.

machine, " steadiness " is obtained at the expense of pitching and rolling with a fairly low period of movement, and the centrifugal effect of turning causes the weight to swing outwards like a pendulum.

In many present-day machines the centre of resistance is below

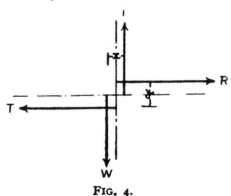

FIG. 4.

the centre of propeller thrust, in order to obtain sufficient propeller clearance from the ground under the worst landing conditions; there is also a stabilizing effect from the propeller.

In Case I. it was stated that for perfect equilibrium the lines of action of the weight and lift should coincide. This condition of equilibrium can only be true for one angle of incidence of the aerofoil, or wing, of present-day practice, since the position of the centre of pressure changes with the angle of incidence; the use of auxiliary surfaces, such as the longitudinal V-tail or rider plane arrangement, negative wing tips, etc., ensure a more or less steady position of the centre of pressure at all flying angles.

Some data for design purposes in connection with the stability of aeroplanes is given in the separate volume of this series, entitled "Stability and Control," in which the principles of stability are discussed, and corresponding particulars are furnished for the design of all control surfaces, etc.

In the case of the lines of action of the resistance and of thrust, these will only coincide at one particular angle of incidence, since the centre line of resistance varies with the angle of incidence and the speed.

CALCULATION OF THE POSITION OF RESULTANT FORCES.

It is necessary, in applying the principles already given to the case of an actual aeroplane, to be able to compute the exact positions of the centres of pressure, gravity, and head resistance respectively from a knowledge of the component forces acting in each case.

A concrete example will exemplify the method.

It is required to find the centre of (vertical) pressure of a complete aeroplane (Fig. 5) at a given speed and incidence. If the vertical forces due to the air pressures upon the component parts, such as the main planes, fuselage, tail planes, and elevator planes, be denoted by L_P, L_F, L_T, and L_E respectively, acting at distances X_P, X_F, X_T, and X_E from some given datum vertical line O O; then, by taking moments about O O, the following relation is obtained:

$$(L_P + L_F + L_T + L_E)X = L_P X_P + L_F X_F + L_T X_T + L_E X_E,$$

where X is the distance from O O of the line of action of the resultant vertical pressure.

That is—

$$\bar{X} = \frac{L_P X_P + L_F X_F + L_T X_T + L_E X_E}{L_P + L_F + L_T + L_E} = \frac{\Sigma L \cdot X}{\Sigma L};$$

or, is equal to the sum of the moments of the component forces, about O O, divided by the sum of the forces acting. It is assumed that the actual forces due to the air pressures at the given speed and incidence of the machine are obtainable from experimental data or by calculation.

This general method is equally applicable to the cases of centres of gravity and resistance respectively.

In estimating the positions of the C.G. and C.R. it is usually convenient to take some fixed plane, such as the engine-plate, fuselage end, or in the latter case the propeller-thrust line, fuselage top, etc., and to reckon all moments as positive to one side of the chosen plane and negative to the other; the moments should then be added algebraically, and divided by the total weight in order to obtain the position of the resultant force.

When considering the position of the C.G., allowance must be made for any variation in the loads themselves, due to such causes as an extra passenger being occasionally carried, the fuel consumption during a flight, release of bombs, etc.

It is usual to situate the passenger's seat and fuel tanks over the C.G. in order to preserve balance; and in the case of it being inconvenient to place the tanks over the C.G., for constructional

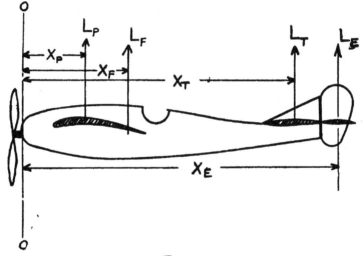

FIG. 5.

or other reasons, the tanks may be arranged on either side of the C.G., so that their distances are inversely proportional to their relative fuel consumptions.

In the case of air-cooled engines this ratio is about 5 : 1, and for water-cooled engines about 10 or 12 to 1. In all cases it should be arranged, if possible, for " variable " weights to be placed as near to the C.G. as possible. In the case of the petrol tank the variation in the position of the C.G. will be very serious if this point is not observed. An 80-h.p. engine requires 240 pounds of petrol for a six hours' flight, which is very nearly the weight of the engine, so that unless the C.G. of the tank and fuel be on the C.G. a difference in balance will occur as the fuel is used up.

THE GYROSCOPIC TORQUE OF ROTARY ENGINES.

When an aeroplane propelled by a rotary engine (that is, one in which the cylinders and crankcase revolve as a whole) is made to deviate from a straight course, a gyroscopic couple is called into play, which to some extent affects both the steering and the stresses upon the engine mounting.

The actual amount of the gyroscopic couple in most cases is small compared with the couples which can be brought into action by the warp or ailerons, and the effect upon the steering is comparable " with that produced by a small gust of known direction, and should cause no difficulty to the flyer," to use the words of the Monoplanes' Accidents Investigation Committee's Report of February 8, 1913.

In the case of a tractor machine, fitted with an engine which rotates anti-clockwise when viewed from the front of the machine, if the aeroplane makes a turn to the left hand (from the pilot's point of view) the effect of the gyroscopic couple, brought into action and due to the angular change in the plane of rotation of the engine, is to tend to bring the tail down or the nose up; a right-hand turn tends to bring the tail up and the nose down.

Again, when the aeroplane dives, the gyroscopic couple will cause a tendency to steer to the left-hand side, whilst an upward change in direction will give a right-hand steering tendency.

The amount of the gyroscopic torque called into play in any specific case depends upon the angular velocity of the change in position of the plane of rotation of the engine, and will also vary as the square of the radius of gyration of the engine about its axis of rotation, and with the mass of the engine.

Expressed symbolically,

$$\text{Gyroscopic torque} = I \, w \, \theta,$$

where I = moment of inertia of engine about its axis of rotation;
$\quad w$ = the angular speed of rotation of engine;
$\quad \theta$ = angular speed of movement of engine's plane of rotation.
This expression can be written in a more useful form thus:

$$\text{Gyroscopic torque} = 0 \cdot 0048 \, \frac{M \, V \, N \, k^2}{R},$$

where M = weight of engine in pounds;
$\quad V$ = velocity of aeroplane in feet per second;
$\quad k$ = radius of gyration of engine about axis of rotation expressed in feet.
$\quad N$ = revolutions per minute of engine;
$\quad R$ = radius of turning circle of aeroplane in feet.

Example.—In the case of a 100 h.p. Gnome engine weighing 290 pounds, and revolving at 1,200 revolutions per minute, the radius of gyration of the engine may be taken as 15 inches. If the aeroplane whilst travelling at 80 miles an hour turns in a circle of 300 feet radius, then the gyroscopic torque called into play will amount to 696 pounds feet.

In a biplane fitted with such an engine the torque which can be produced by the ailerons may reach 2,000 pounds feet, so that the gyroscopic torque (about the same axis) is well within the pilot's control.

THE PROPELLER TORQUE.

In considering the forces acting upon the framework of an aeroplane, the effect of the reactive propeller torque should be allowed for. In the case of similar twin propellers symmetrically situated, these torques may be easily balanced by making them revolve in contrary directions.

The amount of propeller torque acting when the engine is revolving uniformly is given by:

$$\text{Mean propeller torque in pounds feet} = 5{,}250 \cdot \frac{\text{H.P.}}{\text{N}},$$

where N =revolutions per minute and H.P. =horse-power of engine.

The reaction of the propeller torque is taken by the engine-bearers, which must therefore be made strong enough in torsion to resist not only the uniform torque, but sudden fluctuations in the torque due to the variation in the engine torque through misfiring, small number of cylinders, etc.

In the case of a 100 h.p. engine running at 1,250 revolutions per minute, the torque to be taken by the engine-bearers will be 420 pounds feet, which is less than the gyroscopic torque previously calculated.

It should be remembered that, more especially in the case of small horse-power engines, there is an appreciable torque caused through starting the engine by swinging the propeller. Thus, in the case of a mechanic exerting a pull of 40 pounds at a radius of 3 feet, the starting torque will be 120 pounds feet, and will act in the opposite sense to the reactive engine torque when running; a 35 h.p. engine running at 1,000 revolutions per minute gives a uniform torque equivalent to 184 pounds feet; the engine-bearer and fuselage must therefore be designed to take the torque in both directions.

The effect of the reaction of the torque upon the equilibrium of the aeroplane is to cause a banking couple, unless twin propellers are used. The amount of this couple is well within the pilot's control, and it is only its variation which requires attention.

Attempts are often made to counteract this torque reaction effect by introducing some kind of permanent surface fixed at an angle of incidence to the relative direction of travel, which will experience an air-pressure and give a twisting moment opposite in effect and amount to the reactive torque. Thus, an aileron, fin, or wing tip may be permanently flexed or tilted, or the whole tail unit given a twist, as proposed in one of Cody's patent specifications.

CHAPTER II

THE ESTIMATION OF AEROPLANE WEIGHTS

HAVING decided upon the type of machine required and the conditions of flight, such as the number of people to be carried, the fuel for a given number of hours' flight, the speed range, useful load, and other factors, it is always necessary for design purposes to estimate the weights of the various parts with a fair degree of accuracy, in order to fix the total weight and position of the C.G.

In a new-type machine these processes are largely a matter of prediction by analogy with existing machines, and of calculations

In all cases it is useful, and advisable, to check the weight of each finished part of the machine before assemblage, and to correct one's estimates with this information.

It is often advisable, in order to allow for errors in weight estimates, to provide for some adjustment of the positions of the C.G. and C.R. by the provision of adjustable pilot's or passengers' seats, fuel tanks, etc., and in some cases the exact position of the C.G. may be verified by the following method:

(a) Obtain by measurement or component weighing the weight of the whole loaded machine.

(b) Suspend from an accurate spring balance a point of the tail situated at a distance x (Fig. 6) from the point of contact of the wheels with the ground; then, if P be the spring-balance pull in pounds, say, and W the weight of machine in pounds, the distance y of the C.G. of the whole machine from the wheels is given by

$$y = \frac{P\,x}{W}.$$

From a knowledge of the weights per unit volume of various substances, and from the published weights given in the manufacturers' catalogues, the component weights may be fairly closely predicted.

It is usual first to make a rough lay-out of the proposed machine, showing approximately the positions assigned to the various parts; from this the total weight may be estimated and

9

the approximate position of the C.G. obtained. In connection
with the total estimated weight, it is advisable to allow an increase
of between 10 and 20 per cent.

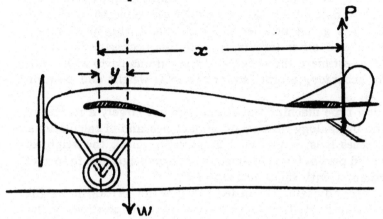

FIG. 6.—METHOD OF FINDING C.G. OF AN AEROPLANE.

From the estimated weight, the sizes of the wings and control
surfaces can be fixed more accurately, and by a process of trial
and error more exact weights may be estimated, and more correct
location of the C.G. will be possible.

DATA FOR WEIGHT ESTIMATES.

1. The Pilot's weight, in full flying kit, may be taken as being
from 160 to 180 pounds.

2. The Engine—(a) *Air-cooled Engines*.—These weights vary
with the type of motor, from 1·95 to 7·0 pounds per b.h.p.

In the case of the Gnome engine, the weight varies from 1·95
pounds in the 160 h.p. type up to 3·4 pounds in the 50 h.p. type.

For the stationary Anzani type, the weight varies from 3·4
pounds in the 200 h.p. model up to 4·72 pounds in the 25 h.p.
model.

A good average figure for the motor alone, in the absence of
exact data, is to allow 4·5 pounds per h.p. for sizes between
30 and 70 h.p., with a proportionate decrease to 3·5 pounds up to
200 h.p. types.

(b) *Water-cooled Engines*.—These engines are invariably heavier
than the corresponding sizes of air-cooled types, and the weight
varies from 3·0 up to 9·0 pounds per b.h.p.

A good average figure for the best types of water-cooled engine
is to take 5·75 pounds per h.p. for sizes between 30 and 70 h.p.

The higher horse-powered engines here also show a reduction
in the weight per h.p.

Thus, the 85 h.p. Benz motor, without radiator, weighs 4·3

pounds, the 100 h.p. type 4·25 pounds, and the 150 h.p. type 3·5 pounds per h.p.

In reckoning the weight of the engine unit, it is advisable to verify whether the manufacturer's figures include the weight of the flywheel, carburettor, magneto, starting device, piping, etc., as the published figures are generally upon the light side.

The weight of a good make of radiator may be taken as 0·75 pounds per h.p., and a magneto for a seven-cylinder engine weighs from 15 to 20 pounds complete.

In estimating water-cooled engine radiator weights, the weight of cooling water should be reckoned; the weight of cooling water per B.H.P. varies from ·300 pound in the case of very high horse-powered engines, to ·500 pound for low-powered engines. Good average figures to assume are as follows :

(a) For H.P. less than 50, weight of water per H.P. =0·500 pound.
(b)   ,,   ,, between 50 and 100 ,,   ,,   ,,   =0·400 ,,
(c)   ,,   ,, above 100,   ,,   ,,   ,,   —0·350 ,,

FUEL WEIGHTS.

For either petrol or benzole the fuel consumption per b.h.p. hour may be taken as:

1. For air-cooled engines, fixed type ..   =0·65 pound.
2. For air-cooled engines, rotary type ..   =0·70 ,,
3. For water-cooled engines   ..   =0·50

Oil consumption per b.h.p. hour:

1. For fixed air-cooled types (without auxiliary
    exhaust ports)   ..   ..   —0·10 pound.
2. For rotary air-cooled types (without auxiliary
    exhaust ports)   ..   ..   —0·25 ,
3. For water-cooled engines   ..   ..   ..   —0·05 ,

FUEL TANKS.

The weight of petrol tanks in copper is slightly heavier than those in tinned steel, but the following figures represent the average results of a large number of measurements:

1. Petrol Tanks, complete with filler and cock:

Weight per gallon capacity = 2·0 to 2·5 pounds for sizes up
                 to 10 gallons.
   ,,   ,, = 1·5 to 1·0 pounds for sizes from
                 10 gallons to 50 gallons.

2. The weight of oil tanks may be taken as being about 15 per cent. heavier than for petrol, but in many cases they are the same weight for the same capacity.

TOTAL MOTOR WEIGHTS.

It is always advisable, when considering the question of engine selection, to remember that for short flights the air-cooled engine is the lighter, in spite of its relatively heavier fuel consumption, but that for long journeys the better fuel economy of the water-cooled type enables a saving in the total power unit weight to be effected.

In considering the weight of the power unit of the machine, which includes the engine, tanks, fuel, and engine mounting, it is often useful to tabulate the available data somewhat in the manner indicated in Table I., in order that the weight for a given h.p. and period of flight may be rapidly determined.

The data given refers to the engine, fuel, tank, and engine-mounting weights. The engine is considered to be working at full power in each case.

The engine weights, unless otherwise stated, include the radiator and magneto, but in the case of the Green engine the optional flywheel weight is included.

ENGINE FITTINGS.

Engine plates and bearers vary considerably in weight, and depend largely upon the fuselage design. An engine plate for a fixed radial type of from 40 to 70 h.p. weighs from 10 to 20 pounds, inclusive of bolts, bracing, and struts; for a radial rotary type this figure varies from 15 to 30 pounds, and the weight goes up approximately as the square root of the h.p. of engine.

The weight of the engine shield or " cowling " also varies as the square root of the h.p., and is about twice as great for rotary as for fixed type engines. Thus, for a 50 h.p. fixed radial engine the " cowling " weight would be about 12 pounds, whereas for a rotary type of the same h.p. the weight would be from 20 to 24 pounds.

An approximate figure for the engine-mounting weight is to take one-eighth of the engine weight for a rotary type and one-twelfth the engine weight for a fixed type engine.

PROPELLER WEIGHTS.

The weight of a 7 feet 6 inch diameter two-bladed propeller for a 50 to 70 h.p. engine varies from 15 to 18 pounds, and goes up as the square root of the h.p. for other engines.

A good rule for approximate purposes is to take the propeller weight W as:

$$W = 2 \cdot 5 \sqrt{\text{h.p.}}$$

The weights of 3- and 4-bladed propellers are in proportion to the number of blades for the same h.p. Thus, a 3-bladed propeller of 7 feet 6 inches diameter weighs from 24 to 32 pounds.

TABLE I.—MOTOR UNIT WEIGHTS.

Type of M.	Max. B.H.P.	R. per Min.	Weight in lb.			Tanks for One Hour's Fuel + Engine Mounting.	Total Weight for Flight of—		
			Motor Complete.	Petrol per Hour.	Oil per Hour.		Two h.	Six Hours.	Ten h.
						lbs.	lb.	lb.	lbs.
70-h.p. Renault, air-cooled	72	1,800*	350	49	5·0	70	550	830	,900
100-h.p. Renault, air-cooled	110	1,800*	640	70	9·5	110	930	1,280	1,650
60 to 65-h.p. Anzani, air-cooled	65	1,250	250	36	12·0	65	420	640	850
125-h.p. Anzani	125	1,250	470	68	20·0	97	770	1,150	1,560
200-h.p. Anzani	200	1,250	690	105	30·0	130	1,120	1 0	2,300
50-h.p. Gnome (air-cooled)†	40	1,200	170	36	10·0	70	350	580	810
80-h.p. Gnome†	67	1,200	200	54	16·0	85	450	800	1,140
100-h.p. et	95	1,200	290	70	20·0	110	610	1,030	1,450
160-h.p. et	145	1,200	340	110	29·0	150	790	1,420	2,030
80-h.p. Le Rhone	85	1,200	250	61	18·0	95	500	880	1,250
30 to 35 h.p. Green‡	40	,900	225§	21	4·0	55	340	0	1, 00
50 to 60-h.p. Green‡	65	,900	400§	39	6·0	68	570	800	1,490
90 to 100 h.p. Green‡	110	,900	580§	60	10·0	90	830	1,150	1,570
120 h.p. Austro-Daimler‡	125	1,200	600	68	6·0	100	870	1,220	1,420
100-h.p. Benz‡	0	1,200	540	60	6·0	100	800	1, 0	1,420
90-h.p. Salmson†	85	1,250	450	54	6·0	85	0	0	1,130
200-h.p. Salmson†	210	1,250	900	115	10·0	150	1,320	1,880	2,450
300-h.p. Salm†	310	1,250	1,350	160	15·0	186	1,920	2,720	3,500
135-h.p. Sunbeam†	135	2,000*	590	80	14·0	105	90	1,370	1,790
90-h.p. Wolseley†	90	1,800*	480	60	10·0	90	720	1 90	1,400
150-h.p. N.A.G.‡	150	1,300	800	85	16·0	108	1,140	1 0	0

* Propeller driven off cam shaft at half engine speed.   † Rotary air-cooled hp.   ‡ Water-cooled hp.

§ Weight includes flywheel, magneto, and radiator.

AEROPLANE WING WEIGHTS.

From the design of a wing, it is an easy matter to calculate the weight of the components, and to allow from 10 to 20 per cent increase for unforeseen additions.

The following table gives the weights of the wings of a few typical machines of standard practice. These weights are in-clusive of all internal clips, bracing, strut and cable clips, fabric, etc.

TABLE II.—WING WEIGHTS.

Type.	Wing Area in Sq. Ft.	Wing Weight in Lbs.
(1) 80-h.p. monoplane	204	176
(2) 80-h.p. ,, ..	175	154
(3) 50-h.p. ,, ..	150	110
(4) 70-h.p. ,, ..	215	120
(5) 80-h.p. biplane, scout ..	220	{ top plane = 88 { lower ,, = 54
(6) 100-h.p. biplane, single seater	250	{ top ,, = 90 { lower , = 70
(7) 70-h.p. biplane, two-seater ..	350	{ top ,, = 190 { lower , = 120
(8) 70-h.p. biplane, two-seater..	400	{ top ,, = 100 { lower ,, = 80

From these figures it will be seen that the wing weight varies from about 0·5 up to about 1·0 pound per square foot of wing area.

The wing weight varies, approximately as the span, in similar types of machine, and in different types as the wing loading per square foot of surface. In the examples given the loading is about the same in each class, but about 30 per cent. greater for the monoplane class.

An instance is given in the Advisory Committee's Report, 1911-12, of a certain biplane of about 1,000 pounds body weight, the area of the upper wing of which is 180 square feet, and its weight 190 pounds, of which 30 pounds is accounted for by the fabric.

From this it follows that the weight of similar wings, exclusive of the fabric, is given by

$$W_1 = 12 \sqrt{A} \text{ pounds where } A = \text{area in square feet,}$$

and inclusive of the fabric by

$$W_2 = 12 \sqrt{A} + \frac{A}{6}.$$

From a consideration of the stresses in similarly loaded wings, the following formulæ have been deduced for the weight of aeroplane wings:

(a) Weight of Monoplane Wing: $w = 0.017 \ W \sqrt{A} + 0.16 \ A$;

(b) Weight of Biplane Wing: $w = 0.012 \ W \sqrt{A} + 0.16 \ A$,

where W = the body weight of the machine in pounds (that is, the total less the wing weight) and A = the area in square feet of the wings. It will be seen from these relations that monoplane wings weigh from 30 to 40 per cent. more than biplane wings; the second term represents the fabric weight in the above expressions.

WEIGHT OF FABRICS.

The weight of undoped aeroplane fabric varies from 3 to 8 ounces per square yard (single), according to its quality and strength—the heavier seaplane fabrics approach the higher figure, whilst lightly loaded biplane fabrics give the lower figure. For doped and varnished fabric the weight varies from 7 ounces to 1 pound per square yard. A good figure to take is 0.7 pound per square yard single surface.

A useful number used by the French designers is 0.5 kilogramme per square metre for single surface. The weight of four coats of ordinary dope, including the finishing varnish, is about 4 ounces per square yard.

WEIGHT OF CONTROL SURFACES.

The methods of construction for the rudder, elevators, tail, etc., are necessarily lighter than those for the wings. The results of a number of measurements give the following data:

For wooden structures: $w = 0.3$ to 0.5 pound per square foot,
For steel structures: $w = 0.5$ to 0.7 pound per square foot,

inclusive of all clips, fittings, and control arms. All-metal frames weigh about 10 to 15 per cent. more than all-wood ones.

FUSELAGE WEIGHTS.

It is not possible to give exact figures for the fuselage, as the weights will vary with the type of machine, number of passengers, h.p. of engine, and type.

Fuselage weights vary from about 60 pounds in the case of light scouts and monoplanes to 200 pounds for large, high-powered biplanes carrying large loads.

A rough average figure of 85 pounds may be taken for small biplanes and monoplanes of about 700 pounds net weight, and 100 pounds for ordinary monoplanes with engines up to 80 h.p., and 1,000 pounds net weight. For two-seater biplanes up to 1,600 pounds net weight 150 pounds is a good working figure.

It is a fairly easy matter to compute the weights of any particular type of fuselage from its dimensions and design. The above figures apply only to the long fuselage type, in which the engine, pilot and passenger, and the rudder, elevators, and tail planes are all carried on the same structure, and not by outriggers as in the Farman, Caudron, and other machines; further, the fuselage weights include all clips and fittings, seats, instrument boards, engine bearers and coverings, engine cowls, etc., but not the tanks and landing chassis, engine, and propeller.

For hydroplane fuselages of copper-sewn mahogany, metal sheathing, etc., the weights are higher; thus a 100 h.p. machine weighing loaded 2,200 pounds will have a " body " weight of between 180 and 240 pounds.

If the fuselage be considered as a girder loaded downwards with the various component weights, such as the engine, fuselage itself, control planes, and supported at the C P's of the wings and tail planes, it follows that the weight of similar fuselages of equal strength will vary as $\dfrac{W \cdot l}{b \cdot d^2}$, where w = the total weight of machine less the wing weights, l = the fuselage length, b its breadth, and d its depth.

In the case of a biplane $W = 1,500$, $d = 27$ feet, $b = 2$ feet, and $d = 2$ feet 6 inches, and the weight $wf = 130$ pounds, from which is obtained the formula for estimating the weights of similar fuselages:

$$wf = \frac{1}{27} \cdot \frac{W \cdot l}{b \, d^2}.$$

LANDING CHASSIS.

As in the case of the fuselage, the weight depends largely upon the design, and therefore it should, where possible, be estimated or checked from the design.

In the case of the Bleriot type of undercarriage the weight for an 80 h.p. machine is about 95 pounds, whilst for the simplest type of V undercarriage, consisting of five ash struts, a pair of 26-inch diameter wheels, and steel axle, the weight can be reduced to about 55 or 60 pounds.

The undercarriage weight will vary with the total machine weight, and with the lowest landing speed. It may be fairly correctly assumed, however, that in well-designed machines the total machine weight and the lowest landing speed will vary as the square root of the h.p.

This leads to the relation for the undercarriage weight— namely:

$$w = 9\sqrt{\text{h.p.}},$$

which will be found to give fairly correct results.

In estimating the weights of undercarriages, the following table of wheel weights (Table III.) will be found useful. The weights given are for the weights of fully inflated tyres complete for fixture to the chassis axles:

TABLE III.—WEIGHT OF PALMER AEROPLANE WHEELS.

Size of Tyre.	Weight complete, with Shields.
600 × 75 mm.	.. 9 lbs. 13 ozs.
700 × 75 mm.	.. 12 lbs. 7 ozs.
750 × 125 mm.	.. 21 lbs. 3 ozs.
800 × 150 mm.	.. 23 lbs. 1 oz.

INSTRUMENT WEIGHTS.

The weights of the instruments usually carried upon aeroplanes should be taken into account; the total weight varies from 12 to 20 pounds, being on the average 2 pounds per instrument. In a specific case the total weight of revolution counter, air-speed recorder, altitude meter, compass, inclinometer, clock, oil and petrol gauges, was exactly 16 pounds 2 ounces.

MISCELLANEOUS WEIGHTS.

In the tables given at the end of the book will be found data for estimating the weights of the various parts from a knowledge of the design and materials used; the weight tables of strainers, piano-wires, cables, metal sheets, steel and aluminium tubing, etc., will also be found useful in the above connection.

Although the weight of an individual strainer, small clip, or bolt is not in itself appreciable, yet when the total number of these parts in the machine be taken into consideration the total weight may become important.

EXAMPLE OF AEROPLANE COMPONENT WEIGHTS.

The figures given below are for a typical case of a biplane of wing area 340 square feet and engine h.p. = 70, fitted with seating for two people:

(A) Dead Loads.   *Weight in pounds.*

70 h.p. engine, complete with radiator pipes and all accessories	410
40 gallon petrol and oil tank	40
Upper wing, with clips	100
Lower wing, with clips	85
Control surfaces	35
Fuselage, complete with engine-bearers, seats, controls, and fittings, instruments, etc.	140
Landing chassis and tail skid	80
Miscellaneous:	
Propeller and plates	17
52 strainers	6
240 feet cable	14
80 feet of struts	56
Clips and fittings, piano-wire, and bolts ..	25
Total dead load ..	1,008

(B) Live Loads.

Petrol for six hours' flight..	240
Oil for six hours' flight	20
Passenger and pilot..	320
	580

Then—   Dead load = 1,008 pounds.
                Useful load = 580   ,,

Total   1,588 pounds.

The useful load carried by a well-designed aeroplane varies from about 0·25 to 0·40 of the total weight of the machine, the useful load being taken to include the live loads, as defined above.

CHAPTER III

GENERAL DESIGN CONSIDERATIONS AND DATA

General Characteristics.

It is desirable that an aeroplane should possess the following qualities:

1. It should be efficient—that is, it should be able to carry the maximum load for a given distance with the least expenditure of energy. Expressed symbolically, the ratio $\dfrac{\text{Weight} \times \text{Velocity}}{\text{Horse Power}}$ should be as large as possible, consistent with the usual factors of safety adopted.
2. It should have a low minimum safe flying speed and a large speed range, and, further, the maximum flying speed should be aerodynamically safe.
3. It should be stable under all conditions of the weather.
4. It should exhibit a good climbing rate.
5. It should be capable of being easily controlled and flown, with the least expenditure of physical energy upon the part of the pilot.
6. It should possess a good gliding angle, in order to obtain, from a given height, the maximum available alighting area.

Further minor requirements are that it should be easily dismantled and re-erected for transporting, silent when in flight, all parts should be weatherproof, it should be able to rise from " plough " land quickly, and should be provided with landing brakes.

Special Characteristics.

These will depend upon the purpose for which the machine is designed. Examples of these special qualities for certain types of machine are given below:

1. *Scouting Aeroplane.*—Designed to carry pilot only at a high speed, with a high climbing rate. Capable of being started and manipulated single-handed. Built very light; good distance range. (Fig. 7, *A*.)

19

2. *Reconnaissance Aeroplane.*—Designed to carry passenger and pilot, with signalling appliances, fuel capacity for a wide radius of action, large speed range for reconnaissance at a minimum speed, able to land and get off from rough ground, silent and as invisible as possible,

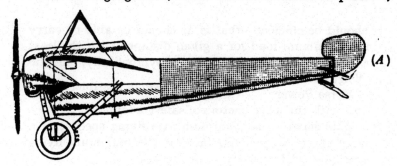

(A)

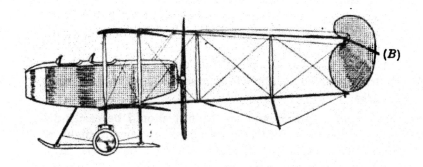

(B)

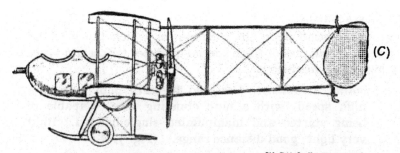

(C)

["*Flight.*" *Copyright.*]
FIG. 7.—TYPES OF AEROPLANES.

both on ground and in the air, wide field of view, stable, easily transported, and weather-proof.　(Fig. 7, *B*).

3. *Fighting Aeroplane.*—Designed to carry pilot and gunner, quickfiring gun (preferably in front), or bombs, for overtaking other machines and destroying, high speed, good

field of fire and vision, armoured on sides and beneath vital parts, as, for example, the pilot, engine and tanks; it should also be silent.   (Fig. 7, *C*.)

4. *Hydroplanes.*—Designed to carry pilot, passenger, and fuel

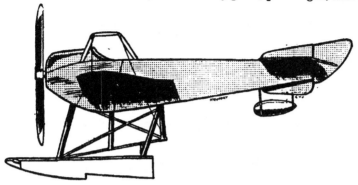

The 100 h.p. Nieuport seaplane.

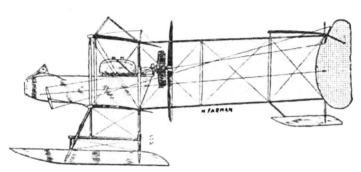

The 80 h.p. H. Farman seaplane.

The 200 h.p. Sopwith flying boat.

["*Flight.*" *Copyright.*
Fig. 8.—Types of Aeroplanes.

for a wide radius of action, capable of alighting on and getting off from fairly rough seas, seaworthy and protected against external influences, easily dismantled and stowed away.   (Fig. 8.)

Machines accepted by the British Military Authorities must fulfil the following conditions (March, 1914):

Military Tests for Aeroplanes.

1. The Chief Inspector of Military Aeronautics is prepared, at the request of an aeroplane constructor, to put an aeroplane through the ordinary military acceptance test under the following conditions:

(1) The test consists of examination of workmanship and materials, speed test, fast and slow, climbing, weight of load carried, rolling test, and one hour's flight. The constructor must supply the pilot and passenger. For purposes of calculation weights of pilot and passenger will be 160 pounds each.

(2) Stress diagrams in duplicate for the aeroplane must be sent with or before the machine. A minimum factor of safety of 6 throughout is essential.

(3) No machine will be tested for military purposes unless it fulfils the conditions of one of the types used for military purposes. These are given in attached table.

(4) The instructor, when applying to have his machine tested, should state his reasonable expectation of the performances of the machine.

(5) Aeroplanes submitted for test must be put through the whole of the tests unless damaged before their completion, or unless the Chief Inspector considers that the tests should be stopped for reasons of safety.

2. The Chief Inspector of Military Aeronautics is also prepared to examine and test aeroplanes which may be designed not for purely military purposes, but to demonstrate some practical or theoretical improvement in design of construction. The tests imposed in such cases will be at the discretion of the Chief Inspector.

3. Results of any test will be supplied to the constructor by the Chief Inspector, and will be kept secret, if desired by the constructor. Should the constructor wish to publish the result of the test, it is to be understood that the result should be published complete. Should only part of any report of the test be published, the Chief Inspector reserves the right to publish it in full.

4. The satisfactory performance of the tests laid down in paragraph 1 does not constitute a guarantee that the aeroplane in question will be purchased by Government.

5. These tests may be altered from time to time; notice will be given as early as possible of any alteration.

TABLE IV.—STANDARD

	Light Scout.	Reconnaissance Aeroplane (A).	Reconnaissance Aeroplane (B).	Fighting A plane (A).	Fighting Aeroplane (B).
Tankage to give an ... of ..	300 mls	300 mls	oo mls	oo mls	300 miles
To carry ..	Pilot only	Pilot and observer, *plus* 80 lb. for wireless equipment	Pilot and r..r, *plus* 80 lbs. for wireless ...	Pilot and gunner, *plus* 300 lbs. for gun and ammunition	Pilot and gunner, *plus* 300 lbs.
Range of	50 to 85 m.p.h.	45 to 75 m.p.h.	35 to 60 m.p.h.	45 to 65 m.p.h.	45 to 75 m.p.h.
To climb 3,500 ft. in	5 mins	7 · mts	10 mins	10 mins	8 ms
Miscellaneous qualities	Capable o being started by the pilot sing e-...		To land over a 30-ft. vertical obstacle, and pull up within a ... of 100 yds. from that obstacle the wind not being more than 15 m.p.h. A very good view ...	A ... field of fire in every li... up to 30 degrees from the line of fight	A ... field o fire in every direction up to 30 ... from the line o flight

Note.—Instructional aeroplanes with an endurance of 150 miles will also be ...ted ... special ... tions; safety and ease o handling will be of fir t importance in this type

Wing Loading.

The weight of an aeroplane is governed largely by its special function, and having once been estimated as correctly as possible, the wing area for supporting this load can be obtained as follows:

If C_L be the absolute lift coefficient corresponding with the section of wing chosen from speed range, power, etc., considerations,

$$\text{then } W = C_L \cdot \frac{\rho}{g} \cdot A \cdot V^2, \text{ where}$$

W = weight of machine, fully loaded, in pounds;

ρ = density of the air in pounds per cubic foot = 0·0807 pound at 32° F.;

g = acceleration due to gravity in feet per second = 32·18;

A = area of wings in square feet;

V = velocity corresponding to normal flying angles (usually between 3 degrees and 5 degrees) in feet per second.

The value of the constant $\frac{\rho}{g}$ is 0·00236, or $\frac{1}{424}$. If the velocity V be expressed in miles per hour, the value of the constant becomes 0·00510, or $\frac{1}{196}$.

In order to facilitate calculations, values of $\frac{\rho}{g} \cdot V^2$, referred to as " conversion factors," have been calculated, and are given in a table at the end of the book.

It is then only necessary to multiply the absolute lift coefficient by the area and by the conversion factor corresponding to the chosen speed, in order to obtain the load lifted.

$$\text{The wing loading per square foot} = \frac{W}{A} = C_L \cdot \frac{\rho}{g} \cdot V^2$$

$$= C_L \times \text{Conversion Factor.}$$

METRIC UNITS.

If W be in kilogrammes, A in square metres, V in metres per second, and further, if ρ be the density of 1 cubic metre in kilo. grammes, and g be expressed in metres per second,

$$\text{then } g = 9·81, \text{ and } \rho = 1·25,$$

so that $W = C_L \cdot \frac{1·25}{9·81} \cdot A \cdot V^2$ where C_L is the absolute lift coefficient, as before.

(The lift and drift coefficients K_y and K_x employed by Eiffel in his published results can be converted into absolute coefficients by multiplying them each by 8·0.

Thus $C_L = \frac{1·25}{9·81} K_y = 8·0 \ K_y$ and $C_D = 8·0 \ K_x$.)

* The density at other temperatures is given in a table at the end of this book.

TABLE V.—LIFT COEFFICIENTS FOR 1,000 POUNDS LOAD.

Speed in M.P.H.	30	40	50	60	70	80	90	100	110	120	130
Speed in Ft. per Sec.	44	58·7	73·4	88	102·8	117·4	132	146·8	161·4	176	190·8
Areas in Sq. Ft.											
150	1·460	0·8210	0·5240	0·3660	·678	0·2057	0·1624	0·1316	0·1090	0·0911	0·0778
175	1·250	0·7020	0·4485	0·3138	0·2294	0·1762	0·1391	0·1130	0·0931	0·0784	·666
200	1·095	0·6140	0·3930	0·2742	·910	0·1542	0·1220	0·0971	0·0816	·685	0·0585
225	0·9740	0·5470	0·3495	0·2441	0·1787	0·1370	0·1083	0·0876	0·0724	·68	0·0520
250	0·8770	0·4810	0·3142	0·2198	0·1606	0·1234	0·0974	0·0790	0·0651	0·0547	0·0469
275	0·7960	0·4465	0·2857	0·1995	0·1459	0·1120	0·0885	0·0716	0·0592	0·0497	0·0424
300	0·7307	0·4100	0·2622	0·1831	0·1341	0·1030	0·0813	0·0659	0·0544	0·0456	0·0389
325	0·6738	0·3780	0·2421	0·1691	0·1236	0·0949	0·0749	0·0606	0·0502	0·0421	0·0359
350	0·6250	0·3513	0·2244	0·1569	0·1147	0·0881	0·0696	0·0563	0·0466	0·0390	0·0334
375	0·5840	0·3278	0·2100	0·1463	0·1071	0·0823	0·0649	0·0526	0·0434	0·0364	0·0312
400	0·5478	0·3075	0·1969	0·1373	0·1006	0·0772	0·0610	0·0494	0·0408	0·0342	0·0292

CALCULATION OF WEIGHTS, AREAS, AND SPEEDS.

In order to facilitate the process of the selection of wing areas to suit different conditions of loads and speeds, the curves in Fig. 9, and the values in Table V., are given, and have been calculated from the relation—

$$C_L = \frac{W \cdot g}{A \cdot \rho \cdot V^2}.$$

There are four possible variable factors in this relation, namely, the load, area, velocity, and lift coefficient; if any three are known, the fourth can be at once ascertained.

Example 1.—Required the wing area to support a load of 1,000 pounds at a speed of 80 miles per hour for the Bleriot XI.A section wing having a lift coefficient of 0·159 at 2·0 degrees incidence.

From the table it will be seen that this value for $C_L = 0·159$ gives a wing area of about 195 square feet.

Example 2.—Required the speed necessary to support an aeroplane of 800 pounds weight, with a wing area of 175 square feet, and for which at the normal flying angle of 4 degrees $C_L = 0·314$.

The speed for 1,000 pounds weight will be seen from the table to be about 60 miles per hour, and therefore the speed corresponding to 800 pounds weight will be $60 \sqrt{\dfrac{800}{1000}} = 54$ miles per hour.

GENERAL USES OF TABLE V. AND FIG. 9.

For properly defined conditions of loading, speed, and wing area, this table enables one to select the proper wing sections which give the required values of the lift coefficient.

Values of C_L for all known types of wings vary from $C_L = 0·00$ at 0 degree, or a small negative angle of incidence, to $C_L = 0·80$ in the extreme cases at angles of incidence of about 10 or 14 degrees, and the range of values for C_L chosen must lie between these limits, and, further, must not be associated with any unstable position of the centre of pressure, or with the value of the lift coefficient at the critical angle of incidence (usually beyond 14 degrees), at which C_L becomes less.

Obviously the values given in Table V. for C_L, which are greater than 0·80, are inapplicable to all ordinary types of aeroplane wing of the present day.

For further information upon the subject of wing sections, lift and drift coefficients, and wing selection for design purposes, the reader is referred to the volume of this series entitled " The Properties of Wing Sections and the Resistance of Bodies," to Eiffel's works, and to the Advisory Committee's Reports.

The speed range of a machine can be roughly estimated from

6·0   7·0   8·0   9·0   10·0

er square foot.

To face page 26.

LATION CHART.

the table; thus, if the wing section chosen gives values of C_L of 0·097 at +0·5 degree incidence, and 0·481 at 12 degrees incidence, and, further, if these extreme flying angles are aerodynamically sufficiently " safe," then for a wing area of 250 square feet and load of 1,000 pounds, the range of speeds (from the table) will be 40 to 90 miles per hour; numerous other examples of the application of the table might be given.

The maximum speed theoretically obtainable will depend upon whether for the chosen load, the horse-power corresponding to the included engine weight is sufficient to overcome the head resistance, after allowing for the propeller " inefficiency "; this subject is further considered later on.

THE APPLICATION OF THE RESULTS OF MODEL TESTS TO FULL-SIZED MACHINES.

It is of great importance to know how far the results of wind-tunnel tests upon model aeroplane wings are applicable to the full-sized machine; the models are generally made from one-tenth to one-twentieth of the full size, and the wind-tunnel speeds have usually been considerably lower than the true flying speeds of the machines themselves. The wind-tunnel speeds vary from 25 to 45 miles per hour (although the latest wind tunnels give higher speeds), whilst the full-sized machines have flying speeds varying from 45 to 125 miles per hour.

In his earlier researches, Eiffel, with the limited data at his disposal, found that the performances of actual machines could be fairly accurately predicted by increasing both the lift and the drift coefficients by 10 per cent.; this correction being based upon the results of measurements of the normal pressure upon flat plates of different area, the normal pressure coefficients varying from 0·576 in smaller planes to 0·640 for large planes. It should be here mentioned that the wind tunnel and the actual aeroplane speeds were not the same, the former being the slower. Eiffel's later experiments upon models of aeroplanes, when compared with the results worked out from readings of recording instruments placed upon aeroplanes exactly similar to the models, flying in still air, showed that the lift and drift coefficients agreed within 1 per cent., when the speeds (15 to 17 metres per second) were about the same.

The model was here tested at the same speed as the aeroplane readings were taken; other comparisons between scale and actual machines showed the same results.

In the case of the Tatin and Nieuport machines, it was found that the lift/drift ratio was greater than that of the model, owing, no doubt, to increase of speed in the former case.

Tests made at the N.P.L. indicate that the lift coefficients of models may be applied without correction to the full-sized machine, but that the drift coefficients of the model may be

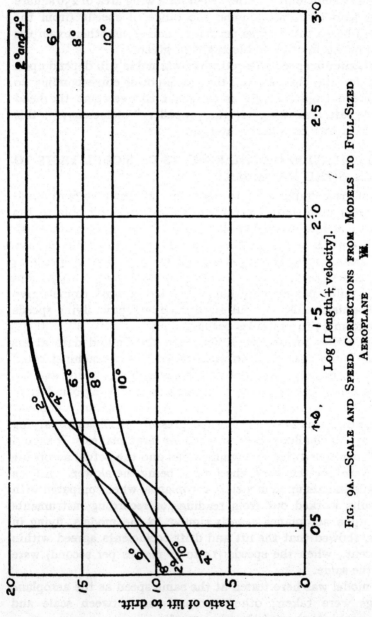

FIG. 9A.—SCALE AND SPEED CORRECTIONS FROM MODELS TO FULL-SIZED AEROPLANE 🌳.

expected to be from 15 to 20 per cent. too great at the angle of maximum lift/drift, the difference being smaller at the other angles.

It has been demonstrated that the results of model tests may be applied to full-sized machines, if the product $\dfrac{V \cdot L}{r}$ is the same in the two cases, where V is the velocity, L the length, and r is the ratio $\dfrac{\text{viscosity}}{\text{density}}$ (or the kinematic viscosity) for the fluid or medium in which the model or full-sized machine is tested. If both are tested in air, then the product $L \cdot V$ should be the same for each case.

The results of N.P.L. investigations upon the effects of model size and speed are shown in Fig. 9A, and the curves shown may be regarded as conversion factors from which the lift/drift of the full-sized machine may be estimated from the model tests.

The difference in the drift coefficients of scale and full-sized machines is probably due to the lower skin friction of the latter, for it is known that the skin friction of surfaces both in air and water decreases with increase in area and speed.

In applying corrections to model results for the full-sized machine, it must be remembered that insufficient experimental data has as yet been accumulated in this direction.

WING-LOADING DATA.

In current practice the wing loading expressed in pounds per square foot for biplanes is about $0 \cdot 0005\ V^2$, and for monoplanes is about $0 \cdot 007\ V^2$ where V is the maximum designed speed in feet per second.

Light loadings correspond with large wing areas for a given load, and generally necessitate larger engine powers to fly at a given high speed, but give a larger margin of safety against excessive loadings due to manœuvring, wind gusts, etc.

In biplanes the loading varies from values as low as $2 \cdot 6$ up to the limiting value of about $7 \cdot 0$ pounds per square foot, the average value being about $4 \cdot 5$.

For monoplanes the loading varies from $4 \cdot 5$ up to $9 \cdot 0$ for normal type machines, a good average figure being $5 \cdot 5$.

The 1913 Gordon-Bennett Deperdussin monoplane of 107 square feet wing area, and 1,500 pounds weight, fitted with a 160 h.p. engine, gave a wing loading of $14 \cdot 0$, and another machine, the 100 h.p. Ponnier, gave a wing loading of $12 \cdot 75$, the speeds attained in both cases being well over 100 miles per hour. These loadings, however, are quite exceptional for normal flight conditions in ordinary machines.

For hydroplanes of the normal type, the average wing loading figure is about $4 \cdot 8$.

Values of wing loading are given for various types of machine in Table VI.

TABLE VI.—TYPICAL WING LOADINGS.

MONOPLANES.

Type.	Max. Speed, M.P.H.	Min. Speed, M.P.H.	Wing Area in Sq. Ft.	Total Load in Lbs.	Wing Loading per Sq.Ft in Lbs.
2-seater, 80-h.p. Gnome	70	40	252	1,500	5·90
2-seater, 80-h.p. Gnome	72		248	1,388	5·60
1-seater, 50-h.p. Gnome	70		194	927	4·80
2-seater, 100-h.p. Mercedes	65		407	1,870	4·60
2-seater, 50-h.p. Gnome	58		236	1,200	5·10
2-seater, 80-h.p. Gnome	70	50	200	1,887	9·40
1-seater, 60-h.p. Le Rhone	84		156	947	6·10
1-seater,100-h.p.Gnome	100	—	86	1,100	12·75

BIPLANES.

Type.	Max. Speed, M.P.H.	Min. Speed, M.P.H.	Wing Area in Sq. Ft.	Total Load in Lbs.	Wing Loading per Sq.Ft in Lbs.
2-seater, 100-h.p. Mercedes	70	40	500	2,240	4·48
1-seater, 80-h.p. Gnome	95	35	235	1,165	4·95
2-seater, 80-h.p. Gnome	65	35	468	1,800	3·85
2-seater, 70-h.p. Renault	72	42	360	1,530	4·25
2-seater, 80-h.p. Gnome	62	40	390	1,930	4·85
2-seater, 80-h.p. Gnome	62	33	420	1,665	4·00
2-seater, 100-h.p. Mercedes	68	40	520	2,200	4·25
2-seater, 80-h.p. Gnome	62	—	378	1,800	4·75
2-seater, 70-h.p. Renault	65	—	560	1,980	3·54
1-seater, 80-h.p. Gnome	92	36	244	1,050	4·30
2-seater,100-h.p.Gnome	100	45	270	1,200	4·45
2-seater, 50-h.p. Gnome	65	—	270	850	3·14

WATERPLANES.

Type.	Max. Speed, M.P.H.	Min. Speed, M.P.H.	Wing Area in Sq. Ft.	Total Load in Lbs.	Wing Loading per Sq.Ft in Lbs.
Tractor biplane, 2-seater,150-h.p.Sunbeam	70	—	600	2,800	4·66
Tractor biplane, 2-seater, 135-h.p. Salmson	75	45	464	2,200	4·74
Tractor biplane, 2-seater, 120-h.p. Austro-Daimler	85	45	450	2,240	4·97
Pusher biplane, 2-seater, 80-h.p. Gnome	60	—	460	2,000	4·35
Tractor biplane, 2-seater, 100-h.p. Gnome	85	45	290	1,800	6·20
Tractor biplane, 2-seater, 100-h.p. Gnome	80	60	350	2,190	6·26
Bat-boat, 2-seater, 200-h.p. Sunbeam	75	48	600	3,180	5·30
Aero-boat, 2-seater, 60-h.p. Wright	60	38	430	1,800	4·20

MONOPLANES AND BIPLANES.

It will be seen from the foregoing considerations that the wing loading of monoplanes is generally higher than that of biplanes for the same performances; both types can, however, be designed quite satisfactorily as regards strength and stability, but each type of construction has its own peculiar advantages, which may be enumerated as follows:

Monoplane.

1. Possesses a lower head resistance due to the absence of separate struts, ties, etc., and thus higher speeds are capable of being attained upon this account; the most successful racing machines have hitherto been monoplanes.

2. More easily controlled, and therefore require less physical exertion on the pilot's part; this is chiefly owing to the relatively smaller moments of inertia about axes of symmetry.

3. More efficient than biplanes in effective lifting capacity, on account of absence of interference with the second plane (as in a biplane).

4. Cannot be made in very large sizes, on account of the excessive wing weights, etc.; the largest monoplanes in use have wing areas varying from 240 to 280 square feet, the usual sizes being from 150 to 200 square feet.

5. Can be easily packed and transported.

During 1912, as a result of a number of accidents to monoplanes, a Government Committee instituted an inquiry into the causes of these accidents.

In the Report issued it was made clear that the accidents were not due to any causes connected with this type of machine, and that the monoplane could be made just as strong as the biplane; the following are the chief conclusions of the Report:

1. The accidents to monoplanes specially investigated were not due to causes dependent on the class of machine to which they occurred, nor to conditions singular to the monoplane as such.

2. After considerations of general questions affecting the relative security of monoplanes and biplanes, the Committee have found no reason to recommend the prohibition of the use of monoplanes, provided that certain

---

* *Vide Aeronautics* (March, 1913), " Report of the Government Committee on Monoplane Accidents."

precautions are taken, some of which are applicable to both classes of aeroplane.

3. The wings of aeroplanes can, and should, be so designed as to have sufficient strength to resist drift without external bracing.

4. The main wires should not be brought to parts of the machine always liable to be severely strained on landing.

5. Main wires and warping wires should be so secured as to minimize the risk of damage in getting off the ground, and should be protected from accidental injury.

6. Main wires and their attachments should be duplicated. The use of a tautness indicator to avoid overstraining the wires in " tuning up " is recommended. Quick release devices should be carefully considered and tested before their use is permitted.

7. In view of the grave consequences which may follow fracture of any part of the engine, especially in the case of a rotary engine, means should be taken to secure that a slight damage to the engine will not wreck the machine. Structural parts, the breakage of which may involve total collapse of the machine, should, so far as possible, be kept clear of the engine.

8. The fabric, more especially in highly loaded machines, should be more securely fastened to the ribs. Devices which will have the effect of preventing tears from spreading should be considered. Makers should be advised that the top surface alone should be capable of supporting the full load.

9. The makers should be required to furnish satisfactory evidence as to the strength of construction, and the factor of safety allowed. In this, special attention should be paid to the manner in which the engine is secured to the frame.

In further connection with the comparison of monoplanes and biplanes, it has been estimated that for planes of the same aspect ratio, span, section, and incidence, the monoplane has from 10 to 15 per cent. more lift at the same speed than the biplane, and it is generally considered that for machines of wing area below 250 square feet the monoplane is the more efficient.

A higher landing chassis is required with a monoplane, in order to obtain sufficient propeller clearance, as compared with the biplane,

As regards the weights of monoplane wings, it is generally

recognized that the methods for bracing the wings are inferior from the point of view of strength to the deep girder system of the biplane, and therefore the wing spars are made stronger in themselves, and therefore heavier, in order to obtain the necessary safety factor.

Biplanes.

1. The wing areas can be made as large as desirable owing to the light girder construction of the biplane system; further, large spans and higher aspect ratios may be used.

   The wing areas vary from 250 square feet for light scouts, 300 to 500 for weight-carrying biplanes, 500 to 3,000 for hydroplanes, flying-boats, and large passenger-carrying machines.

2. Owing to the large areas available, the wing loading can be made as small as desired, the landing and rising speed can be reduced, and a small engine can be used if it is not desired to fly at fast speeds.

3. The design of a biplane adapts itself much better for military purposes; thus it is easy to place the engine and propeller behind the pilot, to stagger the top plane forwards, and to leave a clear field of view or of gun-fire ahead.

BIRD FLIGHT DATA.

Dr. Magnan, as the result of a systematic study of bird flight and measurements, gives the following empirical results for monoplane design (*Compte Rendus*, 1914):

If P = total loaded machine weight in grammes,

S = area of body in square centimetres,

l = total length of bird in centimetres,

$l = \sqrt[3]{P}$, and $S = \sqrt[3]{P^2}$.

Then

$$\frac{\text{wing area in square centimetres}}{\sqrt[3]{P^2}} = 23 \cdot 2;$$

$$\frac{\text{weight of wings (in grammes)}}{P} = 197;$$

$$\frac{\text{span of wings (in centimetres)}}{\sqrt[3]{P}} = 13 \cdot 3;$$

$$\frac{\text{chord of wing (in centimetres) at centre}}{\sqrt[3]{P}} = 2 \cdot 36;$$

$$\frac{\text{length of tail (in centimetres)}}{\sqrt[3]{P}} = 2 \cdot 6;$$

$$\frac{\text{real length of body (in centimetres)}}{\sqrt[3]{P}} = 5 \cdot 9.$$

The proportions for any monoplane can be worked out from these relations.

Thus, if P = 400 kilogrammes (for a fully loaded monoplane), we have:

Area of wings = 12·6 square metres, chord = 1·74 metres, span = 9·8 metres, weight of wings = 78·8 kilogrammes, length of tail = 1·92 metres, length of machine = 4·35 metres.

These results correspond with a wing loading of 6·5 pounds per square foot.

It should be mentioned in passing, that the design of the successful Ponnier racing monoplanes has been based upon these methods of application of Dr. Magnan's results.

DISTRIBUTION OF WING LOADING.

The previous remarks upon wing loading have been confined to the average values of the loading for the whole area of wing, and in estimations of this mean wing loading it is assumed that the lift coefficient is constant over the whole area of wing.

Actually, the value of the lift coefficient for an aerofoil of constant section varies along the span of the aerofoil. Thus the greatest lift coefficient, and therefore wing loading, occurs at the central section, and falls off towards the tips, and the value of the load per square foot at the centre section of the wing span may become more than twice that at, or near, the wing tips.

The ratio of the loadings per unit area at the centre section of the span, and for the section near the wing tip, will depend upon the aspect ratio of the aerofoil and also its plan-form, being smaller for the larger aspect ratio, and smaller for rounded off and graded, or washed-out, wings towards the tips.

Fig. 10 illustrates an aerofoil tested by the N.P.L., with an aspect ratio of 6, and at a wind speed of 30 feet per second. The values of the pressures at different points over the wing were measured, and the results of these measurements are shown plotted in this figure for the case of the more important negative pressures, at points situated at a distance of 0·200 of the chord from the leading edge. The values of the pressure are about a maximum at the given angle of 4 degrees, and for the points situated at 0·200 of chord from leading edge. The values of the pressures per square foot at any given speed V feet per second, for the full-sized wing, are obtained from the Absolute Coefficients given in the graphs, by multiplying the ordinate at any point along the span by $0·00238 V^2$; thus, if the ordinate, as measured off, be 0·424, then the pressure in pounds per square foot at 60 miles per hour (= 88 f.s.) will be $0·00238 \times 88^2 \times 0·424 = 7·72$.

The values for the lift coefficients and lift/drift ratios for the sections designated by the letters A, B, C, D, and E are given in Fig. 11.

The data given in these curves will indicate the nature of the distribution of the wing loading along the span. In calculations of wing stresses, account should certainly be taken of the varia- tion of the loading along the span of the wing.

The above results are directly applicable to the upper wings of most biplanes and the " parasol " type monoplanes, where the fuselage and its fittings does not interfere with the nature of the air-flow (and consequent pressure distribution) along the surfaces.

The effect of fitting the body or fuselage at or near the centre

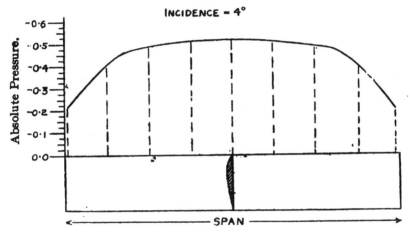

FIG. 10.—PRESSURE DISTRIBUTION ALONG AN AEROFOIL (TOP SURFACE).

of the wing, as in the case of the lower wings of most biplanes and in most monoplanes, is to interfere with the air-flow at and near the central section, and so reduce the efficiency of the whole wing. In some cases, however, the fuselage or body resistance is reduced by attaching the wings. The propeller will also depreciate from the wing efficiency if the slip stream pass over the wing surface at the centre, on account of its helical motion.

When it is remembered that a one-sixteenth scale model aerofoil showed a lift/drift of 24·0 at 4 degrees incidence at the mid- section, whereas the average lift/drift for the whole wing, as measured directly, was about 15·0 for the same angle, it will be seen that the central portion of the aerofoil or wing is very important in contributing to the efficiency of the whole wing.

The wing loading per unit area for any given section along the direction of the line of flight also varies along the chord of wing; this will be apparent from the pressure distribution diagrams shown in Fig. 12 for Eiffel's Bleriot XIII.A. At sections near the centre of the span the point of greatest intensity of loading

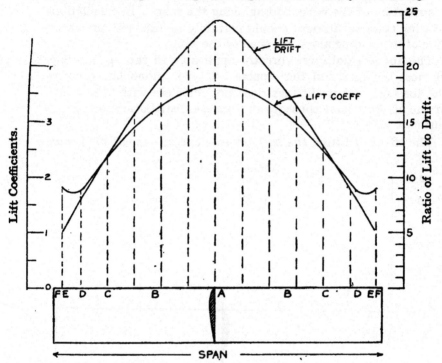

FIG. 11.—LOAD VARIATION ALONG THE SPAN OF AN AEROFOIL.

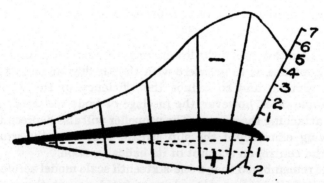

FIG. 12.—DIAGRAM OF PRESSURE DISTRIBUTION
OVER AN AEROFOIL.

is near the leading edge and upon the top surface, usually situated between the leading edge and 0·3 of the chord from the leading edge.

The greatest pressure (or suction) occurs at the large flying angles of incidence, in ordinary flight conditions. The fabric upon the upper surface near the leading edge is under the greatest stress, and the worst stress that can occur is when there is a leakage of positive pressure from the under surface, in addition to the suction upon the top surface. It can be shown that ratio of the maximum to the mean pressure per unit area for the whole wing can be as high as 10·0 for normal flying conditions.

The value of the maximum negative pressure or suction which is realized under normal flying conditions upon the upper surface near the leading edge—that is to say, between the leading edge and a point situated at 0·3 of the chord from the leading edge—lies between 20 and 30 pounds per square foot at small angles of incidence. As the angle of incidence increases, the ratio of the maximum to mean pressure decreases, as reference to Table VII. will show.

TABLE VII.

Angle of Incidence (Degrees.)	Ratio of Max. Pressure to Mean Lift per Sq. Ft.
0	10·00
2½	4·20
5	2·90
7½	2·70
10	2·95
12½	3·10
15	1·20
20	1·20

For ordinary angles of incidence as used in practice this ratio is about 3 to 1.

LOADING OF UPPER AND LOWER SURFACES.

In connection with the proportion of load carried by the upper and lower wing surfaces, Table VIII. gives the percentage of the total lift contributed to, by each surface for a type of wing section resembling Eiffel's Bird Wing No. 9, although the results are generally applicable to most aeroplane wing sections.

TABLE VIII.—LOADING OF UPPER AND LOWER SURFACES.

Angle of Incidence.	Upper Surface Load.	Lower Surface Load.
0	92 per cent.	8 per cent.
2	82 ,,	18 ,,
4	74	26
6	74	26
8	72	28
10	69	31

From this table it will be seen that at small angles the upper surface carries about four-fifths of the load, and that even at large flying angles it carries two-thirds; it is general to design the wing of an aeroplane upon the assumption of the whole of the load being carried upon the upper surface.

It follows from the preceding considerations that for design purposes it is necessary to take into account the variation of load distribution both along the span and along the chord.

The method employable, in the absence of more definite data, is to assume a load variation or distribution along the span, somewhat similar to that shown in Fig. 11, so that the mean loading of the whole wing will be the same as if a uniform load were assumed.

CHOICE OF FLYING ANGLES.

The choice of the normal and extreme flying angles of incidence depends greatly upon the purpose of the machine. Generally speaking, a high-speed type of machine requires a totally different wing section and incidence to a low or moderate speed type. The actual wing sections of aeroplanes of to-day must therefore be a kind of compromise between fast and slow speed sections, in order to insure safe landing and " getting-off."

Where the greatest maximum speed is the first and foremost consideration, a flat approximation to a streamline wing section, at a small angle of incidence, varying from o degree to 2 degrees, is necessary. Further, it is essential that the position of the centre of pressure for the fastest flying angle shall be quite stable, and with a margin of safety in case of unforeseen circumstances causing a further decrease of angle of incidence.

For slow flying a wing section, characterized by good upper and lower surface cambers, and comparatively large angles of incidence, are necessary; further, it is essential that the angle of incidence shall not be too near to the critical angle at which the lift coefficient decreases and the drift increases, and that the centre of pressure has a stable position at the maximum incidence. An example of the wing section of a high-speed " scout " type, and a moderately powered medium-speed machine, similar to those used for flying-school tuition purposes, are given in Fig. 13. For a good speed range the wing sections chosen should possess the following qualities:

    1. The centre of pressure for the range of flying angles used should have a stable position, and, further, the range of movement along the chord should be a minimum. The centre of pressure in a good wing section should

lie between 0·3 and 0·45 of the chord distant from the leading edge at all incidences used in flying, alighting, etc.

2. The lift coefficient should continuously increase over a wide range of angles (from a negative or zero angle to 15 degrees or so), and should then remain constant, and finally decrease at a slow rate, without exhibiting a marked " critical angle "; the maximum safe lift coefficient should not be less than 0·65, whilst the maximum drift coefficient should, preferably, not exceed 0·100.

3. At the small angles of incidence corresponding with the highest speeds, the drift coefficient should be a minimum; published data shows that a drift coefficient lying between 0·005 and 0·010 is attainable at angles

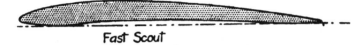

Fast Scout

Medium Speed Biplane

FIG. 13.—EXAMPLES OF FAST AND SLOW-FLYING WING SECTIONS.

between 0 degree and 1·5 degrees incidence. A further requirement for maximum speed, for minimum expenditure of horse-power (for the wings alone), is that the lift coefficient at the minimum value of the drift coefficient should be sufficient for the wing area chosen to support the load at that speed.

The subject of wing sections and resistances of various aeronautical bodies is treated fully in the volume of this series entitled " The Properties of Wing Sections and Resistance of Bodies."

ASPECT RATIO CORRECTIONS.

Models of aerofoils of the same chord and wing section (of approximately the Bleriot XI. *bis* section), but of different spans, have been tested for lift and drift by the N.P.L.

The chords of the models were 4 inches, and the aspect ratios varied from 3 to 8.

The general conclusions drawn from the results of these tests are as follows:

1. That the angles of zero lift occur earlier as the aspect ratio becomes smaller.
2. That at the angles of maximum lift/drift the lift coefficients are only slightly affected by change of aspect ratio.
3. That the maximum lift coefficient is unaltered by change of aspect ratio, but occurs at larger angles of incidence with smaller aspect ratios.
4. That the most important effect of aspect ratio is in connection with the values of the maximum lift/drift ratios obtained, as shown in Table IX. It will be seen that the lift/drift ratio increases rapidly with the aspect ratio; this effect is due almost entirely to the reduction in total drift which occurs with larger aspect ratios.

TABLE IX.—EFFECT OF ASPECT RATIO UPON MAXIMUM LIFT/DRIFT VALUES.

Aspect Ratio.	Maximum Lift/Drift Ratio.	Angle of Incidence.	Lift Coefficient.
3	10·1	5·5	0·305
4	11·5	4·7	0·310
5	12·9	4·7	0·312
6	14·0	4·5	0·314
7	15·1	4·7	0·315
8	15·5	5·7 (?)	—

From the results of aspect ratio tests upon model sections, the correction curves given in Fig. 14 have been drawn. The upper curve gives the percentage increase in the lift coefficients for different aspect ratios, taking the aspect ratio of 3 as the basis of comparison; similarly the lower curve gives the percentage reduction in the drift coefficients for different aspect ratios.

Thus, if it is required to know the percentage increase in the lift/drift in changing from an aspect ratio of 4 to one of 6, then from the curve

$$\text{at aspect ratio } 4 \begin{cases} \text{Lift Coefficient} = 110 \cdot 0 \\ \text{Drift} \quad \text{,,} \quad - \ 95 \cdot 5 \end{cases}$$

$$\text{at aspect ratio } 6 \begin{cases} \text{Lift} \quad \text{,,} \quad = 118 \cdot 5 \\ \text{Drift} \quad \text{,,} \quad = \ 87 \cdot 0 \end{cases}$$

Hence increase in lift drift from aspect ratio 4 to aspect ratio $6 = \dfrac{100 + (118 \cdot 5 - 110)}{100 - (95 \cdot 5 - 87)} = \dfrac{108 \cdot 5}{91 \cdot 5} = 118 \cdot 5.$

That is, the lift drift is increased by 18·5 per cent.

The above curve applies to all wing sections resembling the Bleriot XI. bis type, and for all angles between 4 degrees and 14 degrees, there being no correction for the zero angle, and low lift and drift angles.

Evidently aspect ratio corrections will depend upon the effi-

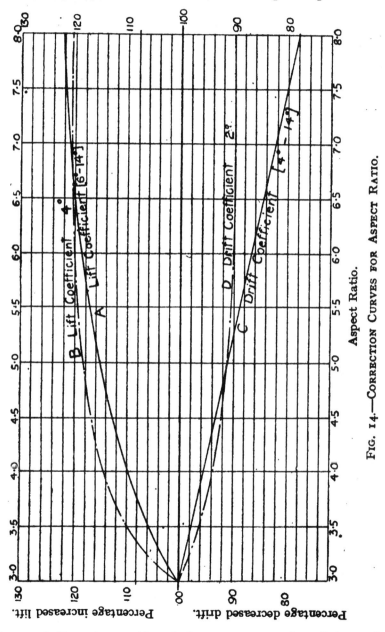

FIG. 14.—CORRECTION CURVES FOR ASPECT RATIO.

ciency of the wing section, being greater as the efficiency increases; also upon the plan-form, being greater for tapered, graded, and washed-out wings.

EFFECT OF BIPLANE SPACING.

The results of wind-channel tests upon exactly similar aerofoils arranged as in a biplane, but with the line joining their leading edges always at right angles to the chords, shows that there is a disadvantageous interference between the air flows caused by the gap between the planes, unless the gap is at least two and a half times the chord.

With gaps of less than this proportion there is a steady reduction in the lift coefficient as the gap becomes smaller, the drift coefficients being only slightly affected.

In most aeroplanes the gap is, for constructional reasons, made equal to the chord, and tests by the N.P.L. show that for angles of incidence of 4 degrees and above, the lift coefficient of the biplane arrangement is only 80 per cent. of that of a monoplane, the lift/drift ratios being reduced in the same proportion for small angles of incidence, and in greater proportions for larger angles of incidence.

The figures given in Table X. enable corrections to be made to the lift coefficients and lift/drift ratios of single aerofoils for different biplane spacings, and is based upon the results of N.P.L. tests.

TABLE X.—CORRECTIONS FOR BIPLANE SPACING.*

Ratio Gap/Chord.	Lift Coefficient.			Lift/Drift.		
	6°.	8°.	10°.	6°.	8°.	10°.
0·4	0·61	0·62	0·63	0·75	0·81	0·84
0·8	0·76	0·77	0·78	0·79	0·82	0·86
1·0	0·81	0·82	0·82	0·81	0·84	0·87
1·2	0·86	0·86	0·87	0·84	0·85	0·88
1·6	0·89	0·89	0·90	0·88	0·89	0·91

The best arrangement of biplane spacing is largely a matter for practical consideration, for although both the lift and the efficiency increase as the gap is increased, yet the increase in the weight and resistance of the extra length of struts and cables generally counterbalances these gains after a spacing of gap equal to the chord is reached.

* Single aerofoil coefficients are multiplied by the numbers given for biplane spacing coefficients.

EFFECT OF STAGGERING.

The effect of staggering the top plane forward is to improve the lift coefficient and the lift/drift ratio.   When the top plane is staggered forwards through a distance equal to about two-fifths of the chord, the lift and lift/drift are both increased by about 5 per cent.   This improvement is equivalent to that which would accrue if the biplane spacing were increased from 1·0 to 1·25 of the chord.

If the top plane be staggered backwards the lift and the lift/drift are reduced, but not by so much as these quantities are increased in staggering the top plane forwards.

If the requirements of design necessitate a backward stagger of the top plane, it can be assumed that the lift and lift/drift will only be slightly affected for moderate degrees of stagger. .

It is generally advantageous to stagger forwards for practical reasons connected with the range of vision of the occupants, and also because of the somewhat reduced resistance of the obliquely set struts, although the strengths of inclined struts under vertical load are smaller.

EFFECT OF DIHEDRAL ANGLE.

The employment of a dihedral angle between the wings for stabilizing purposes for the moderate angles employed in present-day practice—that is, up to 6 degrees—has no detrimental effect upon the lift or lift/drift.

Experiments made with wings in which both positive and negative dihedral angles were given, up to about 7 degrees, have shown that no appreciable difference in either the lift or lift/drift occurs.

It should be mentioned that by a dihedral angle of 7 degrees is meant a total angle between the wings of 180 degrees minus 14 degrees = 166 degrees for the upward dihedral, and 180 degrees plus 14 degrees = 194 degrees for the downward dihedral.

THE CHARACTERISTIC CURVES OF AEROPLANE PERFORMANCES

The wing section is generally chosen to suit the wing loading, speed range, and type of machine.

The wing section having been decided upon, the wing area for the given speed range and load can be obtained from a knowledge of the lift coefficients at different angles of incidence of the section selected, either by direct calculation or more readily by making use of the values given in Table V. and the graphs in Fig. 9.

The engine power must also be sufficient to overcome the total resistance of the whole machine at the two extremes of the speed range, and its total weight with fuel must not cause the total load to exceed the load assumed for the calculated wing area. This, as previously mentioned, is often a case of trial and error in selecting engine types for a given speed range.

WING RESISTANCE CURVES.

Knowing the lift coefficients required for the load to be supported at the given speeds, the corresponding values of the drift coefficients at these speeds are known from the lift and drift curves for the wing section chosen, and the total wing resistance at the same speeds can be estimated.

Thus, if C_L be the lift coefficient required to support the load W pounds at the given velocity V (in English units) at an angle of incidence θ degrees and with a wing area A square feet,

$$\text{then } W = C_L \cdot \frac{\rho}{g} \cdot A \cdot V^2.$$

If the lift/drift ratio $= n$ for the incidence θ degrees,

$$\text{then } C_D = \frac{C_L}{n} \text{ where } C_D = \text{the absolute drift coefficient.}$$

44

Then the total wing resistance R, in pounds, at the given speed V f.s. is given by

$$R = C_D \cdot \frac{\rho}{g} \cdot A \cdot V^2$$

$$= \frac{C_L}{n} \cdot \frac{1}{424} \cdot A \cdot V^2$$

since $\dfrac{\rho}{g} - \dfrac{1}{424}$.

This expression assumes that the resistance of a cambered wing varies as the square of the velocity. This is very nearly true for all the normal flying speeds of present practice, but for

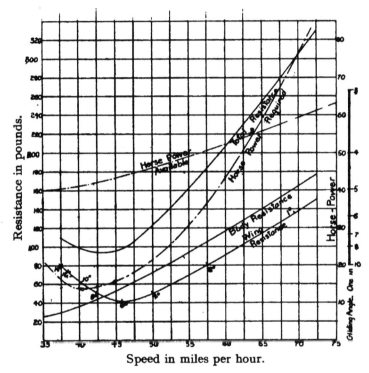

FIG. 15.—CURVES OF PERFORMANCE FOR MONOPLANE.

very high velocities the resistance may vary as $(V)^n$ where n is an index greater than 2.

Values of R can similarly be calculated for all corresponding values of C_L and V over the whole range of flying angles of incidence chosen.

The wing resistance at various speeds having been calculated, the curve of wing resistance can be plotted. The general shape of this curve is indicated in Fig. 15, which represents to scale typical monoplane wing resistance and other curves.

BODY RESISTANCE CURVES.

Before the horse-power required to propel the machine at the given speeds can be calculated, it is necessary to know the re.

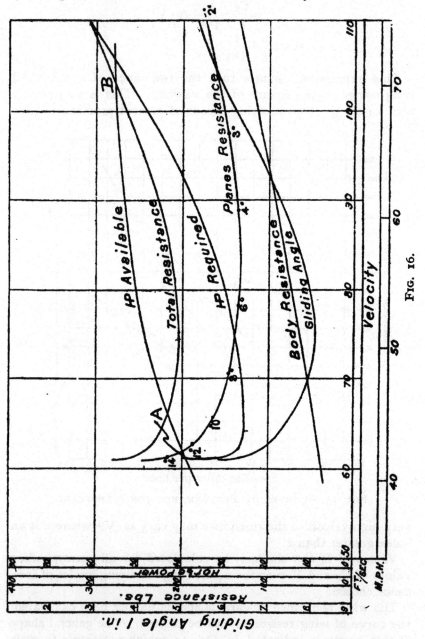

FIG. 16.

sistance] of, the] other parts of the machine exclusive of the wings.

For a fairly accurate estimation it is necessary to calculate the separate resistance of each part of the machine at some given speed.

The experimental data given in another book of this series, entitled " Properties of Wing Sections and Resistance of Bodies," enables the resistance of the important parts of an aeroplane to be computed accurately.

Having found the component resistances at some given speed, the resistance of the whole :" body " can be obtained by summation, and as the body resistance follows a law of variation very nearly proportional to V^2 a curve of body resistance with speed can be drawn.

The total resistance of the aeroplane at any speed V is then the sum of the wing and body resistances. A new curve of " total resistance " can then be plotted by adding the two ordinates of the wing and body resistance curves at each speed.

As an illustration of the method of calculating the total body resistance, values of the component resistances of a monoplane body, chassis, wires, etc., for an actual machine of the Bleriot type are given in Table XI., and for a biplane of the B.E. 2 type in Table XII.

Curves of " body resistance " and " total resistance " are given in Fig. 15 for a similar monoplane, and in Fig. 16 for a biplane similar to the B.E.2 considered in Table XII.

TABLE XI.—RESISTANCES FOR BLERIOT TYPE MONOPLANE.

No.	Particulars of Parts.	Resistance in Lbs. at 60 M.P.H.
1	Fuselage 20 feet by 2·2 feet square, with exposed area of engine and pilot included ..	41·50
2	Bleriot undercarriage, complete with struts, forks, wheels, shock-absorbers, etc. ..	37·54
3	Pylons and cabane (or masts)	5·92
4	100 feet of 5 mm. cable	16·80
5	Rudder and elevator control levers and tail skid	1·00
6	Skin resistance of control surfaces	2·00
	Total	104·76

Note.—Resistance of above at 100 M.P.H. would be 290 pounds.

TABLE XII.—RESISTANCES FOR B.E. 2 BIPLANE.

No.	Part.	Equiv. Normal Area in Sq. Ft.	Value of Section per Bent of Normal Plane.	Resistance in Lbs. at 60 M.P.H.
	Struts :			
	Eight 6′ × 1¼″ ..	5·00	16·5	4·2
	Four 4′ × 1¼″ ..	1·70	16·5	1·4
	Six 3′ × 1¼″ ..	1·90	16·5	1·6
	Wiring :			
	220 feet cable ..	3·20	83·0	29·5
	70 feet high-tension wire diameter = 12 S.W.G. ...	0·60	75·0	5·6
	52 strainers	0·36	75·0	3·0
3	Two wheels, 26″ diameter ..	1·50	33·0	3·5
4	Two skids	0·20	50·0	1·0
5	Axle, 5′ × 1¼″	0·63	65·0	2·0
6	Engine and propeller boss ..	2·00	67·0 ⎫	
7	Fuselage	5·40	10·0 ⎬	40·0
8	Exposed pilot and passenger	0·50	48·0 ⎭	
9	Rudder, 12 square feet ..		Skin friction	0·5
10	Elevator, 25 square feet ..		Ditto	1·5
11	Skid	0·25	20	0·5
12	Wing-skids, plates, silencer, etc.	—	—	10·0
	Total resistance	..	..	104·3

Note.—This biplane has a wing area of 374 sq. ft., an overall length of 29·5 ft., weight of 1,650 lbs. fully loaded, and fitted with a 70-h.p. Renault engine with Tractor propeller. This machine had a speed range of from 39·5 to 73 M.P.H., a climbing rate of about 430 ft. per min., and a gliding angle of 1 in 7·5.

It will be noticed that the method of obtaining the "body resistance" by the process of analysis and summation, is the same as that employed in the estimation of the total load. Similarly, the position of the centre of resistance may be found, as in the case of the centre of gravity.

The body resistance can also be obtained from resistance tests in a wind channel of a model of the complete machine, either by making an allowance for the resistance of the wings from the known wing drift-coefficients and their area, or by supporting the wings separately from the body, but very close to same, and measuring the resistance of the body alone. This method, if it can be employed, is more accurate, as the mutual interference of the air flows for the body and wings is allowed for.

The value of the "body resistance" of the full-sized machine can be independently obtained by subtracting the estimated resistance of the wings from the estimated or measured propeller thrust at the given speed. This method is usually the more accurate one, for it has been found, from the performances of actual machines, that the estimated " body resistance " is usually higher than the observed, even after due allowance has been made for the increased resistance due to the slip stream of the propeller, which may be taken as being at about 25 to 30 per cent. greater velocity.

In calculating the wing resistance of a biplane, due allowance must be made for the following factors:

1. The interference between the two wings due to " biplane spacing " effect.
2. The stagger of the planes.
3. Aspect ratio of full-sized wings and models.
4. Interférence between fuselage, or cabane, *or any other near objects*, and the wings, for in most biplanes the fuselage occupies the centre of the lower wing, and destroys the continuity of the air flow at the most efficient portion. This is a problem which can only be solved by wind tunnel experiment.
5. Scaling-up error from the model to the full-sized machine, if the wing and body characteristics are taken from model test results.
6. Propeller draught and body resistance. The relative velocity of the air to the fuselage or body is increased by as much as 30 per cent. by the propeller slip stream.

Items 3, 4, 5, and 6 are also applicable to monoplanes.

The total resistance of a machine can be obtained, as previously mentioned, by testing a complete model of the machine in a wind channel, if the scale and speed corrections be known.

The larger the model and the nearer the wind-channel velocity to the full-sized velocity, the more accurate will the results be.

It is also essential that the relative roughnesses of the surfaces be proportional, or known, in order that the measured drift values be comparative.

HORSE-POWER CURVES.

From the total resistance curve the values of the h.p. required to overcome the total resistance at the various speeds can be estimated by the relation—

$$\text{H.P. required} = \frac{R \cdot V}{550},$$

where R = total resistance in pounds at the velocity V feet per second.

The Table of values for $\dfrac{V}{550}$ at the end of the book* will be found useful for this purpose.

The " horse-power required " curve can then be drawn. From a knowledge of the power output of the chosen engine and of the propeller efficiency, the available " horse-power " curve can be plotted. The available h.p. is not easy to obtain with a very near degree of accuracy, since the brake horse power of the engine under flight conditions, and the propeller efficiency at different engine revolutions and air-speeds, cannot be readily and accurately obtained.

If the efficiency of the propeller be represented by E, and the b.h.p. at the engine speed for which E is known be denoted by the letters b.h.p.,

then available h.p. = E × b.h.p.

The efficiency E of an air propeller varies from 60 per cent. to 80 per cent. The average value for a well-designed propeller may be taken at from 70 per cent. to 75 per cent.

The h.p. available curve can be approximately estimated; an example is shown in Figs. 15 and 16. The curves of h.p. required and h.p. available are only strictly true at one altitude, the effect of an increase in altitude being twofold—namely, to decrease the available h.p. and to increase the h.p. required, due to the effect of the air-density decrease causing a decrease in the lift of the wings, and therefore requiring an increased speed.

A difference in height of 10,000 feet will cause a difference of about 25 per cent. in the engine power.

It will be seen from the curves Figs. 15 and 16 that the " h.p. required " and the h.p. available curves cut in points A and B. The abscissæ of these points fix the minimum and maximum speeds of the machines respectively. In the case of the biplane these are 42·5 and 70 miles per hour respectively.

RATE OF CLIMBING.

The vertical ordinates intercepted between the two h.p. curves represent the available h.p. for climbing and manœuvring.

In Fig. 16, the maximum available or surplus h.p. is 21, and occurs at 50 miles per hour.

The maximum rate of climbing is then obtained from the relation—

$$V_R \text{ (in feet per minute)} = \frac{\text{H.P.} \times 33,000}{W}$$

where H.P. is the greatest intercept between the h.p. required and h.p. available curves (expressed in horse-power), and W —

* Table A, Appendix II.

weight in pounds of fully loaded machine. In the biplane·
considered, W = 1,500 pounds, and the climbing rate is therefore
450 feet per minute.

The rate of climbing is an important factor in aeroplane design.
Certain types of machine require high climbing rates, whilst
with other types it is a secondary factor.

The climbing rates attained in aeroplane practice vary from
300 feet per minute to as much as 1,200 feet per minute, a good
value for a well-designed machine of moderate h.p. and speed
being 400 to 500 feet per minute. Some values for the climbing
rates measured in the case of the machines entered for the Military
Competition of 1912 are given in Table XIII., together with
values for the later R.A.F. machines; the rate of climb for the
scout type of these latter machines is well defined.

TABLE XIII.—CLIMBING SPEEDS OF AEROPLANES.

Type of Machine.	Rate of Climb in Feet per Minute.	Percentage of Total H.P. employed in Climbing.
Hanriot I. ..	365	26·5
Hanriot II.	333	24·0
Bleriot tandem	250	17·7
Bleriot sociable	236	16·6
Avro	105	8·6
Bristol Monoplane..	200	14·9
Deperdussin	267	20·6
Maurice Farman	207	16·8
B.E. Improved, 1913	400–450	40·0*
R.A.F. Scout, B.S. 1	900 (at 65 M.P.H.)	50·0*
R.A.F. Reconnaissance Type, R.E. 1	600	40·0*
R.A.F. Fighting Type, F.E. 3	350	40·0*

The lowest point of the curve of h.p. required gives the most
economical speed of the machine, which in the case of the
example illustrated is 44 miles per hour.

The effect of running the engine at full power, when an aeroplane is flying horizontally and at a given incidence, is to cause the
machine to climb at such a rate that the surplus h.p. is absorbed.

Thus if H_0 = h.p. required for horizontal flight at V feet per
second,

W = weight of machine in pounds,

θ = angle of slope or climb,

then b.h.p. at propeller at full throttle = $H_0 + \dfrac{V \cdot W \sin \theta}{550}$,

* Values assumed from characteristic curves.

so that the climbing angle θ is governed by the power output of the engine. This angle may be varied, however, by introducing an artificial wind resistance, so as to vary H_0.

THE GLIDING ANGLE.

From the curves given in Figs. 15 and 16 the gliding angles at the different speeds can be readily obtained and plotted. For if R be the total resistance in pounds at a given speed V, and W is the weight of the machine in flying order, then the gliding angle at the speed V is given by $\sin a = \dfrac{R}{W}$, where a is the angle made by the direction of the " glide" with the horizontal. In other words, when the machine is gliding freely, and with the engine stopped, the gravity component $W \sin a$ in the direction of flight must be equal to the head resistance.

Hence the curve of " total resistance " is also a curve of corresponding gliding angles to a different scale—that is, the ordinates, divided by W, give the sines of the gliding angles.

A gliding angle of $\sin^{-1}\dfrac{1}{6}$ is usually expressed as 1 in 6—that is to say, the machine will drop 1 foot vertically for every 6 feet glided.

It will be seen that the flattest gliding angle occurs at the speed where the total resistance ordinate is a minimum. This angle is often termed the " gliding angle par excellence." The smaller this latter angle, the greater is the available area for landing from a given height, should engine failure occur—a desirable attribute in modern aeroplanes. The real gliding angles attained in practice vary from about 1 in 5 to 1 in 8 in the best examples.

Table XIV. gives the measured gliding angles of the aeroplanes entered for the Military Competition in 1912, and for the improved B.E. machines.

TABLE XIV.—GLIDING ANGLES AND SPEEDS.

Type of Machine.	Gliding Angle, One in — n.	Gliding Speed, M.P.H.	Gliding Resistance $=\dfrac{W}{n}$ Lbs.
Hanriot	6·6	61	291
Hanriot	5·9	68	332
Bleriot tandem	5·6	—	267
Bleriot sociable	5·3	52	280
Avro	6·5	—	270
Bristol Mon.	6·5	64	284
Deperdussin	6·2	—	328
Maurice Farman ..	6·6	38	284
Cody	6·2	60	432
B.E. (improved) biplane, 1913	7·4	50	224

The gliding angles attained in practice are generally greater than the theoretical, on account of the propeller effect in increasing the total resistance during gliding and wind effects.

With a favourable up-wind small gliding angles up to 1 in 9 can be obtained for short periods.   The above considerations refer, of course, to calm air conditions.

CHAPTER V

THE STRESSES IN AEROPLANES

The average loading per foot run of the span can be ascertained by the foregoing methods; but before the actual load in at any part of wing can be found, it is necessary to know two things:

1. The distribution of wing loading along the span of the wings, assumed concentrated along the line of centres of pressure, say, and
2. The distribution of the average load for any given wing section over the section.

Factor (1) can only be obtained by measurements of the actual pressures existing under the worst conditions of flight and incidence, by wind channel, or full-size model experiments.

Alternatively a load distribution has to be assumed which will give the same average loading for the whole machine. This method is set forth in the example considered in the proceeding pages.

Factor (2) can be obtained from a knowledge of the pressure distribution over the two surfaces of the wing section at different incidences, an example of which is given on page 36.

The average load over the whole wing section (assumed constant per unit of span) must equal the sum of the distributed loads over the section. The proportion of the load carried by each spar (in a two spar wing) can then be obtained.

An example of the method of finding the load borne by each spar is given herewith for the case of a monoplane of total loaded weight = 800 pounds, and effective wing area = 175 square feet. The wing section selected is Eiffel No. XIII. *bis* (or Bleriot No. 11 *bis*) [see Fig. 12]. The position of the C.P. at the best flying angle (of maximum lift;drift)—namely, at 6 degrees incidence—is 0·32 of the chord from the leading edge. For large incidences the C.P. travels forward, and for smaller incidences backwards. At the highest speed position of 2 degrees incidence, the C.P. is 0·4 of chord

from the leading edge, and at the largest incidence of 12 degrees
it is 0·29. The position of the two wing spars is shown in
Fig. 17—namely, at 0·16 and 0·66 of chord from leading edge.
[In the case of a single spar machine (or control surface) the
spar is generally placed at one-third of the chord from the leading edge, this being the best average position.]

The proportions of the average wing load *w* pounds per foot

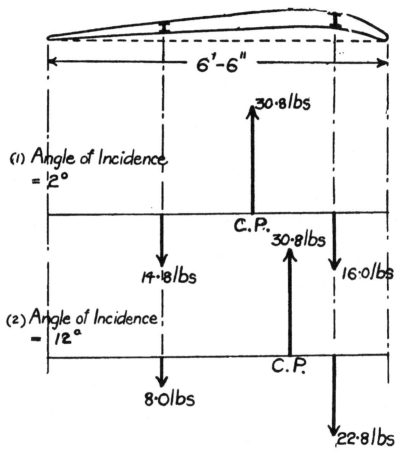

FIG. 17.—DIAGRAM SHOWING THE EFFECT OF THE TRAVEL OF
THE CENTRE OF PRESSURE UPON THE WING SPAR LOADING.

span carried by the two spars for the extreme cases are given
in the lower dragrams of the same figure.   It is important to take
into account the effect of the travel of the C. P. (due to change in
distribution of the loading) upon the loads carried by the front
and rear spars respectively, and to take the most unfavourable
loadings in stress calculations.

FACTORS OF SAFETY.

The working stresses are generally calculated for the case of the aeroplane flying horizontally in still air, the normal "load" in this case being equal to the weight. The usual method hitherto adopted has been to choose a "factor of safety" of, say, 6 upon the normal loading stresses to allow for abnormal stresses; it will be shown that this factor of safety is inadequate, and misleading.

The normal loading of a machine may be increased to many times its value under different conditions of flight. Thus the effects of banking, diving, and flattening-out, sudden or irregular gusts, etc., all impose higher loadings upon the machine.

The following figures, based upon careful estimates of the loadings under the stated conditions, show the ratios of the loadings under the given conditions to the normal loading upon the planes:

For banking, 1·5; for wind gusts, 4 to 5; for flattening-out after a steep dive, 5 to 7.

For any combination of these conditions, the values given must be multiplied together. Thus for a sudden unfavourable wind gust, whilst banking, the value would be 1·5 × 4·5 = 6·7.

The figures given for flattening-out after a steep dive represent an extreme case, which would not be realized by a careful pilot. The maximum abnormal loadings in practice could hardly exceed about *five* times the normal. Under these conditions the dimensions of the members subjected to stresses due to these loadings should be such that there is still a margin of safety in the material itself.

It is advisable to allow an initial factor of safety of about 5, to allow for the maximum abnormal loading, and a second factor of safety of between 2 and 3 to allow for material strength; the overall factor of safety will then lie between 5 × 2 = 10 and 5 × 3 = 15.

The Government at present accept aeroplanes with overall factors of safety not lower than 6, but state that future machines accepted will require factors of safety of double this figure—that is, 12.

In considerations of factors of safety, the nature of the loading should be taken into account. Thus if the load is a steady or "dead" load, the factor of safety for the material may be as low as 2. For live loads, which come on frequently and vary in value, the factors of safety require to be much higher—say, from 3 to 6—in aeroplane work. As an example, from engineering practice, may be mentioned the three following cases for steel structures:

(a) Steady load, F.S. $= 4$.

(b) Load varying from zero value to a maximum, frequently, F.S. $= 7$.

(c) Load varying from a negative maximum, through zero, to a positive maximum, F.S. $= 13$.

The question of lightness of construction is always more or less bound up with that of the margin of safety, and the modern tendency is to adopt larger safety factors at the expense of the weight carrying capacity, although the increased general efficiency of the machines favours this procedure.

The greatest stresses in practice are usually associated with the wing spars. In all cases the effects of the aileron or warp loading, treated as a frequently occurring load varying from zero to a maximum, should be allowed for.

As an acceptance or check test for contract aeroplanes, it is the usual practice of the purchasers to select at random one machine in every eight or twelve, and to support this machine upside down upon trestles, and to load the under-cambered surfaces of the wings with shot or sand in bags until they break down. If W^1 be the total breaking load upon the wings, and $2w$ the weight of the wings, and if W is the total loaded weight of the machine in flight, then the overall factor of safety is given by—

$$\text{Overall F.S.} = \frac{W^1}{W - 2w}.$$

In connection with this method of testing the machine to destruction, it is advisable to introduce, artificially, a loading equivalent to the " drift load "; and, further, to load the planes along the span, and along the chord in accordance with the accepted lift distribution or pressure distribution curves for the wing aspect ratio and section.

In many cases it is usual to subject the machines to a sand-bag test, representing an abnormal loading of between four and five times the normal, before proceeding to fly the machine.

BENDING MOMENTS AND SHEARING FORCES ON WING RIBS.

From a knowledge of the principles of graphical statics, dealt with in another chapter, the B. M. and S. F. diagrams may be constructed for any of the wing ribs.

The load distribution along the span being known (or assumed),

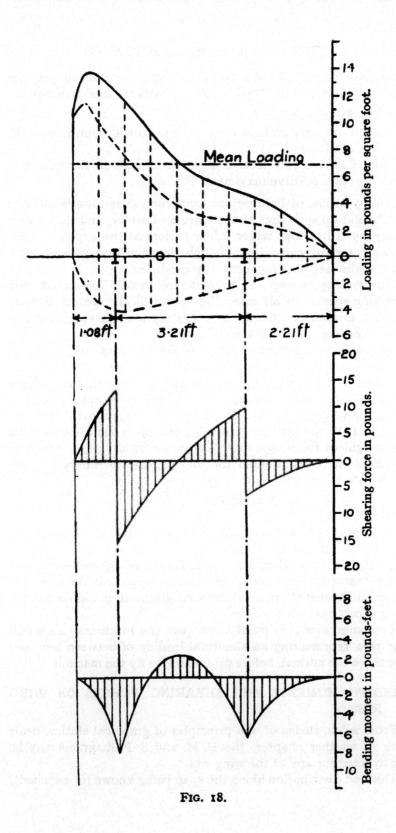

FIG. 18.

the total load carried by any given wing rib can be ascertained. If the rib spacing be denoted by n feet, and w be the load intensity per foot along wing span, $n \cdot w$ will be the total load per rib, and this in turn must equal the total distributed load over the rib section at the angle of incidence considered.

The distribution of load over the chord is obtained, as previously indicated, from the pressure distribution curves of the wing section, by adding together the upper surface suction and the under surface pressure ordinates. The most unfavourable conditions of incidence and velocity should be taken under normal conditions, the abnormal conditions being considered in the factor of safety allowed. As a rule it is advisable to draw the rib-loading diagrams for the extreme and normal incidences.

An example of the wing loading B. M. and S. F. diagrams is given in Fig. 18 for the case of an aerofoil rib similar in general features to that shown in Fig. 17 for an incidence of 12 degrees, the worst case. The greatest B. M. occurs at a point 0·16 of the chord, or where the front spar is, from the leading edge, and the greatest S. F. is also at the same place.

The height of the rib at the point of maximum B. M. being fixed by the wing section, the shape and area of the flanges must be proportioned to give the requisite strength with the given factor of safety.

The proportions of the flanges and webs can be obtained as follows:

Draw the B. M. and S. F. diagrams for the most heavily loaded portion of the wing span (usually near the centre of machine) under the worst normal conditions of speed and incidence. From the B. M. diagram obtain the value of the B. M. at any place in pounds, inches. Call this M pounds-inches.

$$\text{Then } I = \frac{M \cdot y}{f_c},$$

where I is the required moment of inertia in (inches)[4], y the distance of the outermost fibre of the rib section from the neutral axis of bending, in inches, and f_c the permissible working stress in pounds per square inch, to cover abnormal loading conditions and material strength. It is usual to assume that the flanges of rib take all of the bending moment, whilst the web resists the shear. For I sections, if A_1 and A_2 be the respective areas of the upper and lower flanges, d_1 and d_2 their respective distances from the neutral axis, and f_c and f_t the working compressive and tensile stresses, then

$$f_c \cdot A_1 \cdot d_1 = f_t \cdot A_2 \cdot d_2.$$

For example, f_c for ash is about 8,500 pounds per square inch, whilst f_t is about 12,000 pounds per square inch.

If the centres of area of the upper and lower flanges be at equal distances from the neutral axis, then the areas of the upper and lower flanges will be as 12,000 : 8,500—that is, as 1·41 : 1—for equal strengths; conditions of reversal of the loading must also be considered.

The total area of section must give the requisite moment of inertia to resist the maximum B. M. with the given margin of safety.

SHEARING FORCE ON RIBS.

Where the web of rib is thin compared with the flanges the whole of shear may be supposed to be taken by it. Actually the intensity of the shearing force varies as a function of the distance from the neutral axis, but for all practical purposes may be assumed uniform over the whole web section. If $d =$ depth of web in inches at place of maximum S. F. denoted by $S_{max.}$, $t =$ its width or thickness in inches, and f_s the permissible working shear stress, then

$$S_{max.} = f_s \cdot d \cdot t$$

This relation fixes the web proportions, or, rather, the web thickness, since the wing section fixes the depth d; but it will usually be found that other practical considerations fix the actual proportions, which, if tested for strength, will be found to be considerably stronger than is necessary for the best economy of weight and material.

STRESS IN WING SPARS.

The area of the wings will be fixed by considerations of permissible loading and weight.

If W be total weight of machine loaded in pounds, and w the wing loading per square foot in pounds,

$$\text{then area of wings } A = \frac{W}{w} \text{ square foot.}$$

The proportions of span to chord are fixed by considerations of wing weight, efficiency, convenience, etc. Let the aspect ratio be denoted by n,

$$\text{then the chord } C = \sqrt{\frac{W}{nw}} = \sqrt{\frac{A}{n}} \text{ feet,}$$

$$\text{and the Span } S = \sqrt{\frac{nW}{w}} = \sqrt{nA} \text{ feet.}$$

In a biplane, if the lower wing be of shorter span than the upper wing, and if $x = \dfrac{\text{upper wing span}}{\text{lower wing span}}$,

$$\text{then lower wing span} = \frac{1}{x+1}\sqrt{n \cdot A} \text{ feet,}$$

$$\text{and upper wing span} = \frac{x}{x+1}\sqrt{n \cdot A} \text{ feet.}$$

In the case of a lifting tail or float section, the proportion and loading of this tail will determine the fraction of the total weight borne by it, and the remainder must be regarded as the value of W given above.

STRESSES IN MONOPLANE WING SPARS.

The average wing loading per foot run of span being known, it is necessary to fix the distribution of the load.

For approximate calculations for wings of aspect ratio $=6$, if one of the wings be divided into four equal parts, and if the average loading over the inner section (Fig. 19) be taken as 100, then the proportionate loadings of the other sections for normal flight conditions will be as shown.

The case for three equal divisions is also shown in the same

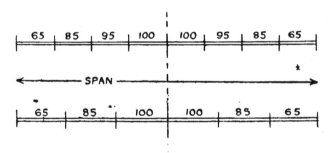

FIG. 19.—DIAGRAM OF LOAD DISTRIBUTION ALONG THE SPAN OF AN AEROPLANE WING.

diagram. For exact purposes, however, it is necessary to know the variation of the lift coefficient along the span.

The effect of warping and of wind gusts upon the outermost sections must be taken into account. Thus in warping the angle of incidence may be increased to three times its normal value, and the loading of the portion of wing warped will be increased in the same proportion. Similarly with wing ailerons the loading near the wing tips will be increased.

In the first example considered in Fig. 19, if the outer one quarter be warped (evenly) from an incidence of 3 degrees to 9 degrees, the loading will become, approximately, $3 \times 0.65w = 1.95w$ pounds per square foot nearly, where w is the loading of inner section.

As the use of the warp or aileron during flight is frequent, it is better to include the effect of these in the normal loading stresses, and not in the factor of safety.

It is usual to express the loading per foot run at any part of the span in terms of the mean loading. Thus, if the wing span for a monoplane of the parasol type be divided into eight equal parts, and if w_m = the average loading per foot run, say, then the loadings per foot run expressed in terms of w_m, will be—

$$1.16w_m, \quad 1.10w_m, \quad 0.986w_m, \quad 0.754w_m$$

from the centre to the wing tips. For a monoplane of the usual type, in which the continuity is interfered with by the body, the approximate loadings will be $1.12\ w_m$, $1.06\ w_m$, $0.96\ w_m$ and $0.86\ w_m$ respectively.

It is further necessary, in the case of a two or three spar wing, to know the proportion of this loading borne by each spar, under the worst conditions; this may be done by the method mentioned upon p. 55.

METHODS OF MONOPLANE WING BRACING.

The lift forces and the weight of the wings are taken by means of wires or cables anchored to king-posts or masts fixed to the fuselage. Three principal methods of wing bracing are shown in the diagrams in Fig. 20. Diagram A represents the most general method in which two or three cables are employed upon each side of each wing. The load cables are anchored to a mast or " cabane " above the fuselage, except in the case of machines employing the " warp " method of lateral control, when these cables pass over pulleys at the " cabane." The lift cables are anchored, or pass over pulleys fixed to a lower mast or "pylon" of such length that the cables make as great an angle as possible with the wing spars. Examples of machines employing this method of bracing are to be found in the Bleriot, Morane-Saulnier, and others.

Diagram B represents a king-post bracing method employed upon large span monoplanes.

The stresses in the king-post cables are equal, and are usually from $\frac{1}{4}$ to $\frac{3}{8}$ of the stress in the main lift cable anchored to pylon; the Martinsyde machine employs this bracing method.

Diagram C illustrates the girder method, somewhat on biplane lines, employed in the German Taube machines, in the Deperdussin hydro-monoplane, and others. It has the advantage of

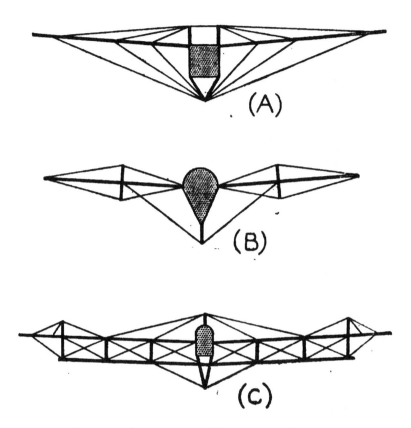

FIG. 20.—METHODS OF MONOPLANE BRACING.

taking both lift and load forces usually without any interference with the efficiency of the top surface, but owing to its constructional features introduces additional head-resistance and weight; it is useful, however, where large spans are concerned.

CALCULATION OF STRESSES.

Knowing the loading per foot run, say, of each spar, the stresses in the spars and stay wires can be determined graphically or otherwise. An illustration of the method employed is best shown by considering the case of a monoplane with a mean loading of 5 pounds per foot run of each wing spar; this is a very light loading, but the figure chosen will serve to illustrate the methods employed.

For simplicity of method, the loading will be taken as uniform along the span; later, the more general case will be considered.

The monoplane is represented diagramatically in Fig. 21,

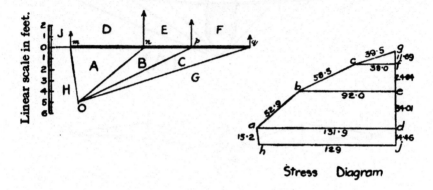

Stress Diagram

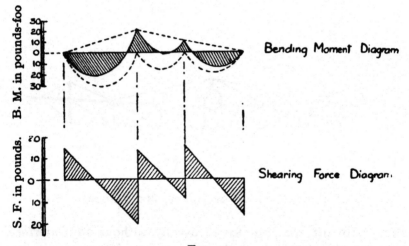

Bending Moment Diagram

Shearing Force Diagram.

FIG. 21.

the lift cables being indicated by On, Op and Oq, and the undercarriage strut by Om.

Employing the notation shown in the figure, let M_m, M_n, M_p, and M_q be the bending moments at m, n, p, and q, respectively, for the front spar; also $mn = 7$ feet, $np = 4.5$ feet, and $pq = 5.5$ feet.

Then—

1. $M_q = 0$, since there is no bending at the extreme tip.
2. $M_n = 0$, at the anchoring of the spar to body.

3. Applying the Theorem of Three Moments to the spans qp and pn :

$$2\,M_p\,(qp+pn)+M_n\cdot pn=\frac{w_m}{4}\,(qp^3+pn^3)\text{ where } w_m =$$
mean loading;

that is, $\qquad 2\,M_p\,(5\cdot5+4\cdot5)+M_n\cdot 4\cdot5=\frac{5}{4}\,(5\cdot5^3+4\cdot5^3)$;

whence $\qquad M_p+0\cdot225\,M_n= 16\cdot06 \qquad\qquad (a)$.

4. Applying the Theorem to the spans pn and nm ·

$$2M_n\,(pn+mn)+M_p\cdot pn=\frac{w_m}{4}\,(pn^3+mn^3)\,;$$

that is, $\qquad 2\,M^n\,(4\cdot5+7\cdot0)+M_p\cdot 4\cdot5=\frac{5}{4}\,(4\cdot5^3+7\cdot0^3)$;

whence $\qquad M_p+5\cdot12\,M_n=120\cdot5 \qquad\qquad (b)$.

From (a) and (b) the bending moments at p and q are given by $M_p=11\cdot3$ and $M_n=21\cdot3$ pounds feet respectively.

SHEARING FORCES.

Denoting the shearing forces to the left-hand by the letters $R_q\cdot L$, $R_p\cdot L$, $R_n\cdot L$, $R_m\cdot L$, respectively, and those to the right hand by $R_q\cdot R$, $R_p\cdot R$, $R_n\cdot R$, and $R_m\cdot R$, respectively, it will be seen that:

1. $R_q\cdot R=0$.
2. $R_m\cdot L=0$.
3. $R_m\cdot R=\dfrac{M_m-M_n}{mn}+\dfrac{w_m\cdot mn}{2}$, where $w_m =$ mean loading.

$$=\frac{0-21\cdot3}{7\cdot0}+\frac{5\times7\cdot0}{2}=14\cdot46\text{ pounds.}$$

4. $R_n\cdot L=\dfrac{M_n-M_m}{mn}+\dfrac{w_m\cdot mn}{2}=20\cdot54$ pounds.

5. $R_n\cdot R=\dfrac{M_n-M_p}{np}+\dfrac{w_m\cdot np}{2}$

$$=\frac{21\cdot3-11\cdot3}{4\cdot5}+\frac{5\times4\cdot5}{2}=13\cdot47\text{ pounds.}$$

6. $R_p\cdot L=\dfrac{M_p-M_n}{np}+\dfrac{w_m\cdot np}{2}=9\cdot03$ pounds.

7. $R_p\cdot R=\dfrac{M_p-M_q}{pq}+\dfrac{w_m\cdot pq}{2}$

$$=\frac{11\cdot3-0}{5\cdot5}+\frac{5\times5\cdot5}{2}=15\cdot81\text{ pounds.}$$

8. $R_q\cdot L=\dfrac{M_q-M_p}{pq}+\dfrac{w_m\cdot pq}{2}=11\cdot69$ pounds.

The shearing forces obtained in the above manner are also

5

shown plotted in Fig. 21, positive shears being taken as to those of the right hand.

From the diagram the places of maximum shear will be seen to be the points of attachment of the lift cables.

REACTIONS.

The reactions at the points of attachment of the cables, etc., can now be obtained in a simple manner.

Denoting the vertical reactions due to the lift at m, n, p, and q by the letters R_m, R_n, R_p, and R_q, respectively, then,

1. $R_m = R_m \cdot R = 14 \cdot 46$ pounds.
2. $R_n = R_n \cdot R + R_n \cdot L = 13 \cdot 47 + 20 \cdot 54 = 34 \cdot 01$ pounds.
3. $R_p = R_p \cdot R + R_p \cdot L = 15 \cdot 81 + 9 \cdot 03 = 24 \cdot 84$ pounds.
4. $R_q = R_q \cdot L = 11 \cdot 69$ pounds.

STRESSES IN CABLES AND STRUT.

Knowing the reactions, the stresses in the various members can be obtained by direct calculation, or graphically

Analytically, the method of sections, as used in lattice girder work, can be applied.

Thus at the joint q, if the members pq and oq be imagined cut through, it will be seen that the forces meeting at q must be in equilibrium.

Calling the angle $pqO = \theta$, then $T \sin \theta = 11 \cdot 69$ from which the tension T in the cable—namely, $39 \cdot 5$ pounds—can be found, and so on.

Graphically, it is necessary to draw the force-diagram for the system of forces shown in Fig. 21. Adopting Bow's notation for the forces, and commencing at the point q, the line of loads *gfedj* can be drawn vertically, and the triangle of forces *gfc* completed; similarly the polygon of forces for the point p can next be completed, namely *fcbe*, and so on for the complete diagram as shown.

The stresses in the members On, Op, and Oq are then represented to scale by the lengths *ab*, *bc*, and *cg*, respectively; these members are in tension.

The compressive forces along the spar in qp, pn, and nm are represented by *cf*, *be*, and *ad*, respectively. The anchoring force JH is denoted to scale by *jh*. The tensile force, due to the lift in Om, is given by the length to scale of *ah*.

Hence the whole of the working loads in the various members are known, and it is a fairly simple matter to determine their dimensions, knowing the factors of safety.

CALCULATION OF WING SPAR DIMENSIONS.

In the case of the main spar $mnpq$, it will be seen that this is subjected to the following:

1. A compressive load due to the lift cables causing at any part a compressive stress $= \dfrac{F_c}{A}$, where F_c is the force obtained from the force diagram or otherwise, and A the area of the section under consideration.

2. A stress due to the bending moment M which varies from a tensile stress $\dfrac{y \cdot M}{I}$ upon the under side of spar (y being the greatest distance from the neutral axis, and I the moment of inertia about neutral axis of the area A), to a compressive stress upon the upper surface of spar, of maximum value $\dfrac{y_2 M}{I}$, where y_2 is the distance of extreme fibre from neutral axis upon compression side.

Methods for calculating the spar dimensions are given in a later chapter.

DIMENSIONS OF MONOPLANE'S SPAR.

Considering the wing spar portion mn, it will be seen from the stress diagram that this is subjected to a compression of 131·9 pounds and a B. M. of 22 pounds feet, the free length being about 6 feet.

The dimensions of the wing spars will depend upon their positions in the wing section, but if it is assumed that three-quarters of the total load comes upon each spar under the worst conditions of the C. P. travel, then a spar section similar to that shown in Fig. 22 will be found to give a factor of safety of about 11 for spruce.* In estimating the size of the spar it is better to select a probable section to suit the depth of section of the wing and to check this selected section for strength as a strut fixed at the ends, of length equal to the " free length "

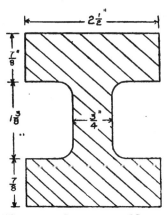

FIG. 22.—SECTION OF MONO-PLANE WING SPAR TO WITHSTAND THE GIVEN STRESSES.

of the spar as given by the B. M. diagram, and laterally loaded with the maximum B. M. shown in the B. M. diagram between the above-mentioned limits of free length; the least radius of gyration must be considered in the strut formula.

* The methods of calculation for wing-spar dimensions are fully considered in Chapter VIII.

STRESSES DUE TO DRIFT.

In ordinary types of aeroplane, the total drift load is about one-sixth of the total weight of machine. This drift load is usually taken by internal bracing between the two spars, and in this case the front spars are put in tension, whilst the rear spars are in compression. It is easy to estimate the amount of these additional stresses by considering the girder formed by the two spars, wing-ribs and internal bracing, to be uniformly loaded with the drift load, in the same way as a biplane system.

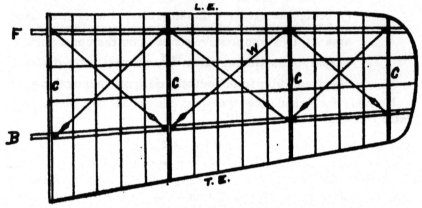

FIG. 23.

If the drift forces are taken by external drift wires from the fuselage or chassis, then the spars, if both are braced externally against drift, are put into compression.

The tensile and compressive stresses due to drift must be added to the lift stresses in the spar.

It is useful to note the usual methods of taking the " drift " of the wings. In the earlier machines it was a common practice to anchor the lift cables to a part of the undercarriage vertically in front of the point of attachment to the wings, so that these cables could take both the lift and the drift of the wings. The disadvantages of this method are that the undercarriage is subjected to shocks which may easily distort it, stretch the cables, and upset the stresses in the cables anchored to it, and that the ratio of lift to drift forces varies considerably over the range of flying speeds, so that the inclination backwards of the lift cable can only be correct for any one ratio.

The other method, now almost universally adopted, is to design the wings strong enough in themselves to take the drift forces; this is usually done as indicated in Fig. 23. The front and back spars F and B, respectively, are provided at intervals with extra strong ribs termed " compression ribs," as shown at C, and diagonal bracing consisting of piano-wire varying in gauge from 12 S. W. G. to 16 S. W. G. is fitted as shown at W, with proper tensioning devices.   This method of construction is equivalent to a deep diagonally-braced girder.

Most machines, whether monoplane or biplane, usually have additional external cables to take the drift, but it is a Government requirement, for machines accepted by them, that the internal bracing shall be strong enough in itself to take the whole of the drift with the given safety factor.

In connection with the member O (Fig. 21), this in flight is usually subjected to a small tensile load, but in landing, and whilst stationary, is subjected to compressive loads.   In the former case the undercarriage strut system must be designed to withstand a compressive load, exceeding from two to three times the weight of the machine, as in bad landings.

GENERAL CASE OF MONOPLANE STRESSES.

In practice the lift wires are attached to the outside of the wing spars, and not to the neutral axis, and consequently the stresses in the spar are a little different from those calculated upon the latter assumption, being generally greater upon this account.

The points of attachment of the lift wires also may not be

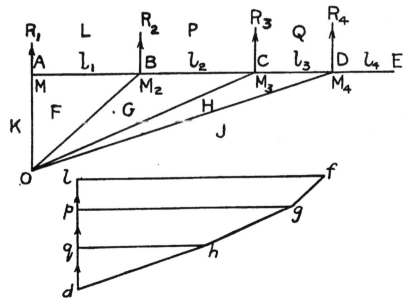

FIG. 24.—STRESSES IN A MONOPLANE WING SYSTEM.

upon the same level, as the Theorem of Three Moments supposes, on account of flexibility of the spars, and stretch or mis-alignment of the wires themselves. The effect of these factors will be mentioned later on. In the general case, consider a monoplane, one wing spar of which ABCDE (Fig. 24) is loaded with average loadings w_1, w_2, w_3, and w_4; these loadings must be chosen for the worst C. P. position—namely, when it is nearest the spar under consideration.

BENDING MOMENTS.

Let M_1, M_2, M_3, and M_4 be the bending moments at A, B, C, and D, respectively.

Then—

    1. $M_1 = O$.

    2. $M_4 = \dfrac{w_4 l_4^2}{2}$.

    3. Applying the Theorem of Three Moments to the points A, B, and C:

$$(M_1 l_1 + M_3 l_3) + 2 M_2 (l_2 + l_1) = \tfrac{1}{4} (w_1 l_1^2 + w_2 l_2^2) \qquad \text{(A)}$$

and

$$(M_2 l_2 + M_4 l_3) + 2 M_3 (l_3 + l_2) = \tfrac{1}{4} (w_2 l_2^2 + w_3 l_3^2) \qquad \text{(B)}.$$

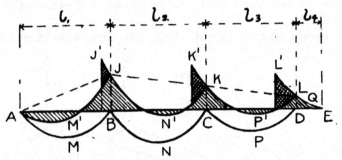

FIG. 25.—BENDING MOMENT DIAGRAM FOR MONOPLANE SPAR.

By substituting for M_1 and M_4 the values given in (1) and (2) in (A) and (B) and simplifying, the following values for the bending moments are obtained:

$$M_2 = \frac{2(l_2 + l_3)(4w_1 l_1^3 + w_2 l_2^3 - 4M_1 l_1) + l_2(4M_4 l_3 - w_2 l_2^3 - w_3 l_3^3)}{16(l_1 + l_2)(l_2 + l_3) - 4l_2^2}$$

$$M_3 = \frac{2(l_1 + l_2)(w_2 l_2^3 + w_3 l_3^3 - 4M_4 l_3) + l_2(4M_1 l_1 - w_1 l_1^3 - w_2 l_2^3)}{16(l_1 + l_2)(l_2 + l_3) - 4l_2^2}.$$

To draw the bending moment diagram (Fig. 25), at the points A, B, C, and D set up ordinates proportional to the values of M_1, M_2, M_3, and M_4 obtained—namely, BJ, CK, DL. Next, upon the base AB, draw the parabola of bending moment, AMB to the same scale, considering the portion AB as a uniformly loaded spar, with loading w_1, and supported at A and B.

The maximum ordinate will be $\dfrac{w_1 l_1^2}{8}$

Similarly for the other sections BC, CD, and DE draw the parabolas BNC, CPD, and EQLD.

Add algebraically the ordinates of the parabolic areas and the diagram AJKL, and the resulting diagram is the bending moment diagram (shown plain shaded) for the wing spar under consideration.

MODIFICATION OF BENDING MOMENT DIAGRAM.

If the points of attachment of the lift wires be B^1, C^1, and D^1, so that the lines OB^1, OC^1, and OD^1 produced meet the neutral axis in B, C, and D (Fig. 26), then if the bending moments at A, B, C, and D be M_1, M_2, M_3, and M_4, respectively, and the diagram of bending moment AM^1J, N^1K, P^1LE be constructed in exactly the same manner as before, the effect of the non-attachment of the lift wires to the neutral axis may be very approximately taken into account (Fig. 25) by producing the parabolas EL to L^1, LP^1K to K^1, and KN^1J to J^1, where the points L^1, K^1, and J^1 are upon the perpendicular ordinates drawn through the points D^1, C^1, and B^1, not shown in the diagram.

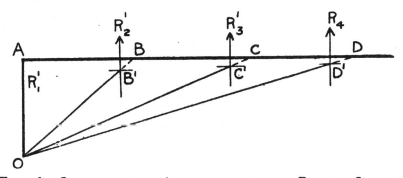

FIG. 26.—CORRECTION FOR ATTACHMENTS OF THE BRACING CABLES.

The shaded area, together with the cross-hatched area, now represents very nearly the new diagram of bending moments.

EFFECT OF NON-ALIGNMENT OF POINTS A, B, C, D, AND E.

If the points A, B, C, D, and E do not lie upon the same straight line, then the results obtained by the Theorem of Three Moments are not true, and therefore require modification. It can be shown that if one of the points is $\frac{1}{4}$ inch out of line, the bending moments will be appreciably modified.

In an example taken, the values of the bending moments at B and C, assuming no distortion of spar, were found to be 144 and 132 pounds feet respectively.

When the points B and C were 0·25 inches above the other points, the bending moments became 170 and 156 pounds feet respectively.

When B and C were at 0·25 inches below the other points, the bending moments were 112 and 103 pounds feet respectively. The effect of the wire breaking at B caused the bending moment to become 520 pounds feet at C, whilst a breakage at C increased the bending moment at B to 515 pounds feet. In the case of a wire breakage at D, the bending moment at C became 1,020 pounds feet, whilst at B the sign of the bending moment was reversed, the value being 80 pounds feet. For a fuller consideration of the methods of taking into account the effects of spar-distortion, wire stretching, and wire fracture, the reader is referred to the Advisory Committee for Aeronautics Report, 1912-13, pp. 218-228.

SHEARING FORCES.

In the general case of monoplane stresses under consideration, if the shearing forces to the left hand be denoted by the letters $R_{A \cdot L}$, $R_{B \cdot L}$, $R_{C \cdot L}$, $R_{D \cdot L}$, $R_{E \cdot L}$, whilst those to the right hand of the points are denoted by $R_{A R}$, $R_{B \cdot R}$, $R_{C \cdot R}$, $R_{D \cdot R}$, $R_{E \cdot R}$, respectively. Then—

1. $R_{E \cdot R} = O$

2. $R_{A \cdot L} = O.$

3. $R_{A \cdot R} = \dfrac{M_1 - M_2}{l_1} + \dfrac{w_1 l_1}{2}.$

4. $R_{B \cdot L} = \dfrac{M_2 - M_1}{l_1} + \dfrac{w_1 l_1}{2}.$

5. $R_{B \cdot R} = \dfrac{M_2 - M_3}{l_2} + \dfrac{w_2 l_2}{2}.$

6. $R_{C \cdot L} = \dfrac{M_3 - M_2}{l_2} + \dfrac{w_2 l_2}{2}.$

7. $R_{C \cdot R} = \dfrac{M_3 - M_4}{l_3} + \dfrac{w_3 l_3}{2}.$

8. $R_{D \cdot R} = R_{D \cdot L} = \dfrac{M_4 - M_3}{l_3} + \dfrac{w_3 l_3}{2} + w_4 l_4.$

Knowing these forces it is an easy matter to draw the S.F. diagrams.

REACTIONS.

The reactions R_1, R_2, R_3, and R_4 at the points A, B, C, and D are as follows:

1. $R_1 = R_A \cdot R = \dfrac{M_1 - M_2}{l_1} + \dfrac{w_1 l_1}{2}$.

2. $R_2 = R_B \cdot R + R_B \cdot L = \dfrac{M_2 - M_3}{l_2} + \dfrac{M_2 - M_1}{l_1} + \tfrac{1}{2}(w_2 l_2 + w_1 l_1)$.

3. $R_3 = R_C \cdot R + R_C \cdot L = \dfrac{M_3 - M_4}{l_3} + \dfrac{M_3 - M_2}{l_2} + \tfrac{1}{2}(w_3 l_3 + w_1 l_1)$.

4. $R_4 = R_D \cdot R = \dfrac{M_4 - M_3}{l_3} + \dfrac{w_3 l_3}{2} + w_4 l_4$.

STRESS DIAGRAM.

Employing the values for R_1, R_2, R_3, and R_4, the force diagram can be drawn, or the stresses existing in the various members c in be calculated. Fig. 24 also illustrates the graphical method in the case under consideration.

The forces in the sections AB, BC, and CD are compressive, whilst in OA, OB, OC, and OD they are tensile.

In connection with the bending moment upon any part of the wing spar, it is necessary in all cases to check the deflexion of the spar in the worst case, and to estimate the effect of the compressive load, due to the bracing, upon the strength of the spar.

Thus, if the centre of a given span BC, say, has a deflexion δ due to the bending moment there, then the compressive load F_c will cause an additional bending moment equal to $F_c \cdot \delta$. For a fuller consideration of this subject, the reader is referred to Chapter VIII.

STRESSES IN A BIPLANE.

Loading.—In normal types of wings the C. P. travels from a position at 0·50 of the chord at 0 degrees to 0·40 at 2 degrees, 0·33 at 6 degrees, and 0·30 at 12 degrees approximately. The loading upon the two wing spars is greatest in each case when the C. P. is nearest the spar; an example is given in Fig. 17 of this effect.

In the case of the upper wing of a biplane, this closely resembles the usual type of model aerofoil tested, and the distribution of loading should be similar to that given for the " parasol " type of monoplane wing shown on p. 61, and based upon pressure distribution tests around an aerofoil.

Where the upper camber is interfered with by king-posts, pylons, fuselage, etc., the efficiency, or loading of the wing, is reduced. On this account, therefore, the lower wing of a biplane, to which the fuselage or body is generally in close proximity and the struts to the top surface, the loading will be necessarily lower than in the upper wing; also, on account of the biplane spacing effect, the efficiency of the lower plane is further impaired.

Fig. 27 illustrates a typical case of biplane loading, taking the above-mentioned factors into consideration; the numbers given representing the relative proportions of the loadings.

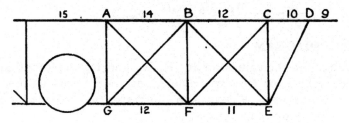

FIG. 27.—DIAGRAM OF LOADING OF BIPLANE.

BENDING MOMENTS.

The method of computing the bending moments is the same as in the cases considered for the monoplane.

The two spars ABCD and GFE are treated separately, the Theorem of Three Moments being applied to the cases of the moments at the joints A, B, C, D, E, F, G, respectively, in order to obtain the moments there.

The shearing forces are next calculated by the methods indicated on p. 72, and from these the vertical reactions, due to the lifting forces upon the wings, can also be found at the above-mentioned places.

STRESSES IN THE SPARS, STRUTS, AND CABLES.

Having found the vertical reactions at these points, the whole frame is assumed to be pin-jointed at the points A, B, C, D, E, F, G, and the stresses in the members are obtained from the stress diagram. An example of the general type of stress diagram for an actual case is shown in Figs. 28 and 29 for a lightly loaded biplane of total weight = 1,370 pounds, the upper and lower wings weighing 120 and 90 pounds, respectively, and the distribution of loading being similar to that given in Fig. 27. In the example given the wing area of the top plane is 240 square feet, whilst for the lower plane it is 180 square feet, the wing loading upon the average being somewhat low. Both forward and rear spar are considered as being equally loaded. The bending moment and shearing force diagrams are not given, as they closely resemble those already considered.

The stress diagram given in Fig. 29 illustrates the following facts, namely·

1. That the stresses in the top wing spar sections AB, BC,

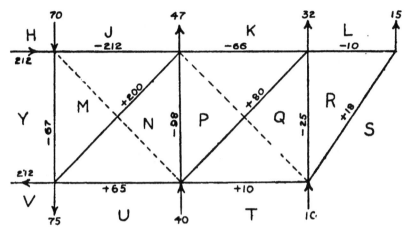

FIG. 28.—EXAMPLE OF THE STRESSES IN A BIPLANE SYSTEM.

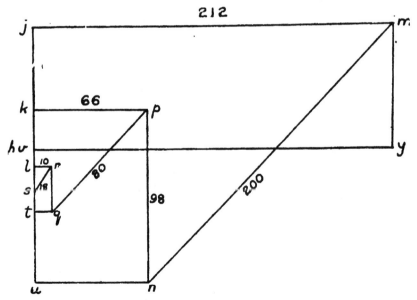

FIG. 29.—STRESS DIAGRAM FOR FIG. 28.

and CD (shown in Fig. 27) are compressive, due to the bracing system.

2. That the stresses in the lower wing spar sections GF and FE are tensile.

3. That in the panel near the centre of top wing spar the compressive loads are greatest, and the cable tensile stress in GB is also the greatest. Further, the maximum tensile load occurs in the lower wing spar in the inner panel.

4. That the stresses near the wing tips are a minimum.

The lift cables GB, FC, and ED are, in practice, usually duplicated for reasons connected with safety and reliance.

The cables AF and BE, shown dotted, are simply the load cables for supporting the weight of the wings when the machine is landing or stationary, and do not take any appreciable part in flying stresses, so are therefore made small compared with the lift cables, although it must be remembered that these cables must be strong enough to take the landing and top-loading stresses.

It should be here mentioned that the above methods assume the points of support to be in a straight line when under load, and that the points of inflexion (or zero bending moment), giving the " free length " of the wing spar under end loading, are unaltered by the superposition of the end loading and bending.

TOP LOADING STRESSES IN AEROPLANES.

1. The Stationary Stresses.

Under some conditions the loading of the wings may be reversed in direction, and in amount may exceed the positive loading during normal flying.

The simplest case of reversal of loading is that which occurs when the machine is stationary upon the ground, and the loading of the wings is simply due to its own weight, together with its struts and bracing.

The weight of the fuselage or body and undercarriage is not borne by the wing bracing system, and so the stresses in the latter are only due to its own weight.

If the weight of the wing system be assumed to be uniformly distributed along the spars, and be denoted by the letter w, whilst the total weight of the complete machine is W, then the ratio of the stresses in the wings during horizontal flight to the stationary stresses is $\dfrac{W-w}{w}$.

In the case of a biplane of 1,500 pounds weight, the wings of which weigh 200 pounds, the stresses in normal horizontal flight will be $\dfrac{1,500-200}{200} = 6\cdot5$ times those occurring upon the wing system whilst the machine is stationary.

2. The Landing Stresses.

The landing stresses, asmentioned in Chapter VII., may easily be from two to three times the stationary stresses, and may become very much higher in an awkward landing.

3. Top Loading Stresses due to Diving.

The other conditions under which top loading may come upon the wing system is when the machine, after a horizontal flight, is suddenly made to assume a steep downward path, greater than its natural gliding path.

Under these conditions the wings will have a negative or top loading, the amount of which will vary as the square of the speed, and inversely as the radius of the vertical circular path.

Thus if W = weight of machine,

$\qquad$ V = its velocity,

$\qquad$ R = radius of circular path,

$\qquad$ L = total loading of the wings reckoned as positive when acting normally outwards from the top surface, as in normal flight,

then $$L = W - \frac{W\, V^2}{g \cdot R}.$$

As an example, consider the case of a machine travelling horizontally at 75 miles an hour, to change its course downwards in a circle of radius 100 feet.

$$\text{Here } L = W - \frac{W \cdot (110)^2}{32 \times 100} = -2 \cdot 8\ W.$$

The negative, or top loading, in this case will be nearly three times the weight of the machine, neglecting the wing weights.

If the machine moved in a circular path of the same radius upwards, the positive loading would be increased to 4·8 times its normal amount.

The above considerations show that the top load wires or cables, which support the weight of the wing system when at rest on the ground, should be designed to cope with these conditions.

It is usual to design the top loading wires or cables to withstand about half the worst loading stresses of the corresponding lift cables, or, in other words, to adopt a factor of safety about half of that used in the lift cables.

Another point to be remembered in connection with this reversal of loading is that whereas the stresses in the spars of monoplanes act in the same sense for both top and bottom loading, and that both positive and negative loadings put the spars in compression, yet in the case of biplanes the stresses are reversed, so that the top spar is no longer in compression, but in tension, whilst the bottom spar is in compression instead of tension, both being subjected of course to bending moments as well.

PRINCIPLES OF CONSTRUCTION OF THE WING SYSTEM

SYSTEMS OF BIPLANE BRACING.

Examples of some typical methods of bracing the wings of biplanes are given in Fig. 30.

It will be noticed that all of these agree in using a combination of struts and diagonal bracing wires or cables; but that where the upper wing overhangs the last strut by a comparatively large amount, an inclined tie-strut member is employed, as in A, which represents the system employed on the D.F.W. biplane and the Farman machines. In some cases an additional king-post is fitted above the last strut, and a series of inclined lift and top load wires take the lift and the top load of the overhung portion, as shown in diagram F, which represents the Farman hydroplane system.

In cases of a small overhang of from one-half to three-quarters of the chord, it is sufficient to make the overhung portion of the spars strong enough as a cantilever, or to add an additional lift cable, as shown in diagrams C and E, which are typical of many existing biplane systems.

Diagrams B and F represent the bracing methods employed for the large spans of flying boats, heavy biplanes, etc., whilst D indicates a typical method of bracing light biplane scouts. Here only one interplane strut pair is fitted to each half of the wing, the span being small.

WING. FORMS.

The plan forms of aeroplane wings vary considerably in shape, sometimes for constructional reasons, in other cases for stability purposes, as in the Etrich Taube, Dunne, and other machines, and in many cases apparently for appearance' sake, but in few cases for reasons connected with the aerodynamic efficiency.

Most successful machines agree in having an aspect ratio of

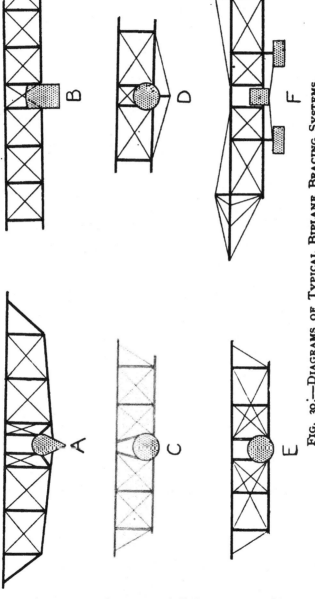

FIG. 30.—DIAGRAMS OF TYPICAL BIPLANE BRACING SYSTEMS.

about 6 or over, except in cases of light scouts, which sacrifice span dimensions for other reasons. The chief differences existing between plan forms of aeroplane wings lie in the shapes of the wing tips and aileron design.

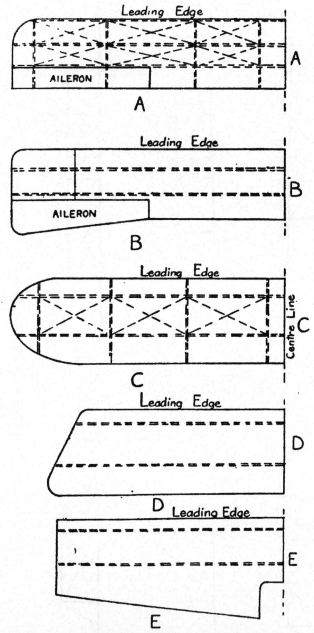

FIG. 31.—SOME TYPICAL WING PLAN FORMS.

The outline diagrams shown in Fig. 31 illustrate a few of the typical wing plan forms of present practice. The diagrams also show the positions along the chord of the wing spars, and in one or two cases the drift bracing system. The wings illustrated in

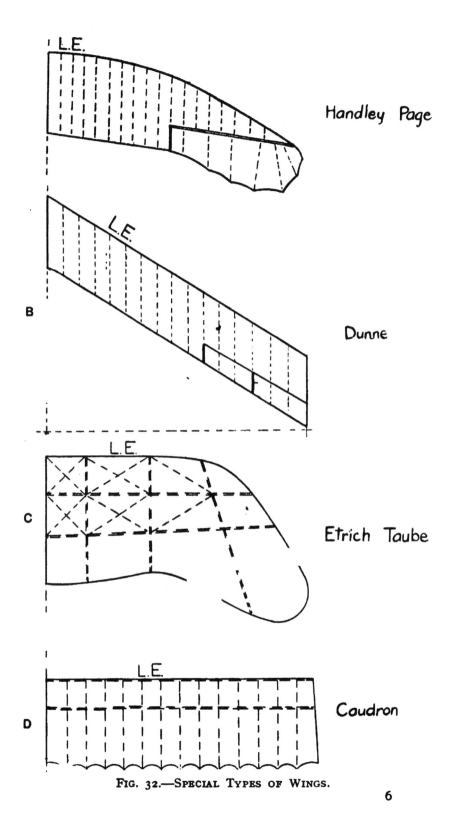

L.E.

Handley Page

B

L.E.

Dunne

C

L.E.

Etrich Taube

D

L.E.

Caudron

FIG. 32.—SPECIAL TYPES OF WINGS.

6

this system belong to the rigid type, except in so far as they require to be warped.

The simplest plan form, much evident in earlier machines, was the plain rectangle. Modern tendency is, however, towards rounded wing tips, with parallel chord along the span.

The B.E. type, as shown in Diagram C, is used in many other machines, either with the major portion of the curve behind, or in front as in the Bleriot, Sopwith, etc.

The plan shape given in D is typical of the Morane-Saulnier monoplane, and Eiffel has shown that this plan form gives a rather higher lift coefficient for the same value of the drift coefficient than the rectangular or rounded forms. The increase in the lift to drift ratio is most marked between 8 degrees and 12 degrees, and amounts to from 4 to 8 per cent.

This type of wing plan is no doubt more efficient on account of the more gradual pressure grading towards the tips, with the consequent diminution in end-losses. A combination of D and E would probably show a still better aerodynamic efficiency.

The plan forms shown in Fig. 32 represent some exceptional wing plan forms, adopted for stability and control purposes. The chief features of A, B, and C, are that the wing tips are negatively warped for stabilizing purposes. In A and C this is obtained by warping the trailing edge upwards, whilst in B the leading edge is warped downwards.

Diagram D illustrates a wing with a flexible trailing edge, also for stability purposes, in which the front edge forms one wing spar; this is also a feature of one or two other machines.

TYPES OF WING SPAR SECTIONS.

1. Wooden Spars.

Wing spars designed to fulfil the requirements of strength may take a variety of shapes and forms, and a large number of different sections are to be found in practice, but this is more especially marked in the machines of a year or two ago than now.

Some typical spar sections are shown in Fig. 33, illustrating different methods of construction.

The spars are usually made of ash, spruce, or poplar, and are made hollow about the neutral axis of the " lift " bending moment, but are left solid where the compression ribs, struts, and external bracing are fixed.

The most common form of section is the I section, which is generally shaped at its outer flange surfaces to conform with the wing section, and is hollowed out as shown in A (Fig. 33).

To avoid warping and distortion, spars have been made in

separate portions, as shown in *B*. The grains of the component pieces are sometimes set at angles with each other, and are glued and screwed (or clamped) together.

Another method, in which economy of weight is aimed at, is shown in *C* and *D*, the vertical webs being made of 3-ply in the former example, which has been employed in the Martinsyde machines.

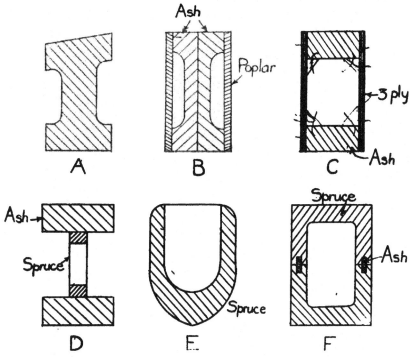

FIG. 33.—EXAMPLES OF WOODEN WING SPAR SECTIONS.

In certain machines, such as the Farman and Nieuport, the leading edge itself forms the front spar, and is shaped (in the former case) as shown in *E*. Needless to remark, in this type the rear spar must be situated well back, in order to withstand the increased stresses due to the backward travel of the C.P. when the angle of incidence decreases; occasionally, however, three spars are employed.

Wing spars are sometimes built up somewhat upon the principle of hollow struts, as shown in *F*, which represents the back spar of a wing of the type in which the front spar is formed by the leading edge.

Armoured wooden spars have been employed in which the greater part of the stresses has been taken by a steel strip (or strips) set with the depth vertical, as in G (Fig, 34), the wooden sides being riveted and bound to the steel, thus giving sufficient rigidity to prevent buckling. Such a spar was fitted to the Caudron machine. In some instances steel tubes of appropriate section have been filled with ash for the wing spars.

2. Steel Spars.

The modern tendency in aeronautical practice is towards the elimination of such materials as wood, as the strength of this

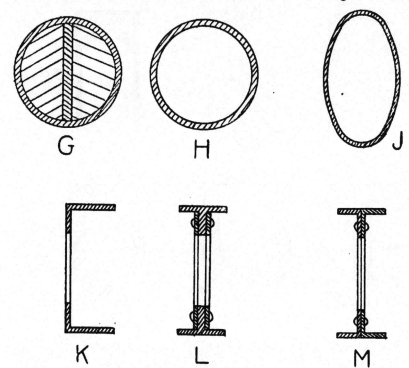

FIG. 34.—EXAMPLES OF METAL WING SPAR SECTIONS.

material depends upon its previous history and subsequent treatment, and is always an unreliable factor. For this purpose steel, and other metals, is replacing these non-homogeneous materials, and successful all-metal wings (and indeed complete machines) have been built.

It is necessary when designing for metals to dispose the material in the best possible way so that the actual weight is a minimum, as one of the reasons for their non-adoption has been-on account of their weight as compared with wood.

The introduction of high tensile alloy steels, modern welding and fusion methods, and the more accurate calculation of the

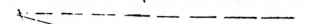

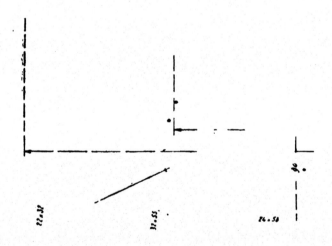

FIG. 35.—THE ETRICH WING WITH

strengths of the parts, may result in the gradual elimination of wooden spars.

The disadvantages of the metal spar as employed up to the present time are, firstly, its rather higher weight; secondly, that in a built-up spar it is difficult to ensure that the union between the component parts will be as strong as the components themselves; and thirdly, that of the protection of the surface of the metal against rust and corrosion. This latter objection has already been largely overcome with the introduction of high tensile non-rusting steels.

Examples of some of the metal spar sections which have been employed are shown in Fig. 34.

Round and elliptic steel tubes have been employed for wing spars, notably in the Breguet machine. For maximum economy of weight, these spars should be tapered in length, or diminished in thickness of section towards the wing tips.

In the Clement-Bayard machine, channel steel section, considerably lightened out in the webs, has been successfully employed for the wing spars (see Fig. 38).

The steel spar, built as a pressing upon this plan, possesses advantages as regards its time of construction, uniformity, and for repetition work.

WING CONSTRUCTION.

The wing is designed to fulfil several objects. Firstly, it must be constructed to give the correct shapes or sections at all places along the span; secondly, it must suitably house the main wing spars and allow means for their external bracing ; thirdly, it must accommodate the lateral control, whether aileron or warp.

The majority of aeroplane wings are now built upon one system, which can be best understood by reference to the Nieuport wing plan in Fig. 23 and the Etrich Taube plan and elevation given in Fig. 35. The two wing spars pass through all the sections, and are internally diagonally braced against drift forces. Suitably shaped ribs are provided at intervals of from 10 to 14 inches to give the fabric its correct profile when stretched over the whole wing framework. These ribs are divided up into two classes: the stronger ribs, to which the drift bracing is attached, are termed "compression ribs," whilst the lighter skeleton ribs, which chiefly serve to give the wing its proper section or shape, are known as "former ribs."

The construction of these ribs is illustrated in Figs. 36 and 37.

Diagram A shows one of the simplest methods of constructing the former ribs, and their attachment to the longitudinal mem-

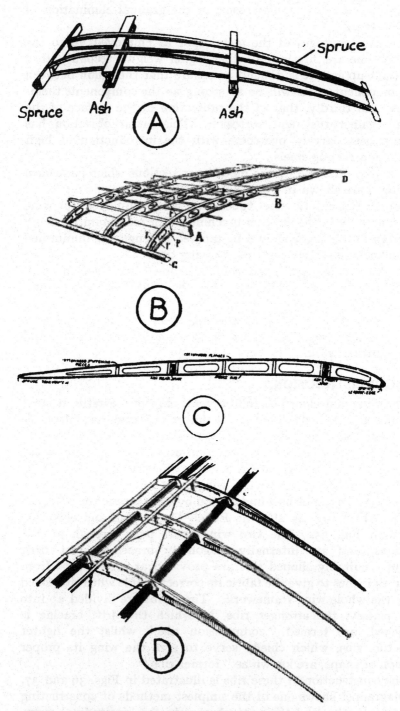

FIG. 36. METHODS OF CONSTRUCTION OF AEROPLANE WINGS.

bers. They are here composed of either spruce or cotton wood, both being very light materials, whilst the leading and trailing edges are of spruce, the main spars being of ash I beam sections.

Diagram *B* shows a perspective view of a portion of the wing structure, with several former ribs in position. In this case the leading edge is composed of an aluminium cup-section bar, whilst the main spars are rectangular in section.

The thin, flat, longitudinal rods S are termed " stringers," and their function is to preserve the shape of the wing between the main spars—that is, to prevent excessive sag in the fabric.

Diagram *C* illustrates a method of constructing a compression rib, details of the materials used being given.

FLEXIBLE WINGS.

In certain types of wing designed for stability purposes, the trailing edge is made flexible. Usually, as in the case of a bird's wing, the trailing portion of the wing offers little resistance to top loading, but is rigid as regards the normal flying loadings.

The Caudron wing is made flexible in the manner shown in *D* (Fig. 36) by splitting the trailing portion of the wing ribs.

In the Taube wings, and in certain experimental machines, bamboo ribs of rectangular section are employed for flexibility. These are made either of solid round cane of about $\frac{1}{2}$ inch diameter, or of portions of split tubular bamboo of from $2\frac{1}{4}$ to $3\frac{1}{4}$ inches outside diameter, the rectangular sections thus obtained measuring about $1\frac{1}{4}$ inches by $\frac{1}{4}$ inch.

Steel wire, in conjunction with an upper and lower rib flange, is employed in the D.F.W. flexible wings.

The materials more commonly employed for the wing construction are birch or ash three-ply, or spruce, for the vertical webs of the ribs, spruce, poplar, white pine or cottonwood for the flanges, and spruce for the leading and trailing edges, although metal is more commonly employed here ; generally ash or an ash-spruce combination for the main spars is employed.

In some machines, notably the Caudron and Farman machines, the leading edge itself forms the front spar, and is then made considerably stiffer.

Full information of these, and other materials used in aeroplane construction, is given in the volume of this series, entitled " Aeroplane Methods and Materials of Construction."

STEEL CONSTRUCTIONS.

Several machines have been fitted with wings constructed entirely of metal, which, whilst usually weighing appreciably more than the wooden constructions, have possessed the advantages of greater strength, homogeneity, and in some cases standardization possibilities.

Some successful wings have been constructed almost entirely of metal tubes welded together, the leading edge being made of about 10 millimetres diameter tubing, whilst the trailing edge was somewhat smaller, the metal thickness being about 22 S.W.G.

The main spars have been made of round tubing of from 30 millimetres to 60 millimetres diameter, and from 20 S.W.G. to 16 S.W.G. in thickness.

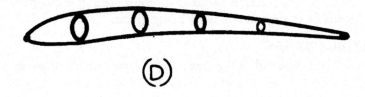

(D)

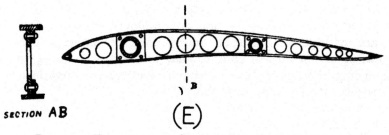

SECTION AB (E)

FIG. 37.—EXAMPLES OF STEEL WING CONSTRUCTION.

In order to preserve the shape of the section, short pieces of elliptical tubing were welded between the outside pieces, as shown in D (Fig. 37); the limit to the thickness of tubing allowable is fixed by welding considerations, 20 S.W.G. being about the smallest workable width.

One interesting French method of constructing metal wings is shown in E (Fig. 37). The spars in this case are of steel tubes; the flanges of the ribs are made of T-section aluminium riveted to the thin steel webs, which are themselves lightened out.

The Clement-Bayard wing construction consists almost entirely of metal, the leading and trailing edges (Fig. 38) being of thin V-section steel, whilst the spars themselves are of channel steel, lightened out around the neutral axis of bending, and are made somewhat thin for flexibility reasons connected with the warping.

The ribs themselves are of wood, whilst the stringers are of very thin flat steel strip.

Another method applicable to the construction of the ribs themselves, especially where reproduction in quantities is important, is to stamp these out of thin steel or aluminium alloy,

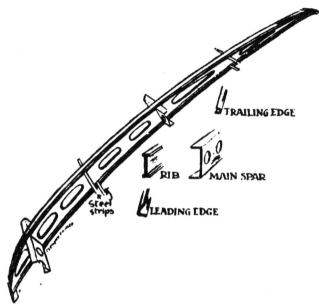

FIG. 38.—THE STEEL CONSTRUCTION OF THE CLEMENT-BAYARD WING.*

such as duralumin, the section being channel and the webs suitably lightened. Lugs can be stamped, or afterwards bent, for affixing the ribs to the spars.

It should be mentioned that even in wing constructions, consisting almost entirely of wood, metal can be employed with advantage. Thus the leading edge can be made of a **C**-sectioned aluminium bar, and the trailing edge of very light gauge streamline tubing (usually about ¾ inch major axis, ¼ inch minor axis, and 22 S.W.G. thickness in steel). The ribs are attached to these metal parts by means of light tinned steel straps, held by one or two wood screws to the ribs themselves.

The advent of nickel chrome and other high tensile steels in the form of tubes of various sections, channels, and other parts, has increased the possibilities of all metal constructions for aeroplanes.

* *Flight* copyright.

CHAPTER VII

PRINCIPLES OF UNDERCARRIAGE DESIGN

The designer should be well acquainted with the actual conditions of rolling and landing, in order to successfully design the undercarriage.

The pilot always endeavours to bring his machine down with its head to the wind, so that its speed relative to the earth is a minimum. It is generally better to glide down at a somewhat greater angle than the natural one, in order to render the controls more sensitive, and for stability reasons. When the machine nears the ground, the tail is gradually brought down in order to increase the angle of incidence to the maximum lift region, until the machine is flying at its minimum speed and gradually drops until the wheels touch earth. The provision of a mechanical brake is of great assistance in bringing the machine to a standstill after alighting; but air-brakes, which depend for their action upon the speed of the machine, are of little use in this respect.

MECHANICAL PRINCIPLES INVOLVED.

When an areoplane is gliding downwards at an angle a, it will have a kinetic energy in the direction of flight given by

$$\text{K.E.} = \frac{W \cdot V^2}{2 \cdot g} \text{ foot-pounds,}$$

where W = the total weight of machine in pounds,
V = its velocity in feet per second,
$g = 32 \cdot 18$.

In the landing operation (Fig. 39), the vertical component F of this energy must be overcome by the springing device of the undercarriage, whilst the horizontal component H is expended in overcoming the rolling and wind resistances.

In order to absorb the vertical component the springing devices (and the tyres) must deflect vertically through a certain distance. The greater this distance the less the mean force acting upon the springing device.

In practice the vertical movement varies from about 4 inches with elastic devices up to 12 inches with pneumatic and hydraulic shock absorbers.

If d = vertical movement of springing device, and F = mean force acting through springing device, then

$$F \cdot d = \frac{W \cdot V^2}{2g} \sin a$$

in the case of a bad landing without flattening out.

To take a concrete example, consider a machine of 1,500 pounds weight with a gliding angle of 1 in 8 to alight at 40 miles per hour at its gliding angle, and further assume that the shock absorbers allow a 12-inch vertical movement, it will be found

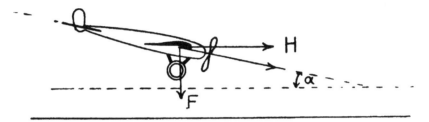

FIG. 39.—THE DYNAMIC FORCES IN ALIGHTING.

that the average force acting through the springing will be 10,000 pounds, or about six and a half times the weight of the machine ; further, if the machine lands upon one wheel, the conditions will be worse.

It is doubtful whether a landing chassis of aeroplane practice would survive such a mean force. The maximum force acting would be much greater than the mean, so that the conditions are even worse than assumed.

In practice it is the object of the pilot to reduce the vertical component of the machine's velocity to a minimum by flattening out as close to the ground as possible.

The undercarriage should be designed to withstand the shock due to a vertical drop of from 12 to 18 inches of the whole machine. In this case the expression for the mean force acting becomes

$$F = [1 \cdot 0 \text{ to } 1 \cdot 5] \frac{W}{d},$$

where d is the deflection in feet of the springing device and W the total load, as before.

It should be noted that the stresses in the wings, struts, and bracings may easily be from two to three times the stresses due to the weights of these parts when the machine is at rest on the ground.

Dealing next with the static forces affecting the stability or equilibrium of the machine during landing, it will be seen that when a machine touches the ground in alighting it is subjected to the forces shown in Fig. 40—namely·

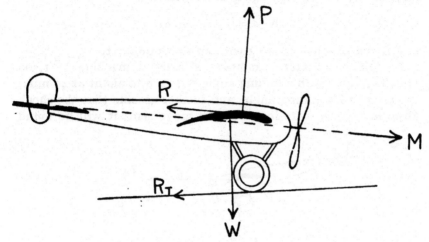

FIG. 40.—THE STATIC FORCES ON ALIGHTING.

1. Its weight W acting through the C.G.
2. The lift P due to its forward velocity [this during the landing operation falls off rapidly].
3. The force M_F, due to the momentum M, depending upon its weight and velocity, which may be considerable in magnitude, but which will depend upon the rate at which this momentum changes; this acts through the C.G.
4. The tractive resistance R_T, at the point of contact with the ground, where $R_T = \mu[W - P]$, the coefficient of rolling friction μ varying with the nature of the ground. Usually for grassy ground, such as found in aerodromes, the resistance may be taken at 80 to 120 pounds per ton.
5. The head resistance R.

The engine is assumed to be switched off in these considerations. If running it will introduce an additional force T at the propeller.

The momentum force brings into play a couple $M \cdot d$ (where d is the perpendicular distance of M from the point of wheel contact) tending to overturn the machine, whilst the lift force P also produces an upsetting moment.

If the C.G. of the machine is behind the point of contact of the wheel and ground, a righting couple is brought into play; the head resistance couple also tends to right the machine.

Calling x_w, x_p, x_m, x_r, and d, the perpendicular distances of the lines of action of the forces W, P, M_F, R, and R_T, respectively, from the wheel centre, the condition for equilibrium during alighting is that $[W \cdot x_w + R \cdot x_r]$ shall be greater than $[P \cdot x_p + M_F \cdot x_m + R_T \cdot d]$.

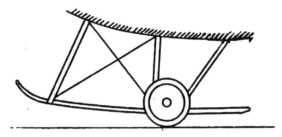

FIG. 41.—TYPES OF UNDERCARRIAGE.

GENERAL DESIGN PRINCIPLES OF UNDERCARRIAGES.

In undercarriage design the position of the C.G. is usually chosen so that it lies behind the point of contact of the wheel and ground when the machine is flying at its greatest angle of incidence (the distance being from 1 foot to 2 feet in most cases), otherwise a forward skid is provided, and the wheels are placed very nearly at the C.G., as shown in Fig. 41, to prevent overturning.

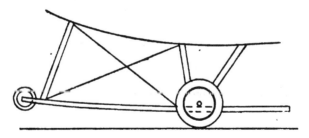

FIG. 42.—TYPE OF UNDERCARRIAGE.

This type of landing chassis sometimes takes the form of a forward skid provided with a single or pair of smaller diameter wheels at its extremity, as shown in Figs. 42 and 42A, suitably strutted and braced. The skid itself is sprung or flexibly connected to the transverse member, and is often extended sufficiently rearwards to act as a tail skid, so that no additional skid or support is required at the tail extremity.

In practically all existing designs of undercarriage the C.G. is placed very near to the centre of wheels when the machine is horizontal, and some form of rear support, either as a light tail skid, or an extension of the main skid, as indicated in Figs. 41 and 42, known as a " kangaroo " skid, is provided.

The nearer the C.G. to the wheel centre, the greater the proportion of weight taken by the main wheels, and the lighter the tail skid may be designed.

FIG. 42A.—TYPES OF UNDERCARRIAGE.

The proportion of the total weight carried by the tail skid in present practice is from 4 to 10 per cent., according to the position of the C.G. relative to the wheels.

The proportion of weight carried by the tail skid, when the machine is running over the ground, depends upon whether the machine has a carrying or a non-carrying tail, being smaller in the former case, and incidentally enabling a much lighter fuselage tail end construction.

If the C.G. is too far behind the wheel centres, the tail will tend to drop during alighting, thus increasing the incidence and causing an increase in the lift, so that the machine " rebounds " several times in coming to rest. Further, the weight upon the tail skid is excessive, and the frictional resistance prevents rapid acceleration when starting off.

The undercarriage should be designed so that when the machine is at rest, prior to starting, the angle of incidence of the planes is from 12 to 20 degrees, in order to provide for rapid rising.

The height of the undercarriage is dependent upon the propeller diameter, as sufficient ground clearance (from 12 to 24 inches) must be given under all conditions, whether the machine is tilted, or whether the wheels sink in a ground depression when the machine is running over the ground. Tractor machines can be designed with lower undercarriages than pushed machines on account of the propeller clearances being less at alighting angles.

It will generally be found that monoplanes require a somewhat higher undercarriage than biplanes.

When considering landing conditions, the effect of the wheels sinking in soft earth or sand should be remembered.

GENERAL REQUIREMENTS FOR UNDERCARRIAGES.

The undercarriage must be designed to suit the following enumerated conditions:

1. It must allow the machine to start and to stop in the quickest possible time consistent with comfort and safety. For this reason the resistance to rolling and sliding of the parts must be minimized. Some form of efficient brake should be fitted.

2. It must be well sprung in order to eliminate both forward and side shocks.

3. It must give both lateral and longitudinal stability whilst travelling over the ground (preferably without the addition of wing-tip skids or wheels).

4. It must be capable of withstanding rolling and side-shocks without serious deflection or fracture. The effects of landing in side winds or upon uneven ground may cause serious side stresses.

5. It must enable the machine to rise off soft ground or " plough." Usually this is a question of sufficient wheel diameter and width.

6. The head resistance must be as low as possible, and the chassis weight as low as possible consistent with safety.

7. It should enable the machine to be steered on the ground without the aid of the propellor blast upon the rudder.

In connection with monoplanes and with certain types of biplane employing lift bracing cables below the bottom plane, no lift or drift bracing cables should be anchored upon any portion of the undercarriage structure, but upon a separate and

specially designed " pylon " or mast.   Many serious and fatal
accidents have occurred through inattention to this point.

In connection with item 3, the fore and aft stability has already
been discussed, but the question of lateral stability will depend
upon the width of the wheel track in relation to the span and
weight of the machine.   Generally speaking, the wider the wheel
track the more stable the machine laterally; if a narrow track is
adopted, then wing-tip skids or wheels become a necessity.

The wheel tracks of aeroplanes vary from about 4 feet in the
case of light biplane scouts and monoplanes to 6 feet for ordinary
biplanes, and up to 12 feet for wide wing span biplanes of large
area.

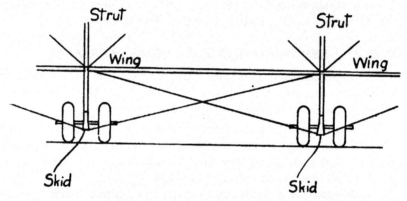

FIG. 43.—UNDERCARRIAGE FOR A HEAVY MACHINE.

The wheel track varies from one-quarter to one-tenth the span
of the machine in extreme cases, but may be taken upon the
average as from one-sixth to one-eighth the largest wing span
(in the case of a biplane).

Many undercarriages have been designed with an intentionally
smaller factor of safety than possessed by the remainder of the
machine, in order that the greater part of the shock of a bad
landing may be taken by the undercarriage, and the resulting
damage confined to that part.

TYPES OF UNDERCARRIAGE.

Many of the earlier machines, including the Wright and Farman
biplanes, possessed rigid skid structures without wheels.   This
system, although disadvantageous for " getting off," gave a rigid
anchoring for the lift cables.

The most popular type of undercarriage for biplanes at the
time present is that outlined in Figs. 41 and 42, consisting of a
pair of single or double wheels, combined with a single central

sprung skid of ash or hickory, or a pair of skids, each situated between and below a pair of wheels, as illustrated in Fig. 43.

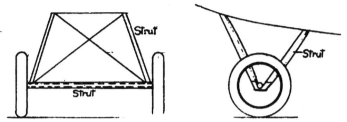

FIG. 44.—UNDERCARRIAGE ARRANGEMENT FOR A LIGHT SCOUT OR MONOPLANE.

This latter arrangement is employed upon the heavier types of machine, and gives a firm undercarriage.

The type of undercarriage employed upon light scouts or monoplanes is illustrated in Fig. 44, and consists of a pair of

FIG. 44A.—THE V-TYPE UNDERCARRIAGE, WITH CENTRAL PIVOTED AXLE.

V-struts, either of streamlined steel tubing, ash, or spruce, each pair viewed in front elevation being splayed out towards the ground and diagonally braced, as shown, with large gauge piano wire or cable to the eight extremities of the struts.

The wheels are usually carried upon plain axles, running on light gunmetal bushes in the wheel hubs.   The main axle may be continuous or divided in the centre, each half being pivoted at the centre, as shown in Fig. 44A.

In the latter arrangement additional staying of the central portion is required, and the head resistance thereby enhanced.

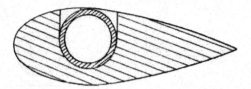

FIG. 45.—STREAMLINE STRUT WHICH IS ALSO USED FOR STREAMLINING THE WHEEL AXLE IN FLIGHT.

In designing the strut system for undercarriages, advantage should be taken of the shielding effect of struts placed one behind the other in the direction of flight, an appreciable reduction in the total head resistance resulting.

FIG. 45A.—STREAMLINING THE AXLE IN V-TYPE UNDERCARRIAGE.

The main axle (or axles) in the V-type chassis, and in those illustrated in Fig. 44, is usually either made in streamline tubing, or, when a transverse strut is fitted between the two V's, it is often grooved out to receive and streamline the plain round section axle when in flight, as shown in Figs 45 and 45A.

In Fig. 44 each system of V-struts is connected along the fuselage extremities by means of a cable or steel strip, to take any outward thrust along the struts.

Other systems of bracing the undercarriage are shown in Fig. 46.

In the Bleriot monoplane (Fig. 47) the undercarriage consists of two wheels of about 6 feet track, each wheel being allowed a vertical travel of 12 inches. The wheels are allowed to swivel through 45 degrees, being held in the normal position by light rubber cables; no front skid is fitted.

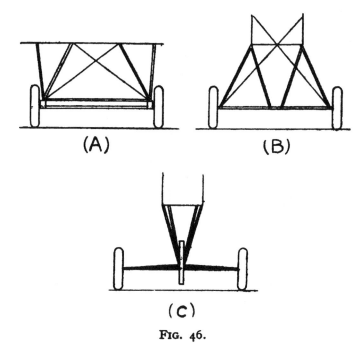

(A)   (B)

(C)

FIG. 46.

The object of the swivelling wheels is to obviate the serious side stresses consequent upon landing in a side wind, as the machine then has a lateral motion relatively to the ground. If the machine can be brought head to the wind, the use of swivelling wheel devices is obviated.

The additional weight and considerable head resistance of this type of undercarriage more than counterbalances any advantages accruing from its distinctive features.

In the Nieuport monoplane (Fig. 46, C) the undercarriage has been designed with the object of reducing head resistance. The wheels are mounted at the end of a transverse laminated spring attached to the single central skid in a position well in front of the C.G. The wheels, axle, and skid are held to the fuselage by means of V-struts in front elevation, and the use of cables is obviated.

The central skid is continued behind the wheels, and the usual tail skid is therefore absent.   This arrangement is similar to that shown in Fig. 41, and possesses the advantage that, being heavily loaded, it acts as braking agency when pulling up after landing. When starting, the lifting effect of the propeller blast upon the

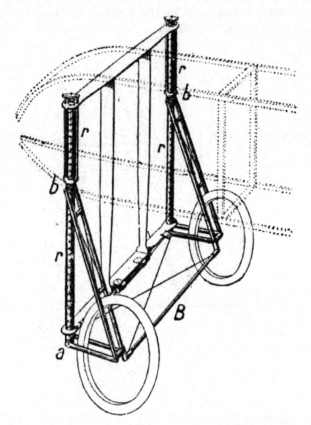

FIG. 47.—THE BLERIOT TYPE OF UNDERCARRIAGE.

tail takes most of the weight off the rear end of the skid, and thus facilitates " getting off." This type of undercarriage gives simplicity of design, low head resistance, and strength.

SPRINGING AND SUSPENSION.

The chief requirements of any springing device are that it should not only absorb shocks of landing and rolling, but that it shall do so in such a way that the energy of the shock shall not merely be stored up by the springing device and then given out again in the form of a rebound, but that it shall absorb the energy without giving it back in the previously mentioned form.

The absorption of vertical shocks is perhaps the chief function of a shock absorber, but a mere energy absorber is insufficient if means are not provided for undamped springing when rolling over uneven ground.   It is usual to allow the wheels a few inches of undamped vertical travel, either by means of compressed air or spiral springs.

For this reason rubber and helical springs are not the most suitable devices, as the energy of shock is not " absorbed " but merely stored.

The common form of laminated or leaf spring of motor-car is a decided improvement upon the two forms of springing men tioned above, in that the frictional resistance due to the sliding of the " leaves " over each other absorbs the energy of springing.

Perhaps the best devices for shock absorbing are the pneumatic and hydraulic systems as used upon the Breguet, R.A.F., and other machines.   When oil is employed, these latter are known as oleo-pneumatic systems.   In these types a dash-pot is provided, which absorbs the " work " of the shock of landing or encountering an obstacle when rolling.

Fig. 48* illustrates a typical oleo-pneumatic and spring shock absorbing device as used on the Breguet machines.

It consists of two telescopic steel tubes, the outer one, or cylinder, being attached to the axle of the wheels, whilst the inner tube, or piston, is attached to the body of the machine.

The piston is provided with a cup-leather and a spring-loaded valve, which can be adjusted to suit the weight and speed of the machine.

Upon landing oil is forced from the cylinder through the spring-loaded valve into the interior of the piston, whence it passes out again through ports in the walls of the piston.

When the machine rests upon the ground the spiral spring takes the load, and the valve is automatically opened by the spring seen in the base of the cylinder; the top spring is used for rolling purposes.

In the R.A.F. oleo-pneumatic shock absorber, which is very similar to the Breguet, the lower telescopic tube contains the oil, and this tube, carrying with it the axle, drops 11 inches when in flight.   Upon the machine striking the ground the oil first passes into a central air chamber, and then through three exit holes, each 4 millimetres in diameter.   When the velocity of impact is sufficiently high, the pressure of the oil due to its resistance in passing through the holes is raised to 640 pounds

---

* Reproduced from " Aeroplane Undercarriages," Proceedings of Institute of Aeronautical Engineers, 1912.

per square inch, and a spring loaded valve is opened to provide an additional oil passage.

The arrangement is designed so that after the first 2 inches of travel of the lower tube the resistance remains constant, and equal to two and a half times the weight of the machine. As the

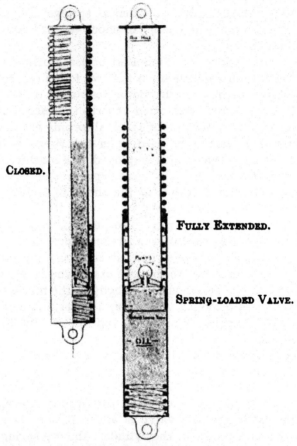

FIG. 48.—BREGUET SHOCK ABSORBER.

total vertical travel exclusive of the first 2 inches is 13 inches, the total energy absorbed at constant pressure works out at 4,300 foot pounds, and this corresponds with a vertical landing velocity of 13 feet per second.

Actually it has been shown that a fully loaded biplane can drop vertically from a height of 18 inches to the ground without injury.

In this form of suspension the rolling shocks are taken by strong spiral springs, as in the Breguet.

The Houdaille hydraulic shock absorber as applied to cars is an additional example of this type, and is very satisfactory in practice.

RUBBER SHOCK ABSORBERS.

Rubber possesses the advantages over steel for undercarriage springing that it will absorb a much greater amount of energy per unit weight and that it is readily replaceable.

"Flight" Copyright.

FIG. 49.—RUBBER SHOCK ABSORBER AND BRAKE.

The amount of energy which good rubber can absorb varies from 500 to 1,000 foot pounds per pound, whilst with steel it varies from 10 to 30 foot pounds, but it absorbs less work the more it stretches.

Rubber is further more easily adaptable to the various systems of suspension in vogue, and signs of deterioration are easily detected.

The rubber is used either in the form of an annular ring of from 6 to 12 inches diameter and from 1 to 3 inches wide and thick, or more generally as a woven fabric-covered cord or rope composed of from 50 to 300 strands of rubber covered with a woven surface, the diameter varying from ¼ inch up to 1 inch.

The method of adapting this cord to aeroplane undercarriage springing is shown in Fig. 49; sometimes, however, the rubber cords are arranged to take the shocks, in direct tension, as distinct from bending.

The amount of cord used will depend upon the weight and alighting speed of the machine, but a rough figure to allow for design purposes is 16 yards per 1,000 pounds weight of ½-inch diameter cord for the two (or more) wheels, *or about* 9 yards of ¾-inch diameter cord.

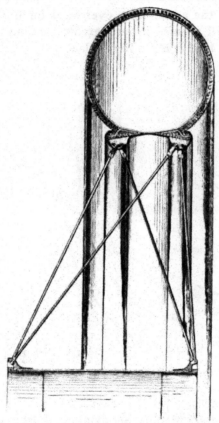

FIG. 50.—SECTION OF THE PALMER AEROPLANE TYRE AND WHEEL.

WHEELS.

The lighter wheels of earlier aeroplane practice are now being replaced by much stronger wheels with wide axles and well-splayed spokes for taking side stresses.

The hubs are invariably made plain, with gunmetal-steel bearings for lightness and quick replacement facilities.

The sizes of aeroplane wheels vary from 10 inches in the case of the wing-skid tip wheels up to 32 inches for very heavy machines, the standard size for monoplanes and biplanes being about 26 inches by 3 inches. (Particulars of Palmer sizes of wheels and tyres are given on p. 17.)

A section of an aeroplane undercarriage wheel is given in Fig. 50, showing the method of taking lateral stress by means of four rows of well-splayed spokes and the long bushed hub for the axle bearing.

The wheels are usually fitted with detachable celluloid metal, or canvas discs, to minimize head resistance. The larger the diameter of the wheel and the greater its width, the better is it adapted to traversing rough ground; the use of wheels in parallel or in tandem enables the machine to travel over rougher ground, owing to the hollows and crests being " bridged " over better.

It should be here mentioned that the lower the normal landing speed in still air, and the lighter the total weight of the machine, the lighter will be the landing chassis, in construction and weight, and the smaller the section, though not necessarily the diameter, of the wheels.

CHAPTER VIII

MECHANICAL PRINCIPLES INVOLVED IN AEROPLANE DESIGN

1. HOOKE'S LAW.

This states that within the limits of elasticity the strain produced by a stress is proportional to that stress. This may be written $\frac{p}{E} = \frac{x}{l}$, where p is the stress, E the modulus of elasticity, x the extension produced in a bar of initial length l, by the stress p.

For mild steel E = 13,000 tons per square inch, so that a stress of 1 ton per square inch produces an elongation in a bar of $\frac{1}{13000}$ of its original length; in the case of wood, the moduli of elasticity vary from 400 to 1,000 tons per square inch.

Thus, for ash   E = 730 tons per square inch,
whilst for spruce   E = 500   ,,   ,,   ,,
[Other values are given in Appendix I.]

2. POISSON'S RATIO.

The transverse contraction e, due to the elongation of a bar under tension, is given by—

$$e = \frac{p}{E} \cdot \frac{1}{\sigma} = \frac{x}{l} \cdot \frac{1}{\sigma},$$

where σ is a coefficient varying from 3 to 4 for metals, the reciprocal of this coefficient being known as Poisson's ratio.

3. SHEAR STRESS.

If ϕ = angle of shear, q the shearing stress producing this, and C the modulus of rigidity, then

$$\phi = \frac{q}{C}.$$

The value of C, which is equal to the shearing stress divided by the shearing strain, is about two-fifths that of E.

4. VOLUMETRIC COMPRESSION.

If three stresses p, acting in directions at right angles upon a body of initial volume V, and cause a diminution in volume by an amount v, then

$$p = K \cdot \frac{v}{V},$$

where K is a constant for the material known as the "bulk modulus."

The cubic strain produced is three times the linear strain in any one direction.

5. RELATION BETWEEN ELASTIC COEFFICIENTS.

The three elastic coefficients E, C, and K, which are concerned with the tensile, shear, and volumetric properties of a body, respectively, are related as follows:

$$\frac{1}{E} = \frac{1}{3C} + \frac{1}{9K}.$$

6. WORK DONE IN EXTENSION AND SHEAR.

Using the same notation as before—

(a) Work done per unit of volume in tension $= \dfrac{p^2}{2E}$.

(b) Work done per unit volume in shear $= \dfrac{q^2}{2C}$.

PROPERTIES OF BEAMS.

1. Simple Bending Stresses.

In the case of a beam subjected at any given section to a bending moment M, the following relation holds:

$$\frac{p}{y} = \frac{E}{R} = \frac{M}{I},$$

where p is the tensile or compressive stress at a point situated at a distance y from the neutral axis (Fig. 51) of bending (which passes through the C.G. of the section), E is the Elastic Modulus, R the radius of curvature of the bent or deflected beam, and I is the moment of inertia about the neutral axis of the area of section.

If M is in pounds-inches, I in (inches)⁴, and y in inches, then p will be in pounds per square inch.

If M is in kilogrammes-centimetres, I in (centimetres)⁴, and y in centimetres, p will be in kilogrammes per square centimetre.

The greatest stress occurring is when y is a maximum; it is equal to half the depth of the section in symmetrical sections, and for materials in which the ultimate tensile and compressive stresses are equal.

The Strength Modulus is the ratio $\frac{I}{y}$, and is usually denoted by the letter Z.

$$\text{Then } p = \frac{M}{Z}.$$

In all beam calculations, the value of p, the working stress is fixed by the factor of safety, and is usually taken as the ultimate stress divided by the factor of safety, but in some cases the elastic limit decides the value of the working stress taken.

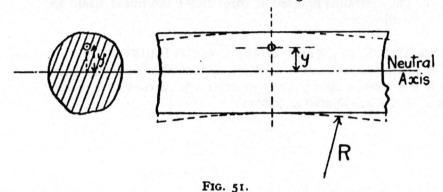

FIG. 51.

Values of the moments of inertia are given in Tables XV. and XVI. for the sections illustrated in Fig. 52.

XV.—MOMENTS OF INERTIA OF SOLIDS.

Type of Body.	Moment of Inertia.	Radius of Gyration.
Circular disc about perpendicular central axis. Mass$=$M, radius$=r$	$\dfrac{Mr^2}{2}$	$\dfrac{r}{\sqrt{2}}$
Elliptical disc about perpendicular central axis. Mass$=$M, major axis$=a$, minor axis$=b$	$\dfrac{Ma^2+b^2}{2}$	$\dfrac{\sqrt{a^2+b^2}}{\sqrt{2}}$
Sphere about a diameter	$\dfrac{2}{5}Ma^2$	$a\sqrt{\dfrac{2}{5}}$
Rod of length l about perpendicular axis through centre	$\dfrac{Ml^2}{12}$	$\dfrac{l}{\sqrt{12}}$
Rod of length l about perpendicular axis through end	$\dfrac{Ml^2}{3}$	$\dfrac{l}{\sqrt{3}}$
Cylinder about perpendicular axis. Radius$=r$	$\dfrac{Mr^2}{2}$	$\dfrac{r}{\sqrt{2}}$
Cone about axis perpendicular to its height l through apex	$\dfrac{Ml^2}{3}$	$\sqrt{3}$

XVI.—PROPERTIES OF SECTIONS.

No.	Moment of Inertia about Dotted Axis I through C.G.	Radius of Gyration $=\sqrt{\dfrac{I}{A}}$	Strength Modulus Z.
	$\dfrac{bd^3}{12}$	$0.289d$	$\dfrac{bd^2}{6}$
2	$\dfrac{d^3[b^2+4bb^1+b_1^2]}{36(b+b^1)}$ $a=\dfrac{d}{3}\left[\dfrac{b+2b_1}{b+b_1}\right]$	$d\sqrt{\dfrac{b^2+4bb_1+b_1^2}{18(b+b_1)(2b_1+b)}}$	$\dfrac{d^2[b^2+4bb^1+b_1^2]}{18(b+b^1)}$
	$\dfrac{bd^3}{36}$ $a=\dfrac{d}{3}$	$0.2357d$	$\dfrac{bd^2}{18}$
	$\dfrac{5\sqrt{3}}{16}a^4$	$0.456a$	$\dfrac{5a^3}{8}$
	$\dfrac{a^4}{12}$	$0.289a$	$\dfrac{a^3\sqrt{2}}{12}$
6	$\tfrac{1}{3}[b(a_1^2-f^4)+b_1(f^3+a^3_2)]$ $a_1=\dfrac{bb_2^2+b_1d_1(d+b_3)}{2[bd-(b-b_1)d_1]}$		$\dfrac{I}{d_1}$ and $\dfrac{I}{d_1-f}$
7	$\dfrac{bd^3-(b-b_1)d_1^3}{12}$ where $d=2a+d_1$	$\sqrt{\dfrac{bd^2-(b-b_1)d_1^2}{12[bd-(b-b_1)d_1]}}$	$\dfrac{bd^3-(b-b_1)d_1^3}{6d}$
8*	$\dfrac{\pi}{64}d^4$	$0.25d$	$\dfrac{\pi d^3}{32}$
9 Ellipse	$\dfrac{\pi}{64}bd^3$	$0.25d$	$\dfrac{\pi bd^2}{32}$
10	$\dfrac{d^4}{16}\left[\dfrac{\pi}{8}-\dfrac{8}{9\pi}\right]=0.0069d^4$ $a=\dfrac{2d}{3\pi}=0.2122d$	$0.132d$	$\dfrac{I}{a}$ and $\dfrac{I}{\frac{d}{2}-a}$
11 Para-bola	$\dfrac{8}{175}bh^3$	$0.2619h$	

* For an annular circular section for which outside diameter$=d$, and inside diameter$=d_1$:

$$I=\frac{\pi}{64}[d^4-d_1^4] \quad \text{and} \quad Z=\frac{\pi}{32}\left[\frac{d^4-d_1^4}{d}\right].$$

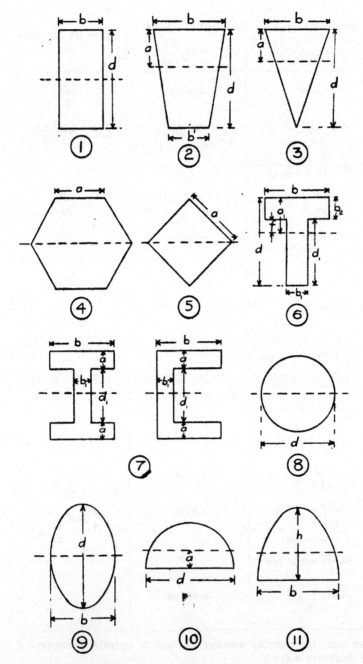

FIG. 52.—MOMENTS OF INERTIA OF AREAS.

METHOD FOR FINDING THE LEAST RADIUS OF GYRATION.

Consider as a concrete case an angle-section as shown in Fig. 53.

Let I_x and I_y be its moments of inertia about axes YY and XX at right angles through the centre of gravity of the area.

Consider any other axis PP making an angle a with OX, then by a well-known Theorem—

$$I_{OP} = I_x \cos^2 a + I_y \sin^2 a - 2 I_{xy} \sin a \cos a,$$

where I_{xy} is the product of inertia about the two axes, and is zero when the axis OP passes through the centre of gravity, as in the case considered.

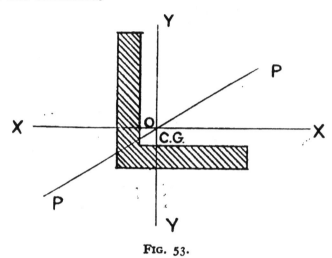

FIG. 53.

If r_x, r_y, and r_p be the radii of gyration corresponding with the moments of inertia I_1, I_y, and I_p, respectively, and if the values $\dfrac{1}{r_x}$, $\dfrac{1}{r_y}$, and $\dfrac{1}{r_p}$ be plotted, each along its axis, as measured from O, then an ellipse can be drawn through the points so obtained; this is called the "momental ellipse." The major and minor axes of this ellipse give respectively the reciprocals of the maximum and minimum radii of gyration.

GRAPHIC METHOD FOR MOMENTS OF INERTIA.

Moments of inertia may be easily obtained for any given section by the following polar method:

Let ABC (Fig. 54) be any area; it is required to find its moment of inertia about any line OO.

Draw a series of lines similar to *ef*, parallel to OO, and take a fixed base line MN parallel to OO at a distance *d* from it.

Project *ef* on to base line MN in *ab*, and from a point E in OO project radially the points *a* and *b* to e_1 and f_1.

If this process be repeated for all points similar to *e* and *f*, a

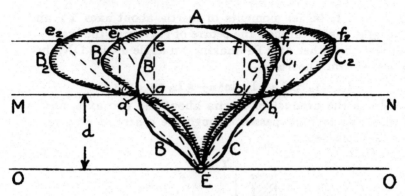

FIG. 54.—GRAPHICAL METHOD FOR MOMENTS OF INERTIA.

closed curve $A_1B_1C_1$ will be obtained, made up of points like e_1f_1. This is called the " first moment curve," and we have

Moment of area ABC about OO = $\begin{cases} \text{area of first moment curve} \\ AB_1C_1 \times d. \end{cases}$

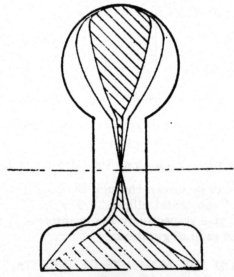

FIG. 55.

If this process be repeated for the first moment curve, a series of points like e_2, f_2 will be obtained, which lie on the closed curve AB_2C_2, which is termed the " second moment curve," and we have—

$$\text{Moment of inertia of ABC about OO} = \begin{cases} \text{area of second moment} \\ \text{curve } AB_2C_2 \times d^2. \end{cases}$$

If the moment of inertia be required about an axis through the C.G. parallel to OO, and if h is the perpendicular distance from the C.G. to OO, then—

$$\text{Moment of inertia of area ABC about C.G.} = \begin{cases} \text{area } AB_2C_2 \times d^2 + \\ \text{area ABC} \times h^2. \end{cases}$$

By choosing the axis OO to coincide with the neutral axis, through the C.G. of section, the method may be simplified, and the fixed base lines can be chosen at the extreme points of the sections away from the C.G.

An example of first and second moment curves drawn in this way is given in Fig. 55.

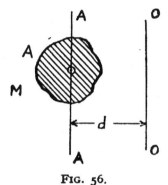

FIG. 56.

The first moment curve gives to scale the strength modulus of the section. If in Fig. 55 A = area of either first moment curves (since these are equal), and d = distance between their respective centres of gravity, then the strength modulus is given by—

$$Z = A \times d.$$

MOMENTS OF INERTIA ABOUT PARALLEL AXES.

If I_G be the moment of inertia of a body of mass M (or an area A) about an axis AA through its C.G. (Fig. 56), then the moment of inertia I_O of the body, or area, about a parallel axis OO, situated at a distance d from it, is given by—

$$I_O = I_G + M \cdot d^2 \text{ for a solid body,}$$
$$\text{and } I_O = I_G + Ad^2 \text{ for an area.}$$

ECONOMICAL BEAM SECTIONS.

The weight of a beam of constant section is proportional to its sectional area, whilst its resistance to bending is proportional to its strength modulus.

8

The most economical form of beam is that in which the ratio $\dfrac{\text{strength modulus}}{\text{area}}$ is a maximum.

For a given area, the greatest strength modulus is obtained by massing the material as far away from the neutral axis as possible, the I and T sections being good examples of economical sections.

In beams of these sections the flanges may be considered as taking all of the direct bending stresses, whilst the vertical web resists the shear.

In the case of cast iron, this material is about five times as strong in compression as in tension; whilst with most timbers the tensile strength is about 50 per cent. higher than the com-

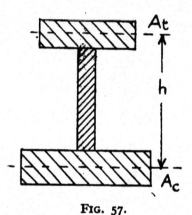

FIG. 57.

pressive strength; for example, in the case of ash $f_t = 12,000$ to $17,000$, whilst $f_c = 8,500$ to $9,500$ pounds per square inch. In order to design the most economical sections for such materials, the following method must be employed:

Let A_t and A_c be the areas of the tension and compression flanges respectively, and f_t and f_c the working tensile and compressive stresses. Further, let h (Fig. 57) be the depth of the section as measured between the flanges. Then if the vertical web is of small area compared with the flanges—

$$f_t \cdot A_t = f_c A_c,$$
$$\text{and } M = f_t A_t \cdot h = f_c A_c \cdot h,$$

where M is the bending moment.

If A = area of the vertical web, and f_s be the working shearing stress—

$$A \cdot f_s = F,$$

where F is the total shearing force on the section.

The area A so calculated has to be made rather greater, for certain practical reasons, connected with the construction; it will generally be found that the web area so calculated gives too thin a web.

In designing beams of the greatest bending strength for a given weight, the working stresses at the outermost fibres for compression and tension should be checked, as one may lie within the working value, and thus give a somewhat heavier section.

From a knowledge of the values of the bending moment at different sections along the beam, the most economical sections to resist these bending moments may be chosen; thus, in the relation $p = \dfrac{M}{Z}$ the greatest economy of weight occurs when p is constant and equal to the working stress, then $Z \propto M$, that is, the Strength Modulus, is proportional to the Bending Moment.

Thus, in the case of a cantilever beam loaded with a weight at the outer end, the bending moment for any section is proportional to its distance from the load, and the strength modulus will also vary as this distance. If the beam is of rectangular section of breadth b and depth d, then the strength modulus will be $\dfrac{bd^2}{6}$; and if the breadth of the beam be constant, its depth will follow a parabolic law, so that in side elevation, or if the top surface be flat, the under surface will be a parabola from the load to the fixing of the cantilever; the vertex of this parabola will be at the load.

In the case of a uniformly loaded cantilever, the most economical beam will be triangular in shape, in side elevation, with the apex at the free extremity, the breadth being constant.

Ordinary parallel beams are extremely uneconomical, and in all cases the depth or breadth of the section should be so chosen within practical limits of construction, that the strength modulus is proportional to the bending moment, in order that the working stresses may be constant for all sections.

INTENSITY OF SHEARING STRESS IN BEAM SECTIONS.

It is of importance in examples of built-up spars, beams, and girders to allow for the shearing stresses in both normal section planes and at right angles to these planes, that is, in planes parallel to the neutral plane of bending. It is the shear stress in this latter longitudinal sense which determines the strength and proportions of the rivets in built-up girders, and of the glued or welded joints in other examples.

The following general expression gives the distribution of the shear stress in any section of a loaded beam, both in the section itself and in a plane at right angles to the section, both values being the same:

$$q = \frac{S \cdot A \cdot y_0}{b\,I},$$

where S = the total shearing force at the section,
 A = area of section above point considered in the section,
 y_0 = distance of the C.G. of the area, above the point considered from the neutral axis,
 b = width or breadth of beam,
 I = its moment of inertia about neutral axis.

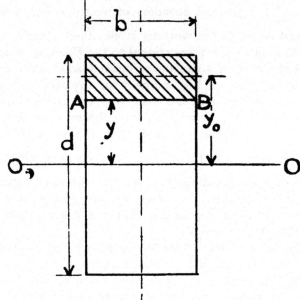

FIG. 58.—DISTRIBUTION OF SHEAR STRESS IN A BEAM SECTION.

Reference to Fig. 58 will serve to make the application of this formula more clear. Here the shearing stress intensity along the plane AB is given by—

$$q = \frac{S \cdot A_0 \cdot y_0}{b \cdot I} = \frac{S \cdot b \cdot \left(\frac{d}{2} - y\right)\left(\frac{y}{2} + \frac{d}{4}\right)}{b \cdot \frac{1}{12} b \cdot d^3} = \frac{6S\left(\frac{d^2}{4} - y^2\right)}{bd^3}$$

This stress is a maximum when $y = 0$, that is, at the centre, and zero the extreme edges distant $\frac{d}{2}$ from centre.

The maximum stress is then $\frac{3}{2} \cdot \frac{S}{bd}$ at the centre, and is one and a half times the mean stress over the whole area.

For a circular section the maximum stress is $\frac{4}{3}$ of the mean.

In I beams, where the web is thin, and the value of b in the formula is small, it will be seen that most of the shear stress comes upon the vertical webs, and is nearly uniform over the web; this is the reason why the flanges are often neglected in considering the shear stresses, whilst the webs are similarly left out of account in dealing with tensile and compressive stresses due to bending.

It should be remembered in considering built-up beams, in which the flanges and web are made separate, but are joined together by rivets, glue, soldering, or welding, that the joint must be made strong enough to withstand with safety the shearing stress in a plane parallel to the neutral plane of bending, as determined quantitatively by the above method.

BENDING MOMENT AND SHEARING FORCE.

The bending moment and shearing force diagrams are given in Figs. 59 and 60 for some typical loaded beams, and the maximum values are tabulated, together with the greatest deflections.

For a beam loaded in any manner, the diagrams of B.M. and S.F. may be obtained graphically by making use of the relation—

$$F = \frac{dM}{dx},$$

where F is the shearing force at a point distant x along the beam, from some chosen fixed point, or origin.

The bending moment curve is obtained by integrating the shearing force curve, and the shearing force curve is obtained by integrating the loading curve; for

$$F = \int w_x \cdot dx, \text{ and } M = \int F \cdot dx = \int\int w_x \cdot dx,$$

where w_x is the loading at x.

An example of the application of this method is given in Fig. 61 for the case of a beam irregularly loaded, as shown in the upper diagram.

To obtain the bending moment curve, divide the loading curve into a number of parts by means of the vertical dotted lines shown. Consider the weight of each part to act at the C.G. of that part, and to be represented by the forces fg, gh, etc.

Let R_1 and R_2 be the reactions at the supports, the magnitude of which are required.

Next draw the polar diagram Ofm shown in the right-hand corner, by drawing the vertical line fm, making fg, gh, hj,

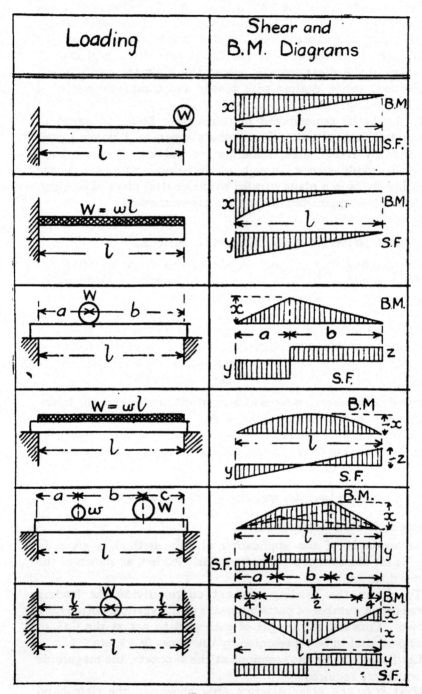

FIG. 59.

TABLE XVII.

Maximum Bending Moment.	Maximum Shearing Force.	Maximum Deflection.
$x = Wl$	$y = W$	$\dfrac{Wl^3}{3EI}$ at W.
$x = \dfrac{wl^2}{2}$ $= \dfrac{Wl}{2}$	$y = wl$ $= W$	$\dfrac{wl^4}{8EI}$ or $\dfrac{Wl^3}{8EI}$ at W.
$x = \dfrac{W \cdot ab}{l}$	$y = \dfrac{Wb}{l}$ $z = \dfrac{Wa}{l}$	$\dfrac{Wa^2b^2}{3EI(a+b)}$
$x = \dfrac{Wl}{8}$ $= \dfrac{wl^2}{8}$	$y = z = \dfrac{W}{2}$ $= \dfrac{wl}{2}$	$\dfrac{5Wl^3}{384EI}$ or $\dfrac{5wl^4}{384EI}$
$x = \dfrac{ac^2}{l}(W+w)$ $+ W \cdot \dfrac{bc^2}{l}$	$y = \dfrac{ac}{l}(W+w)$ $+ W \cdot \dfrac{bc}{l}$	
$x = \dfrac{Wl}{8}$	$y = \dfrac{W}{2}$	$\dfrac{wl^4}{384EI}$ or $\dfrac{Wl^3}{384EI}$

jk, *kl*, and *lm* proportional to the respective forces *fg*, *gh*, *hj*, *jk*, *kl*, and *lm*. Choose any pole O, and join O*f*, O*g*, etc. From O draw O*x* perpendicular to *fm*.

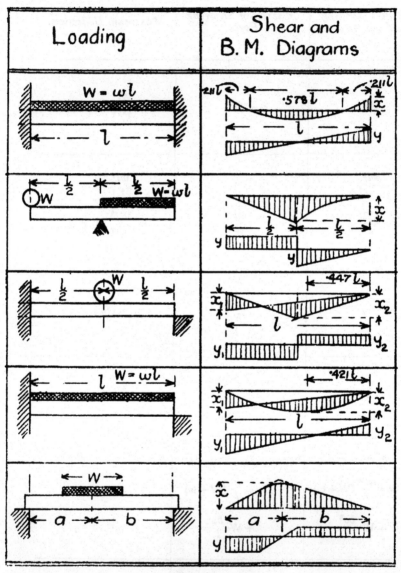

FIG. 60.

To draw the bending moment curve, draw *ab* parallel to O*f*, *bc* to O*g*, and so on until the last line *tv* is parallel to O*m*, and ends on the line of the resultant R₂. Join *av*, and in the polar diagram draw O*r* parallel to *av*.

Then *avtsedcb* is the diagram of bending moments to a certain scale, which is found as follows:

Using English units, let the linear scale of the beam be such that 1 foot is represented by z inches; let the load scale be such

TABLE XVIII.

Maximum Bending Moment.	Maximum Shearing Force.	Maximum Deflection.
$x = \dfrac{wl^2}{12}$ $= \dfrac{Wl}{12}$	$y = \dfrac{W}{2}$	$\dfrac{Wl^3}{192EI}$
$x = Wl$	$y = W$	$\dfrac{Wl^3}{3EI}$ at centre.
$x_1 = \dfrac{3Wl}{16}$ $x_2 = \dfrac{Wl}{4}$	$y_1 = \dfrac{11W}{16}$ $y_2 = \dfrac{5W}{16}$	$\dfrac{Wl^3}{107EI}$ at $0.447l$
$x_1 = \dfrac{Wl}{8}$ $x_2 = \dfrac{Wl}{8}$	$y_1 = \dfrac{5W}{8}$ $y_2 - \dfrac{3W}{8}$	$\dfrac{Wl^3}{185EI}$ at $0.421l$
$W \cdot \dfrac{ab}{a+b} - \dfrac{Wc}{4}$	$W \cdot \dfrac{b}{a+b}$	$\dfrac{Wa^2b^2}{3EI(a+b)} -$ $\dfrac{Wc^3}{8EI}$

that 1 pound is represented by y inches. Then, if x be the polar distance Ox in inches, the bending moment scale will be such that 1 pound foot is represented by $\dfrac{zy}{x}$ inches or, in other words, 1 inch will represent $\dfrac{x}{zy}$ pounds feet.

From the polar diagram, the values of the reactions R_1 and R_2 are represented to scale by fr and mr respectively.

It is usual to replot the bending moment diagram upon a horizontal base.

The line of action of the resultant force R, due to the loading, is given by the intersection at p of ab and vt produced.

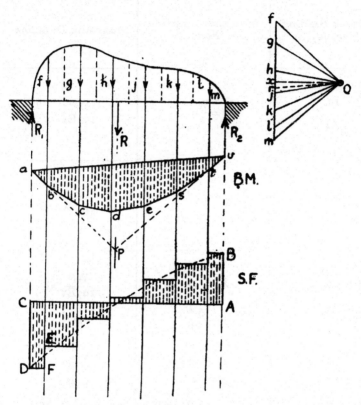

FIG. 61.—GRAPHICAL METHOD FOR B.M. AND S.F.

The shear diagram may be obtained from the load diagram by graphic integration, or more easily obtained by setting CD downwards and equal to R_1, whilst AB is set upwards and equal to R_2. At each line of loads, such as EF, the shearing force is reduced by an amount equal to the load itself (or in the case considered by fg).

The greater the number of vertical load diagram sections taken, the more accurate will be the results, and the more continuous the curves, as shown dotted in the shearing force diagram.

This method is applicable to the case of spars or surfaces under air pressure or load, such as the rib of an aeroplane wing, tail plane, fuselage, or other loaded surface, and the end reactions, centres of pressure, bending moment, and shearing force diagrams may be readily obtained. An example of the use of this method is shown in Fig. 21.

It should be remarked here that the slope and deflection diagrams may be obtained by a similar method to that outlined by treating the bending moment as the load curve, and integrating this graphically; an example is given in the next paragraph.

DEFLECTIONS OF BEAMS.

If the bending moment on a beam be constant, the radius of curvature of the bent beam will also be nearly constant, and will be given by—

$$R = \frac{EI}{M}.$$

If u denote the deflection of a beam perpendicular to its initial length, or span, and if θ be the angle of slope of the beam at any point x along the beam, then

$$\theta = \int \frac{M}{EI}\, dx.$$

$$u = \int \theta \cdot dx = \iint \frac{M}{EI}\, dx.$$

These relations enable the slope and deflection to be obtained for any manner of loading, provided that the bending moment be known at any point along the beam.

Graphical Method.

The deflection at any part of a loaded beam may be calculated from the relations given above, involving the use of the integral calculus; the deflection at each point has to be separately estimated, and this is a tedious process, except in the simplest cases.

The graphical method enables the deflections at all points along a loaded beam, no matter how complicated the loading is, to be determined in a very simple manner.

In Fig. 62 the upper diagram represents the B.M. diagram, for any system of loading, obtained by the graphical method, given upon p. 117.

Divide the B.M. diagram into a number of equal parts by the verticals shown dotted; the greater the number of these parts, the more accurate and continuous will be the deflection curve obtained.

The mid-ordinates AB, BC, etc., of the B.M. diagram divided up by the dotted lines are then set down to a convenient scale along the vector line *abcdefg* (Diagram 1), where *ab* represents AB to scale, and so on. Any pole O is chosen, at a convenient perpendicular distance OH from the vector line. Join O*a*, O*b*, O*c*, etc. Next draw HJ parallel to *a*O (Diagram 2), the point J lying on the mid-ordinate AB produced; then draw JK parallel to *b*O, KL parallel to *c*O, and so on for the other vector lines. Join HQ.

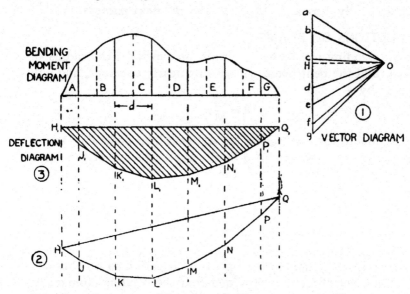

FIG. 62.—GRAPHICAL METHOD FOR DEFLECTION OF BEAMS.

Then HJKLMNPQ is the deflection diagram, and the vertical distances between HQ and the rest of the diagram represent the deflections of the beam at the points considered, under the given system of loading corresponding with the B.M. diagram given.

For convenience the base HQ is usually drawn horizontal, and the diagram then becomes the one shown shaded in Diagram 3.

SCALE OF DEFLECTION DIAGRAM.

The scales, in graphical methods similar to the above, usually give some trouble at first, but a little practice will accustom the student to the methods employed.

In the above method, let d be the distance between the mid-ordinates measured from the diagram itself in inches.

Let the linear scale of the B.M. diagram be 1 inch $=x$ feet, and the B.M. scale be 1 inch $=y$ tons feet.

Further, consider the vector diagram to be drawn, so that each portion, such as ab, is $\frac{1}{n}$ of the B.M. ordinates AB; or, in other words, let $AB = n \cdot ab$.

Then 1 inch on the vector scale represents $n \cdot x \cdot y \cdot d$ tons feet[2]; let this quantity $nxyd = Z$.

Next let OH be the polar distance measured in inches, and E the modulus of elasticity of the material of the beam in tons per square foot; also let the moment of inertia of the section about the neutral axis be I, expressed in $(ft)^4$ units.

Then the scale of the deflection diagram is such that 1 inch $= \frac{x \cdot OH \cdot Z}{EI}$ feet deflection. An example will make the question of the scales more clear.

Example.—A beam of white pine 12 feet long, 1 inch wide, and 2 inches deep, is supported at its ends and loaded with a weight of 60 pounds at its centre. Draw the deflection diagram, and find the deflections at the centre and for a point situated 6 feet from the centre.

For white pine E = 1,900,000 pounds per square inch, and for the given section $I = \frac{1}{12}bd^3 = 0.66$ inches[4].

Hence EI = 1,900,000 × 0.66 = 1,266,666 pounds inches[2] units.

The B.M. diagram is shown in Diagram A, Fig. 63, the linear scale being 1 inch = 2 feet, and the B.M. scale 1 inch = 2,000 pounds inches.

The vector line ag is drawn to the same scale as the B.M. diagram, without reduction or increase.

Then 1 inch down the vector diagram represents

nx, y, d pounds inches[2] = 1 × 24 inches × 2,000 × 1 inch
= 48,000 pounds inches[2] = Z.

Since the polar distance OH = 2 inches, it follows from the previous considerations that the deflection scale for the deflection diagram, drawn as shown in C, is such that

$$1 \text{ inch} = \frac{x \cdot OH \cdot Z}{EI} = \frac{24 \times 2 \times 48,000}{1,266,666} \text{ inches}$$
$= 1.82$ inches deflection.

The maximum deflection in the diagram is at the centre, and scales 1.60 inches. This therefore corresponds with an actual deflection of 1.60 × 1.82 = 2.93 inches at the centre of beam.

For a point situated at 3 feet from the centre the deflection diagram scales 1.15 inches, which gives an actual deflection of 1.15 × 1.82 = 2.09 inches.

FACTORS OF SAFETY FOR BEAMS AND STRUCTURES.

In calculations of stresses upon beams or structures the assumption is made that the strains resulting are proportional to the stresses, and it is the elastic limit of the material which limits the accuracy of the methods based upon such assumptions.

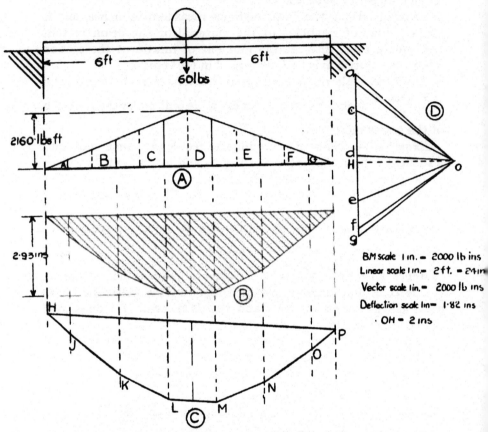

BM scale 1 in. = 2000 lb ins
Linear scale 1 in.= 2 ft. = 24 in
Vector scale 1in.= 2000 lb ins
Deflection scale 1in= 1·82 ins
OH = 2 ins

FIG. 63.—GRAPHICAL METHOD FOR DEFLECTIONS OF BEAMS.

The factor of safety chosen should take into account the relation of the elastic limit to the ultimate breaking strength, and should be also chosen to cover the inaccuracies of construction, deterioration, and the manner of load application.

The table on p. 127 indicates values of the factors of safety under the conditions stated:

In certain materials, such as the high tensile alloy steels, the elastic limit is a higher percentage of the ultimate strength than in ordinary steels, and a lower value for the factor of safety may be used. In the case of timbers the factors of safety are always taken as being higher than in the case of metals; this is owing to the fact that the strength of timber depends upon its previous history, place of growth, seasoning, etc., all of which are uncertain factors.

Tables of working stresses for wires and rods of mild steel are given at the end of the book, to suit the varying conditions of loading.

TABLE XIX.—FACTORS OF SAFETY (PERRY).

	Steady Load.	Varying Load.	Structures subjected to Shock.
Wrought iron and steel ..	3½	5 to 8	10 to 12
Cast iron	5	6 to 10	15
Timber	7	10 to 15	20
Brickwork and masonry ..	20	30	

BREAKING LOADS OF BEAMS.

The breaking load W pounds of a rectangular-sectioned beam of length l feet, breadth b inches, and depth d inches, supported at the ends and loaded at the middle, is found to be fairly accurately represented by the relation $W - \dfrac{c \cdot bd^2}{l}$, where c is a constant which depends upon the material of the beam, and which is usually $\dfrac{1}{18}f$, where f is the weaker of the bending stresses, either tensile or compressive.

The following values of c may be employed with this expression:

TABLE XX.

Material.	C.	Deflection Constant.
Ash	675	0·000260
English oak	557	0·00030
Fir..	370	0·0005 to 0·0002
Larch	284	0·000400
Deal	600	0·000250
Elm	337	0·000600
Red pine	450	0·000230
Pitch pine..	544	0·000350
Beech	518	0·000300
Mild steel	6,400	0·000013
Cast steel	10,000	—

The deflection constant may be employed in place of c to calculate the deflection in inches at the centre at breaking.

CONTINUOUS BEAMS.

When a beam possessing flexibility rests upon more than two supports it is said to be continuous.

The pressure upon the central support in the case of a uniformly loaded beam of uniform section and with equal spans may be computed by first finding the deflection $\dfrac{5wl^4}{24EI}$ of the beam with the central support supposed absent, $2l$ being the span and w the loading per unit length.

Next imagine the central support raised until it lifts the beam off the two end supports, considered as a double cantilever; the deflection as a cantilever will be $\dfrac{wl^4}{8EI}$.

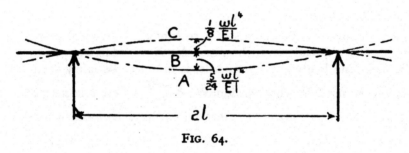

FIG. 64.

The pressure of the central support increases from zero (Fig. 64) in position A to the value required at B, and then to the maximum $2wl$ at C, when it takes all the load. Evidently the pressure on the central support at B will be

$$\frac{\dfrac{5}{24}}{\dfrac{1}{8}+\dfrac{5}{24}} \text{ of } 2wl = \frac{5}{4}wl.$$

The pressures upon the end supports are then $\dfrac{3}{8}wl$ each.

BEAMS WITH SUPPORTS OUT OF LINE.

The method here considered is applicable to cases of continuous beams in which the three points of support are not quite in the same line, as in the case of an aeroplane spar, where cable stretch or misalignment may occur.

If the central support be either above or below the level of the other supports by a small amount denoted by δ, then the pressure upon the central support will be $\dfrac{wl}{4}$ $(5 + 24\delta)$ when the support is above, and $\dfrac{wl}{4}$ $(5 - 24\delta)$ when below the level of the other supports.

THEOREM OF THREE MOMENTS.

If A, B, C be three consecutive supports of a continuous beam, considered as being upon the same level, and if l_{ab} and l_{bc} be the lengths of the spans AB and AC respectively, and further if M_A, M_B, and M_C be the bending moments at the three respective

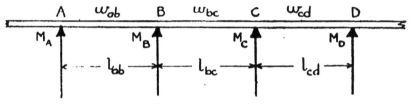

FIG. 66.—CONTINUOUS BEAMS.

supports, then if w_{ab} and w_{bc} be the loadings of the spans AB and BC, there is a general relation between these quantities, expressed thus:

$$(M_A + 2M_B)l_{ab} + (M_C + 2M_B)l_{bc} + \frac{w_{ab}}{4} \cdot l^3{}_{ab} + \frac{w_{bc}}{4} \cdot l^3{}_{bc} = 0.$$

If there be another consecutive support D, then, employing the above notation for the supports B, C, and D the above relation becomes—

$$(M_B + 2M_C)l_{bc} + (M_D + 2M_C)l_{dc} + \frac{w_{bc}}{4} \cdot l^3{}_{bc} + \frac{w_{cd}}{4} \cdot l^3{}_{cd} = 0.$$

From these two relations, and knowing the terminal conditions, the values of M_A, M_B, M_C, and M_D may be determined.

Usually at the extreme supports the bending moments are zero, and the process of finding the other moments is simplified. It will be noticed that if there are n supports, there will be $(n - 2)$ equations for finding the support moments, and 2 terminal conditions.

A continuous beam is usually much lighter than a series of separate beams bridging the same spans, and further, as the greatest bending moments occur near the supports, the weight of the beams may be concentrated there, and thus cause less

9

bending, since in long beams the weight of the beam itself is a serious factor.

The disadvantage of continuous beams is that if the points of support yield, the stresses and moments are altered, and if a beam be designed upon the assumption of the same level serious consequences may arise, since very small changes in level will produce appreciable alterations in stresses.

This defect may be eliminated by hinging the beam at the points of inflexion—that is, where the bending moments are zero—then any change in level of the supports will not produce any change in the stresses.

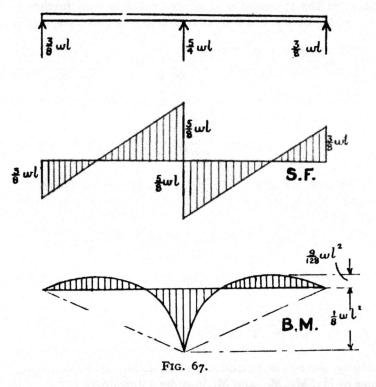

FIG. 67.

Examples of continuous beams with three supports, together with the bending moment and shearing force diagrams, are given in Fig. 67. The pressures upon the supports are also given.*

A useful method of expressing the reactions of the supports and the shearing forces to the right and left hands of the sup-

* The subject of continuous beams is treated in a paper by Perry and Ayrton, Proceedings of the Royal Society, 1879; and in Fidler's " Treatise on Bridge Construction."

ports* is given in Fig. 68. The figures above the lines give the values of the moment coefficients, which, when multiplied by wl^2, give the bending moments. Below the lines are given the shearing force coefficients, which, when multiplied by wl, give the shearing forces to the right and left of the support. The numerical sum of the shearing forces at each support gives the reaction at the support.

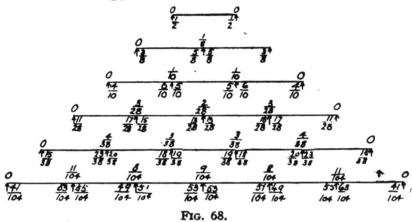

FIG. 68.

From this data the diagrams of bending moment and shear may be obtained for continuous beams with any number of supports.

STRUTS AND COLUMNS.

1. **Short Struts**, in which the ratio of the length to the smallest sectional dimension is small, may be treated as simple compression members, the relation between the crushing load P, the area of cross-section A, and ultimate compressive stress f^c, being $f_c = \dfrac{P}{A}$.

2. **Very Long Struts.**—Euler gives the following formulæ for very long struts, subjected to purely axial loads, straight and homogeneous.

If P be the buckling load, E the modulus of elasticity for the material, I its least moment of inertia about an axis in the cross-section and through the centre of area of the section, and l the length of the strut, then

$$P = \frac{n\pi^2 EI}{l^2}$$

The value of the constant n depends upon the manner of attachment of the ends of the strut.

* *Vide* " The Strength of Materials," by Ewart S. Andrews. (London: Chapman and Hall, Ltd.).

Value of n.

1. If both ends are rounded so that the strut is free to incline in any direction   1
2. If both ends are fixed and forced to remain parallel the direction of thrust..   4
3. If one end is fixed, and one rounded, but not free to move sideways   ..   .. $\frac{2}{1}$
4. If one end is fixed, and one rounded, but free to move sideways   ..   .. $\frac{1}{4}$
5. If both ends are fixed in direction, but one end free to move sideways   1

Euler's formula is only applicable where $\dfrac{\text{length}}{\text{least radius of gyration}}$ is greater than 90; this formula requires modification in practice, but is useful in showing the importance of a large moment of inertia for the strut section, and high Modulus of Elasticity.

THE RANKINE-GORDON FORMULA.

This formula is a modification of the two previous methods, to take into account struts of all lengths, and it may be regarded as an empirical formula with experimentally determined constants, although based upon rational methods. It is generally expressed as:

$$p = \frac{f_c}{1 + c \cdot \dfrac{L^2}{k^2}},$$

where f_c is safe compressive strength for short columns, p the working stress per square inch for the strut, and c is constant depending upon the material, k being the least radius of gyration, values of which for various useful sections are given in Table XXII.

The values for the constant C and for f_c, experimentally found, are as follows:

TABLE XXI.

Material.	C.	f_c.
Mild steel	$\frac{1}{3000}$ to $\frac{1}{9000}$	6 tons per sq. in.
Cast iron	$\frac{1}{1600}$ to $\frac{1}{1800}$	7 ,, ,, ,,
Timber	$\frac{1}{3000}$	$\frac{1}{4}$ ton ,, ,,

The values of the constants vary according to the published figures of different authorities, but the above are given as representing the more reliable of these.

In applying Euler's formula to long struts, it should be remembered that P is the buckling load, and that this requires dividing by a suitable factor of safety in order to give the allowable working stress.

For simple dead axial loads it is usual to take a factor of safety of 5 for iron or steel, 6 for cast-iron, and for wood 10, since the homogeneity of the latter is always a questionable feature. For live loads thesefactors of safety should be doubled.

In employing this formula it is useful to know the values for the least radii of gyration, for the common sections used, and the following table gives some of the more useful results:

TABLE XXII.—LEAST MOMENTS OF INERTIA.

	Least Moment of Inertia.	Least Radius of Gyration.
Circular section [diameter $= D$] ..	$0 \cdot 05\ D^4$	$0 \cdot 25\ d$
Annular section [diameters $= D$ and d]	$0 \cdot 05\ (D^4 - d^4)$	$0 \cdot 25\ \sqrt{D^2 + d^2}$
Rectangular section $\begin{cases} \text{longer side} = d \\ \text{shorter ,, } = b \end{cases}$	$\frac{1}{12}\ bd^3$	$0 \cdot 289\ d$
Square section [side $= b$] ..	$\frac{b^4}{12}$	$0 \cdot 289\ b$
Thin square cell [side $= b$]	—	$0 \cdot 408\ b$
Thin circular cell [diameter $= d$] ..	—	$0 \cdot 354\ d$
Elliptical section $\begin{cases} \text{major axes} = a \\ \text{minor ,, } - b \end{cases}$ ..	$\frac{\pi a b^3}{64}$	$0 \cdot 444\ b$
Equal angle iron [side $= b$]	—	$0 \cdot 204\ b$
Equal cruciform section [sides $= b$] ..	—	$0 \cdot 204\ b$

The following values of the Moduli of Elasticity for timbers may be taken as correct:

$E = 18{,}000{,}000$ for spruce.
$E = 16{,}000{,}000$,, ash.
$E = 1{,}800{,}000$,, hickory.

THE TETMARJERSCHE FORMULA.

This German expression for the strength of struts is given as:

$$\frac{P}{A} = K(1 - a \cdot x) \times 14 \cdot 2,$$

where A = cross-section in square inches at which the greatest stress occurs,

P = breaking or buckling load in pounds,

$x = \dfrac{\text{length}}{\text{least radius of gyration}}$.

K and a are constants whose values are given on p. 134.

TABLE XXIII.

Material.	K.	A.	Range for x.
Wrought iron ..	3,030	0·00426	10 to 112
Cast iron	3,100	0·00368	10 ,, 105
Mild steel	3,350	0·00185	10 ,, 90
Wood	293	0·00662	1·8 ,, 100

The " range for x " column gives the limits between which the formula is applicable.

There are several other strut formulæ employed in practice, but these are more applicable to large steel and cast-iron stanchions.

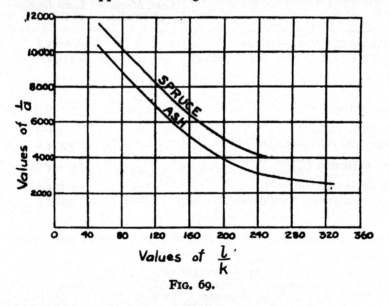

FIG. 69.

CRIPPLING LOADS UPON STRUTS.

R.A.F. Method.

In connection with the compression stresses in the interp ane struts, and in the case of buckling loads upon the " free lengths " of wing spars, the following formula, representing the results of R.A.F. tests upon pin-jointed ash and spruce struts, is given:

$$\text{Crippling load in pounds} = \frac{F \cdot A}{1 + \frac{a \cdot l^2}{k^2}}$$

where F = 5,600 pounds per square inch for spruce,
= 6,250 pounds per square inch for ash,

> A = area of section in square inches,
> l = length of section in inches,
> k = least radius of gyration of the section, in [inches][4].

and a = a constant which depends upon the value of $\frac{l}{k}$.

Values of this contant are given in Fig. 69 for different values of $\frac{l}{k}$.

Another formula, given in the *Aeronautical Journal*, April, 1912, for the crippling load s lbs. of spruce struts is $S = 12,832 \frac{I}{l^2}$,

> where I = least moment of inertia of the section [inches][4],
> l = length of strut [inches].

STRUTS WITH LATERAL AND ECCENTRIC LOADS.

It is well known that a small force applied to a loaded strut in a direction at right angles will greatly reduce the buckling load. For a fuller discussion of the cases of laterally loaded struts the reader is referred to a paper by Perry (*Philosophical Magazine*, March, 1892).

The formula suggested in this paper, and which has been shown to yield accurate results, may be written

$$\frac{Wl}{4f_c Z} = \left(1 - \frac{w}{f_c}\right)\left(1 - \frac{w}{\beta}\right),$$

> where W = the total lateral load or force,
> l = length of strut,
> Z = the least modulus of the section,
> $= \frac{I}{y}$, where y is the greatest distance of a point in the section from the neutral line on the compressive side,
> f_c = maximum compressive stress,
> β = Euler's breaking stress as given by the relation—
>
> $$\frac{n\pi^2 EI}{l^2 \cdot A} = \beta,$$

and w = the actual breaking stress of the strut.

The value of f_c, the maximum compressive stress, is obtained from the relation—

$$f_c = \frac{\mu}{Z} + \frac{F}{A},$$

which expresses the fact that the total stress is the sum of the stresses due to the direct load F and to a bending moment μ due to the lateral loading, where $\mu = \frac{1}{4}W \cdot l \cdot \frac{U}{U-F}$, the symbols being the same as those previously given.

Another method of adapting these results to practical cases is given on p. 136.

In the case of eccentric loads, in which the distance of the line of action of the load F from the symmetrical axes is denoted by e, the following formula may be employed for finding the equivalent central load F_0:

$$F_0 = F\left(1 + \frac{l \cdot y_0}{k^2}\right),$$

where y_0 = distance from C.G. of section to the edge of the section nearest to the load.

In aeroplane practice struts are generally made of streamline section,* and tapered from a maximum cross-sectional area at the centre to a minimum at the two ends; struts of this form do not usually break at the centre, although they are nearly always weaker than parallel struts.

The Euler formula is deduced from considerations of the deflection of the strut at the centre, so that if the deflection is reduced a stronger strut should result.

Aeroplane struts are usually hinged or pivoted at the ends, but in such a manner that bending can only freely occur in the plane offering the most resistance—that is to say, the streamline major axis is in the plane of deflection.

For a fuller consideration of the question of tapering aeroplane struts of equal strength for all sections along the length, reference should be made to an article in *Engineering*, April 24, 1914, p. 566, entitled "Critical Loads for Ideal Long Columns" (Morley), and to the issue for October 2, 1914, for an article entitled "Critical Loads for Long Struts of Varying Section" (Bairstow and Stedman).

APPLICATION OF FORMULÆ TO WING SPAR STRESS DIAGRAMS.

From the diagram of bending moments, the points of zero bending moment (or inflexion) can be obtained.

These points fix the "free lengths" of wing spar. Each free length may be regarded as a strut in the case of a monoplane spar, or the upper spar of a biplane, subjected to a lateral loading due to the bending moment M at its centre.

It can be shown by the method given on p. 135 that in the case of a strut with lateral loading and subjected to end loading due to the compressive load F_c of the bracing, the maximum bending moment produced by the combination of the two loadings is given by

$$M_0 = \frac{M}{1 - \dfrac{F_c}{F_E}},$$

where M = B.M. at centre,
F_c = compressive load.

* In the volume entitled "The Properties of Wing Sections and the Resistance of Bodies," various streamline sections for struts are given, together with their resistances and strut values.

[In the case of a tensile load F_t, as in the lower wing of a biplane, $\dfrac{F_t}{F_e}$ becomes of positive sign in the above relation.]

F_e is the buckling load of the free length under consideration, and is given by Euler's formula:

$$F_e = \frac{\pi^2 EI}{4l^2},$$

where E = the Elastic Modulus for the material,

I = the least moment of inertia of the spar section about an axis in the plane of section through its C.G.,

l = the free length of wing spar.

If the buckling loads for the material of the wing spar be known for various lengths of the spar and for different cross-sections, the processes of calculation may be greatly simplified.

Finally, knowing the equivalent bending moment M_o, the maximum compressive stress in the wing spar due to both bending and compression is given by

$$f_c = \frac{M_o}{Z} + \frac{F_c}{A},$$

where Z = the strength modulus of the section—namely, $\dfrac{I}{y}$, where y is the greatest distance from neutral axis, and A is the area of section.

This relation enables the area and dimensions of the section to be chosen for a given factor of safety.

Approximate Method.

A simpler method of arriving at the wing spar section dimensions is to regard the stress at any part of the section as being due to the compressive load and bending moment separately, and to add the stresses obtained on this supposition.

If M = the bending moment, I the moment of inertia about neutral axis, and y the distance of the extreme fibre or point of section upon the compressive side, then the total compressive stress is given by

$$f_c = \frac{M \cdot y}{I} + \frac{F_c}{A},$$

where F_c = compressive load, and A = area of section.

If, as in the case of the lower wing spars of a biplane, there is a tensile load F_t, combined with a bending moment M (y in this case is the distance from the neutral axis to extreme fibre upon the tension side), the total tensile stress is given by

$$f_t = \frac{My}{I} + \frac{F_t}{A}.$$

If any appreciable deflexion of the wing spar occurs, due to the bending moment, the end load will cause an additional bending moment $= F \cdot \delta$, where δ is the deflexion and F the end load, so that when employing this approximate method it is advisable to check the worst case for deflexion. Generally this deflexion, with the factors of safety now employed, will be found to be negligible.

In practically every case the bending stresses will be found to be of much greater importance than the direct compressive or tensile stresses.

An approximate method of taking into account the additional bending due to deflexion and end loading (compression) is to add to the bending moment M the product $F_c \cdot 2d$, the doubled product being taken to allow for the extra deflexion due to end loading.

The deflexion d can be obtained graphically, as mentioned on p. 123.

The maximum stress at the outermost fibre, taking deflexion into account, is given by

$$f_c = \frac{M + 2F_o \cdot d}{Z} + \frac{F_c}{A}.$$

In wing spar calculations, it is important to include the stresses due to the drift wires or bracing, and to add same to the loading stresses.

STRESSES IN MEMBERS OF STRUCTURES.

Graphical Method.

A convenient method of finding the stresses is to draw the reciprocal figures or force polygons for each set of forces acting at a point. These may be superposed upon one diagram in most cases; the advantage of this method is that it can be applied to structures in general, no matter what the directions of the forces may be.

A simple example for a frame under vertical loads is given in Fig. 70. The notation known as Bow's notation is employed, in which the letters are placed in the spaces between the members and between the lines of action of the forces. Thus AG represents the reaction force, BL the force in the member indicated.

The polygon of forces is drawn for the joint ABL, and is represented by the letters *abl* in the force diagram shown on the right-hand side. Next, having found the force *bl*, and knowing *ed*, the force polygon is drawn for the joint BLJC, and so on, until the diagram is completed for the whole structure.

To determine whether a member is in compression or tension,

the polygon of forces must be examined for one end of each member. If the polygon denotes that the force in the member acts towards the joint considered, then the bar is in compression, but if the force acts away from the joint it is in tension.

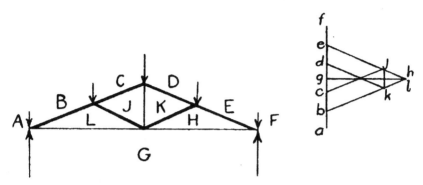

FIG. 70.—STRESSES IN FRAMES.

Compression members are generally shown by double or thick lines, and tension members by thin lines.

When drawing the force polygon it is important to follow the same order in taking the forces, and to construct each side of the polygon in the same rotation, whether clockwise or anticlockwise. Thus, in the example given, at the joint BLJC, the forces are

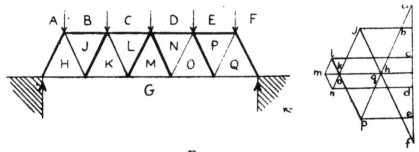

FIG. 71.

considered in the order BL, LJ, JC, and CB, and the force polygon for these forces is drawn in the anticlockwise direction— namely, *bljcb*.

At each joint considered all known forces are dealt with first in drawing the force polygon, and parallel lines are drawn to the unknown forces. The number of unknown forces at any joint must not exceed two, or the diagram cannot be drawn.

An example for the case of a lattice girder is given in Fig. 71, which does not require further explanation.

In aeroplane and airship design the above-mentioned graphical method can be frequently applied. Examples of the use of this method have already been given in the case of aeroplane wing structures.

The Method of Sections.

When the diagrams of bending moment and shearing force have been obtained for any structure or beam, it is a fairly simple matter to find the stresses in the members.

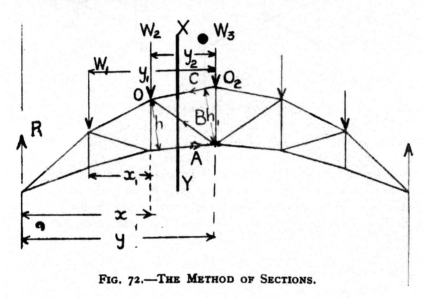

FIG. 72.—THE METHOD OF SECTIONS.

Consider the case of an arched beam (Fig. 72), and imagine it cut by the plane XY, then for equilibrium of the structure forces A, B, and C must be applied to the three dissected members. If moments be taken about the point O, then

$$A \times h = \text{B.M. at O.}$$

This B.M. is obtained either from the B.M. diagram or by direct calculation, thus:

$$A \times h = Rx - W_1 x_1.$$

The other two forces B and C have no moment about O, since they pass through this point.

To find the force C, take moments about O_1, then

$$C \times h_1 = \text{B.M. at } O_1,$$
$$= R \cdot y - W_1 y_1 - W_2 y_2.$$

The third force B may either be found by taking moments about a third point O_2, or by equating the vertical resolutes of the forces A, B, and C with the shearing force at the section as obtained from the shearing force diagram.

Thus if θ_a, θ_b, and θ_c be the angles made with the vertical line XY by the members A, B, and C, and if S.F. denote the shearing force at XY, then

$$\text{S.F.} = A \cos \theta_a + B \cos \theta_b + C \cos \theta \ ,$$

since C and A are known, B can be deduced.

In the case of a built-up girder, as shown in Fig. 73, the forces in the members may readily be found by this method.

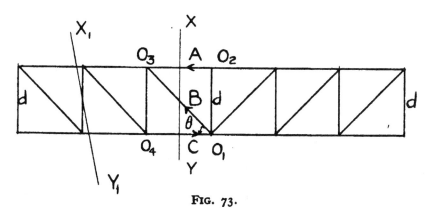

FIG. 73.

Thus if a section XY be taken as shown, then by taking moments about O_1

$$A \cdot d = \text{B.M. at } O_1 O_2.$$

By taking moments about O_3

$$C \cdot d = \text{B.M. at } O_3 O_4.$$

Finally, by taking the vertical resolute of the force B in the plane XY,

$$B \sin \theta = \text{S.F. at XY.}$$

The whole of the forces are thus determinate, and the stresses in the other members may be obtained in a similar manner.

The stresses in vertical members may be obtained by considering the section $X_1 Y_1$ to be slightly inclined, so that it does not quite coincide with the vertical member. It will then be seen that the stress in a vertical member is simply equal to the shearing force at the section.

TORSION OF SHAFTS.

The following formulæ are given for cases of shafts subjected to twisting moment:

1. In the case of a circular shaft subjected to a uniform torque M, the shear stress q_x at any radius x from the centre is given by

$$q_x = \frac{2M}{\pi x^3}.$$

The stress is a maximum when $x = \frac{d}{2}$ the radius, and then

$$q = \frac{16M}{\pi d^3}.$$

In the case of a hollow shaft of internal and external diameters d_1 and d respectively

$$q = \frac{16M d_1}{\pi (d^4 - d_1^4)}.$$

2. The angle of twist in the plane of the cross-section is given by

$$\theta = \frac{32M}{\pi C d^4} \quad \text{and} \quad \frac{32M}{\pi C(d^4 - d_1^4)}$$

respectively for solid and hollow shafts, where C is the modulus of rigidity (see p.   ).

3. The axial twist ϕ along the length l of the shaft is given by

$$\phi = \frac{d}{2l} \cdot \theta = \frac{16M\theta}{\pi C \cdot l \cdot d^3}$$

HORSE-POWER TRANSMITTED BY SHAFTING.

The following formulæ are deduced from the previous considerations:

$$d = 2.88 \sqrt[3]{\frac{H.P.}{N}} \text{ for steel,}$$

$$d = 4.15 \sqrt[3]{\frac{H.P.}{N}} \text{ for cast-iron,}$$

where d is the diameter in inches of a solid shaft which will safely transmit the horse-power H.P. at the revolutions per minute N, a factor of safety of about 5 is employed in these expressions; but in the case of torques of varying magnitude, as occurring in petrol engines, the maximum torques may be twice the mean, and an allowance must also be made for rapid repetitions of the torque. It is then better to use the formula—

$$d = 68.5 \sqrt[3]{\frac{H.P.}{f_q \times N}},$$

where f_q is the safe shear stress fixed by the material, the variation of torque, and its maximum value; usually with the high tensile steels of automobile practice factors of safety lying between 7 and 10 are used.

SOLID AND HOLLOW SHAFTING.

In aeronautical practice, where weight saving is of great importance, hollow shafts may be employed in place of solid ones in all cases of bending and torsion, with the only disadvantage which may occasionally occur, that in exposed positions the wind resistance, even if streamlined or " faired," may be increased.

For shafts in torsion or bending the equivalent hollow shaft to a solid one may be deduced from the relation

$$d^3 = \frac{d_1{}^4 - d_2{}^4}{d_1},$$

where d = solid diameter and d_1, d_2 = external and internal diameters respectively; it is possible to affect a saving of 50 per cent. of the weight in this respect, without a great increase in external diameter.

Table H, Appendix I, given at the end of the book, will be found useful for design purposes where tubing is suitable for use, the full properties of the more generally used tube sections in steel and duralumin being tabulated.

COMBINED TWISTING AND BENDING.

Many instances occur in practice, often in cases of the transmission of power by means of shafting, in which the shaft is subjected to a bending moment M as well as a torque M.

It is usual to express the combined effect of these two factors, either as an equivalent bending moment M_0, or an equivalent torque T_0, thus:

Equivalent bending moment $M_0 = \frac{1}{2}(M + \sqrt{M^2 + T^2})$,

Equivalent twisting moment $T_0 = M + \sqrt{M^2 + T^2}$.

Either of these expressions may be used, but in the former case the shaft must be treated as a beam with a bending moment M_0, and in the latter case as a shaft under a twisting moment T_0. In both cases the maximum stresses are approximately the same, although the resulting stress is a normal stress, whilst that given by the latter method of treatment is a shear stress.

A common instance of the use of this formula is in the case of a propeller shaft driven either direct, by chain or gearing, in which the weight, pull of the chain, or pressure of the teeth give a bending moment in addition to the torque.

APPENDIX I

TABLES OF STRENGTHS AND PROPERTIES OF MATERIALS

A.—Properties of Steels.

B.—Properties of Metals and Alloys.

C.—Elastic Coefficients.

D.—Table of Working Stresses in Metals.

E.—Properties of Timbers.

F.—Moduli of Elasticity for Timber.

G.—Notes upon Timber Strength.

H.—Properties of Steel and Duralumin Tubes.

I.—Working Loads for Mild Steel Rods, Wires, Pins, and Bolts.

J.—Areas of Mild Steel Sections, Plates, etc.

K.—Breaking Loads of Piano Wire.

L.—Table of Relative Strengths for Weights.

10

A.—PROPERTIES OF STEELS.

Material.	Tensile Breaking Stress. Tons per Square Inch.	Elastic Limit. Tons per Square Inch.	Extension. Per ...	Shearing Strength. Tons per Square Inch.	Remarks.
Mild steel plate	24 to 28	16 to 20	20 to 30	17·9	Elongation on 2".
Bright drawn mild steel	30 ,, 40	28 ,, 35	15 ,, 35	19·0	—
Siemens' forged mild steel	29 ,, 35	17 ,, 19	20 ,, 25	—	—
Fluid compressed steel	50 ,, 55	40 ,, 45	—	—	—
Rivet steel	22 ,, 26	15 ,, 20	26	12·5	—
Tool steel (annealed)	45 ,, 55	35 ,, 40	20	—	—
" " (hardened)	60 ,, 70	45 ,, 60	8 to 12	—	—
Axle steel	35 ,, 40	18 ,, 25	20 , 25	—	—
Tyre steel	50 ,, 55	40 ,, 45	10 , 15	—	—
Spring steels (treated)	55 ,, 75	30 ,, 35	5 , 14	—	—
Steel castings	26 ,, 35	12 ,, 17	15 , 20	—	—
Case-hardening steel (annealed)	34	28	44	}	Elongation on 2". as steels.
" " " (case-hard end)	46	35	3·2	}	
Nickel Chrome Steels :					
(1) As rolled	50 to 85	40 to 75	16 to 22	—	Elongation on 2".
(2) Air-hardened	90 ,, 115	80 ,, 100	8 , 12	—	—
(3) Oil-hardened	100 ,, 125	85 ,, 100	8 , 12	—	—
Chrome Vanadium Steels					
(1) As rolled	50 ,, 60	40 ,, 50	25	—	Elongation on 2".
(2) Heat treated	110 ,, 120	100 ,, 105	6 to 8	—	,,
(3) For springs	110	64	4	—	,,
Nickel Steel :					
(1) As rolled, 5 per cent. Ni	40 to 48	30 to 35	25	—	Elongation on 2".
(2) Oil-tempered, 5 per cent. Ni	85 ,, 95	80 ,, 88	12	—	,,
(1) As rolled, 3 per cent. Ni	40 ,, 44	28 ,, 34	25 to 30	—	,,
(2) Oil-tempered, 3 per cent. Ni	75 ,, 85	68 ,, 78	12 ,, 16	—	,,
(1) Case-hardening (annealed)	30 ,, 35	22 ,, 27	30	—	,,
(2) " (hardened)	65 ,, 75	58 ,, 65	14 to 18	—	,,

B.—PROPERTIES OF METALS AND ALLOYS.

Name.	Tensile Strength.	Elonga- tion.	Compres- sion Strength.	Modulus of Elasticity.	Specific Gravity.
	Tons per Square Inch.	Per Cent.	Tons per Sq. Inch.		
Aluminium: sheet	12	—	—	$12 \cdot 5 \times 10^6$	2·67
cast . ..	8	—	—	—	2·56
Duralumin: wire..	40	2	—	—	—
rolled.. ..	25	20	30 to 35	$10 \cdot 5 \times 10^6$	2·80
rivet bar ..	16	25	—	—	—
Navaltum: rolled	25	5 to 10	—	—	—
annealed ..	14	20	—	—	2·50
cast	9	12	—	—	—
Antox: cast ..	12	7	—	—	2·65
rolled.. ..	25	4 to 8	—,	—	—
wire	30	2 ,, 4	—	—	—
Magnalium: cast..	8 to 12	—	—	—	2·50
rolled.. ..	15 ,, 20	—	—	—	—
Aeromin: rolled ..	18 ,, 20	10	⎫	$9 \cdot 3 \times 10^6$	⎫
annealed ..	20 ,, 25	20 to 25	⎬ 39	to	⎬ 2·80
rivet	20	15 ,, 20	⎭	$10 \cdot 3 \times 10^6$	⎭
Copper: cast ..	8·5	—	—	9×10^6	8·60
sheet	13·4	50 to 60	25	12×10^6	8·80
wire	26·0	25	—	16×10^6	8·90
Tin: cast	2·0	—	6·7	$4 \cdot 6 \times 10^6$	7·29
Gunmetal (10 per cent. tin) ..	14 to 17	—	12	$9 \cdot 9 \times 10^6$	8·46
Phosphor bronze: wire	100 ,, 150	1 to 2	—	—	—
soft . ..	20	30	—	—	—
hard	33	5	—	$13 \cdot 7 \times 10^6$	—
Aluminium bronze (90 per cent. copper)	25 to 32	—	58	17×10^6	7·70
Manganese bronze: cast	24	—	—	—	—
rolled.. ..	30	—	—	—	—

C.—Elastic Coefficients.

In Pounds per Square Inch.

Material.	Modulus of Elasticity (E).	Modulus of Rigidity (C).
Cast iron: white	23,000,000	7,600,000
,, ,, grey ..	15,000,000	5,000,000
Wrought-iron bar ..	29,000,000	10,000,000
Mild steel plate ..	30,000,000	13,500,000
Rivet steel	30,000,000	13,000,000
Cast steel (untempered) ..	30,000,000	12,000,000
Copper plate	15,000,000	5,600,000
,, wire	17,000,000	5,000,000
Phosphor bronze ..	14,000,000	5,250,000
Aluminium: cast ..	12,500,000	3,400,000
,, sheet	13,500,000	4,800,000

Note.—The Modulus C is about $\frac{2}{5}$ E for most metals.

D.—TABLE OF WORKING STRESSES IN METALS IN LBS. PER SQ. IN.

(a, FOR STEADY LB.)

Material.	Tension.	Compression.	Shear.	Torsion.
Cast iron ..	4,200	2,000	2,200	,90
Wrought iron ..	15,000	15,000	12,000	,90
Mild steel plate ..	13,00 to 17,00	13,00 to 17,00	10,00 to 13,00	8,00 to 12,000
Nickel steel plate..	16,00 „ 18,00	16,00 „ 18,00	13,00 „ 14,00	10,00 „ 15,000
Cast steel ..	17,00 „ 21,00	17,00 „ 21,00	13,00 „ 17,00	12,00 „ 16,000
Nickel chrome steel (hardened)	17,00 „ 23,00	17,00 „ 23,00	13,500 „ 18,00	11,00 „ 16,000
„ „ (hardened)	35,00 „ 46,00	35,00 „ 46,00	26,00 „ 36,00	20,00 „ 30,000
Chrome vanadium (unhardened)	17,00 „ 21,00	17,00 „ 21,00	13,00 „ 17,00	11,00 „ 15,000
„ „ (hardened) ..	36,00 „ 50,00	36,00 „ 50,00	27,00 „ 40,00	21,00 „ 35,000
Gunmetal ..	4,200	4,000	,90	2,000
Phosphor bronze..	10,000	7,000	,90	40
Aluminium, sheet .	6,000	4,000	4,800	40

(b) For loads varying from a maxim m, frequently as in the case of shocks, etc., ply the above bars by 0·66.

c) For loads varying from a stress of ne sign, through o, to a stress of the opposite sign, frequently, as in the case of a tie-rod, multiply the die numbers by 0·33.

E.— PROPERTIES OF 1 INS (LBS. PER SQ. IN).

Material.	Tensile Strength.		Shear S	Compressive Strength.
	With grain.	Across grain.		
Ash	12,000 to 17,000	1,600 to 2,300	—	8,000 to 10,000
Beech	11,000 ,, 22,000	1,500 ,, 2, 00	—	7,000 ,, 9,000
Birch	15, 00	1,800	—	3, 90
Cedar: West Indian ..	5, 00	1,000 to 1,500	—	5, 90
American	10,800	60 ,, 800	—	6, 00
Lebanon..	11, 00	1,000 ,, 1,400	—	5,800
Elm: English..	13, 00 to 14,000	—	800 to 1,360*	6, 00 to 10, 00
Rock ..	13, 00	—	—	, 90
Silver spruce ..	10,100	400 to 800	—	6, 90
Oak ..	8, 90	—	—	14, 00
Larch	9,000 to 10,000	1, 90 to 1,700	—	3, 00 to 5, 00
Mahogany: Honduras ..	6,000 ,, 20,000	1,800	—	8, 00
Spanish ..	15, 00	1,300	—	8, 00
Maple ..	11,150	1, 90 to 1, 60	2,300	7,150
Oak: English ..	10, 00	1,500	—	6, 90
African ..	21, 00	2, 00 to 2, 90	—	,300
Pine: red	2,000 to 14,000	1,100 ,, 1,300	—	5,500 to 7,500
white	8, 00 ,, 11,000	1, 90 ,, 1, 90	—	4,000 ,, 6,500
yellow	13, 00	1,300 ,, 1, 90	—	5,300
pitch	8, 00	1,200 to 1, 90	—	5, 90
ga	4, 90	—	—	3, 90
nh	12, 60	—	—	8, 00
ad	10, 00	—	90	7,000
Poplar..	7,500	1,600	—	4, 80
Hickory ..	5,000 to 18,000	2,200 to 2,500	—	9,000 to 11,000
Teak ..	90 ,, 15,000	2,000 ,, 2,300	—	8,000 ,, 12,000
Lancewood ..	20,000	2,200 ,, 2,600	—	7, 00
Walnut: French	90 to 8,500	1,600	—	5,000 to 6,000

* Across grain.

F.—Moduli of Elasticity for Timber.

In Pounds per Square Inch.

Material.					Modulus E.
Ash ..	..	..	..	..	.. 1,600,000
Beech	..	..	..	..	.. 1,350,000
Birch	..	..	..	..	.. 1,500,000
Cedar	..	..	..	..	.. 500,000
Elm ..	..	..	..	..	.. 700,000
Spruce	..	..	..	..	.. 1,800,000
Larch	..	..	..	..	.. 900,000
Honduras mahogany		..	..	..	.. 1,250,000
English oak		..	..	..	.. 1,450,000
African oak..		..	..	..	.. 2,280,000
Pine: red ..		..	..	..	·.. 1,850,000
Pitch ..		..	..	..	.. 1,225,000
American		..	..	..	.. 1,600,000
Yellow..		..	..	..	.. 1,600,000

G.—Notes upon Timber Strength.

The strength of timber varies considerably, and is dependent upon the age of the tree, the season at which it is felled, its geographical situation, manner of seasoning, etc.

The factors of safety employed for timber are higher than those employed for metals, in the ratio of 1·5 to 1·8 to 1; for steady loads take 10.

The Crushing Strength of timber may be approximately found from the relation:

Crushing Strength in lbs. per sq. in. = Wt. per cu. ft. × 165.

The Transverse Crushing Strength (that is, across the grain) is about one-quarter of the strength in the direction of the grain.

The Shear Stress of timber may be taken as one-eighth of the tensile strength with the grain, and varies from 1,500 to 2,500 lbs. per square inch.

The Modulus of Rigidity C for timber may be taken as varying from 170,000 to 100,000 lbs. per square inch.

H.—PROPERTIES OF STEEL AND DURALUMIN TUBES

Outside Diameter		3/8"	1/2"	5/8"	3/4"	7/8"	1"	1 1/8"	1 1/4"	1 3/8"	1 1/2"	1 5/8"
Decimal of Inch		0.37500	0.5000	0.6250	0.7500	0.8750	1.0000	1.1250	1.250	1.3750	1.5000	1.6250
24 S.W.G. 0.022	W	0.08400	0.1133	0.1436	0.1719	0.2002	0.2295	0.2588	0.2881	0.3172	0.3465	0.3768
	A	0.02440	0.0339	0.0417	0.0503	0.0590	0.0676	0.0762	0.0849	0.0935	0.1024	0.1108
	I	0.00038	0.0010	0.0019	0.0033	0.0054	0.0081	0.0116	0.0161	0.0215	0.0279	0.0356
	Z	0.00200	0.0039	0.0061	0.0089	0.0123	0.0162	0.0207	0.0257	0.0313	0.0373	0.0438
22 S.W.G. 0.028	W	0.10370	0.1441	0.1785	0.2157	0.2533	0.2907	0.3281	0.3655	0.4029	0.4403	0.4777
	A	0.03050	0.0415	0.0535	0.0635	0.0745	0.0855	0.0965	0.1075	0.1185	0.1295	0.1405
	I	0.00046	0.0011	0.0023	0.0042	0.0067	0.0101	0.0145	0.0201	0.0269	0.0351	0.0448
	Z	0.00250	0.0045	0.0075	0.0112	0.0153	0.0202	0.0258	0.0321	0.0391	0.0468	0.0552
20 S.W.G. 0.036	W	0.13010	0.1782	0.2264	0.2744	0.3223	0.3706	0.4185	0.4555	0.5148	0.5627	0.6110
	A	0.03830	0.0524	0.0666	0.0807	0.0948	0.1090	0.1231	0.1372	0.1514	0.1655	0.1797
	I	0.00056	0.0014	0.0029	0.0050	0.0083	0.0127	0.0183	0.0234	0.0340	0.0442	0.0567
	Z	0.00300	0.0058	0.0093	0.0135	0.0190	0.0254	0.0326	0.0407	0.0495	0.0592	0.0698
18 S.W.G. 0.048	W	0.16760	0.2319	0.2968	0.3601	0.4240	0.4882	0.5522	0.6164	0.6803	0.7446	0.8085
	A	0.04930	0.0682	0.0870	0.1059	0.1247	0.1436	0.1624	0.1813	0.2001	0.2190	0.2378
	I	0.00067	0.0018	0.0037	0.0065	0.0107	0.0163	0.0236	0.0338	0.0440	0.0577	0.0740
	Z	0.00360	0.0072	0.0117	0.0175	0.0245	0.0326	0.0419	0.0524	0.0641	0.0770	0.0911
16 S.W.G. 0.064	W	0.21250	0.2980	0.3834	0.4689	0.5544	0.6399	0.7253	0.8108	0.8962	0.9817	1.0672
	A	0.06250	0.0876	0.1128	0.1379	0.1630	0.1882	0.2133	0.2385	0.2636	0.2887	0.3139
	I	0.00082	0.0021	0.0045	0.0078	0.0135	0.0207	0.0301	0.0421	0.0567	0.0746	0.0958
	Z	0.00420	0.0085	0.0144	0.0218	0.0308	0.0414	0.0536	0.0673	0.0826	0.0995	0.1179
14 S.W.G. 0.080	W	—	—	0.4658	0.5726	0.6794	0.7862	0.8930	0.9998	1.1066	1.2134	1.3202
	A	—	—	0.1370	0.1684	0.1998	0.2312	0.2626	0.2941	0.3255	0.3569	0.3883
	I	—	—	0.0052	0.0096	0.0160	0.0246	0.0361	0.0506	0.0685	0.0903	0.1162
	Z	—	—	0.0166	0.0256	0.0365	0.0493	0.0641	0.0809	0.0997	0.1204	0.1430
12 W. 0.104	W	—	—	—	—	0.8565	0.9953	1.1341	1.2730	1.4118	1.5506	1.6895
	A	—	—	—	—	0.2519	0.2927	0.3336	0.3744	0.4152	0.4561	0.4969
	I	—	—	—	—	0.0191	0.0298	0.0440	0.0620	0.0844	0.1117	0.1445
	Z	—	—	—	—	0.0436	0.0597	0.0783	0.0994	0.1228	0.1490	0.1778
10 S.W.G. 0.128	W	—	—	—	—	—	—	1.3631	1.5439	1.7048	1.8757	2.0466
	A	—	—	—	—	—	—	0.4009	0.4512	0.5014	0.5517	0.6019
	I	—	—	—	—	—	—	0.0506	0.0718	0.0984	0.1308	0.1697
	Z	—	—	—	—	—	—	0.0900	0.1149	0.1431	0.1743	0.2089

W = Weight in pounds per ft. m.   A = area at (D − t).   I = Moment of inertia = $\frac{\pi}{64}(D^4 - d^4)$.

$$Z = \text{Modulus of resistance} = \frac{2I}{D} = \frac{A}{8}\left(\frac{D+d}{D}\right).$$

d = Inside diameter = D − 2t.   t = Thickness.

Weights given are for steel tubes at .283 lb. 1 cu. in.   For duralumin multiply given weight by .61.

Outside Diameter		1¾″	1⅞″	2″	2⅛″	2¼″	2⅜″	2½″	2⅝″	2¾″		3″
Decimal of Inch		1·7500	1·8750	2·0000	2·1250	2·2500	2·3750	2·5000	2·6250	2·7500	2·8750	3·0000
24	W	0·4160	0·4353	0·4646	0·4939	0·5232	—	—	—	—	—	—
S.W.G.	A	0·1194	0·1281	0·1367	0·1455	0·1540	—	—	—	—	—	—
	I	0·0445	0·0548	0·0667	0·0802	0·0955	—	—	—	—	—	—
0·022	Z	0·0509	0·0585	0·0667	0·0755	0·0849	—	—	—	—	—	—
22	W	0·5157	0·5525	0·5899	0·6273	0·6647	0·7021	0·7395	—	—	—	—
S.W.G.	A	0·1515	0·1625	0·1735	0·1845	0·1955	0·2065	0·2175	—	—	—	—
	I	0·0562	0·0693	0·0844	0·1015	0·1207	0·1423	0·1661	—	—	—	—
0·028	Z	0·0642	0·0740	0·0844	0·0955	0·1073	0·1198	0·1329	—	—	—	—
20	W	0·6589	0·7069	0·7551	0·8031	0·8510	0·8993	0·9476	0·9955	1·0438	—	—
S.W.G.	A	0·1938	0·2079	0·2221	0·2362	0·2503	0·2645	0·2787	0·2928	0·3070	—	—
	I	0·0711	0·0879	0·1071	0·1289	0·1533	0·1807	0·2115	0·2456	0·2827	—	—
0·036	Z	0·0813	0·0938	0·1071	0·1213	0·1363	0·1522	0·1692	0·1871	0·2056	—	—
18	W	0·8728	0·9367	1·0001	1·0649	1·1291	1·1931	1·2573	1·3212	1·3855	1·4494	1·5137
S.W.G.	A	0·2567	0·2755	0·2944	0·3132	0·3321	0·3509	0·3698	0·3886	0·4075	0·4263	0·4452
	I	0·0931	0·1150	0·1404	0·1690	0·2014	0·2376	0·2780	0·3227	0·3721	0·4261	0·4851
0·048	Z	0·1064	0·1228	0·1404	0·1591	0·1790	0·2001	0·2224	0·2459	0·2706	0·2964	0·3234
16	W	1·1526	1·2381	1·3236	1·4090	1·4945	1·5800	1·6654	1·7509	1·8364	1·9218	2·0073
S.W.G.	A	0·3390	0·3641	0·3893	0·4144	0·4396	0·4647	0·4898	0·5150	0·5401	0·5653	0·5904
	I	0·1208	0·1435	0·1826	0·2203	0·2628	0·3104	0·3635	0·4224	0·4873	0·5586	0·6364
0·064	Z	0·1379	0·1595	0·1826	0·2073	0·2336	0·2614	0·2908	0·3218	0·3544	0·3886	0·4243
14	W	1·4270	1·5337	1·6405	1·7473	1·8541	1·9609	2·0677	2·1745	2·2813	2·3881	2·4949
S.W.G.	A	0·4197	0·4511	0·4825	0·5139	0·5454	0·5768	0·6082	0·6396	0·6710	0·7024	0·7338
	I	0·1466	0·1821	0·2227	0·2691	0·3215	0·3802	0·4456	0·5180	0·5983	0·6863	0·7825
0·080	Z	0·1676	0·1942	0·2227	0·2533	0·2858	0·3202	0·3565	0·3948	0·4351	0·4774	0·5217
12	W	1·8283	1·9672	2·1060	2·2448	2·3837	2·5225	2·6613	2·8002	2·9390	3·0779	3·2167
S.W.G.	A	0·5377	0·5786	0·6194	0·6603	0·7011	0·7419	0·7828	0·8236	0·8644	0·9053	0·9461
	I	0·1830	0·2277	0·2792	0·3380	0·4047	0·4794	0·5627	0·6555	0·7577	0·8701	0·9931
0·104	Z	0·2091	0·2429	0·2792	0·3182	0·3597	0·4037	0·4502	0·4994	0·5511	0·6053	0·6621
10	W	2·2175	2·3884	2·5592	2·7301	2·9010	3·0719	3·2428	3·4137	3·5846	3·7554	3·9263
S.W.G.	A	0·6522	0·7025	0·7527	0·8030	0·8533	0·9035	0·9538	1·0040	1·0543	1·1046	1·1548
	I	0·2158	0·2694	0·3313	0·4019	0·4821	0·5720	0·6726	0·7843	0·9079	1·0439	1·1929
0·128	Z	0·2466	0·2874	0·3313	0·3783	0·4285	0·4817	0·5381	0·5976	0·6603	0·7262	0·7953

W = Weight in pounds per foot run. A = Cross-section area $\pi t(D - t)$. I = Moment of inertia $= \frac{\pi}{64}(D^4 - d^4)$.

Z = Modulus of resistance $= 2I/D = \frac{A}{8}\left(\frac{D^2+d^2}{D}\right)$. D = Outside diameter. d = Inside diameter $= D - 2t$. t = Thickness.

Weights given are for steel tubes at 0·283 lbs. per cu. in. For duralumin multiply given weight by 0·361

For aluminium multiply given weight by 0·328.

I.—WORKING LOADS FOR MILD STEEL RODS, WIRES, PINS, AND BOLTS, IN POUNDS.

Diam. in Inches.	Diam. in Millimetres.	Dead Load.		Load varying frequently from 0 to Max.		Load varying frequently from − Max. to + Max.	
		Single Shear.	Tension.	Single Shear.	Tension.	Single Shear.	Tension.
1/32	0·79	8·5	9·2	4·9	6·3	2·4	3·1
1/16	1·58	33	39	21	27	10·5	13·5
1/8	3·17	134	158	85	109	42	54
3/16	4·76	304	358	193	248	96	124
1/4	6·34	540	635	343	440	170	220
5/16	7·93	840	995	537	690	270	350
3/8	9·52	1,210	1,430	772	990	390	500
7/16	11·10	1,650	1,950	1,050	1,250	530	630
1/2	12·70	2,160	2,550	1,375	1,770	690	890
9/16	14·30	2,740	3,230	1,740	2,230	870	1,120
5/8	15·90	3,380	3,980	2,150	2,760	1,080	1,380
11/16	17·50	4,080	4,730	2,600	3,340	1,300	1,670
3/4	19·00	4,850	5,730	3,090	3,970	1,550	1,990
13/16	20·60	5,700	6,740	3,630	4,660	1,820	2,330
7/8	22·20	6,600	7,800	4,210	5,410	2,110	2,710
15/16	23·80	7,600	9,000	4,830	6,210	2,420	3,110
1	25·40	8,650	10,400	5,500	7,060	2,750	3,530

J.—Table of Areas of Mild Steel Sections, Plates, etc.

Calculated for Tensile Strength of 25 Tons per Square Inch.

Breaking Load in Pounds.	Area in Square Inches.	Area in Square Millimetres.
50	0·00089	0·574
100	0·00179	1·154
150	0·00268	1·727
200	0·00358	2·308
250	0·00446	2·875
300	0·00536	3·455
350	0·00625	4·030
400	0·00715	4·610
450	0·00804	5·180
500	0·00894	5·760
550	0·00982	6·330
600	0·01072	6·910
650	0·01160	7·490
700	0·01250	8·060
750	0·01340	8·650
800	0·01430	9·240
850	0·01520	9·800
900	0·01610	10·390
950	0·01690	10·900
1,000	0·01790	11·550
2,000	0·03580	23·080
3,000	0·05360	34·550
4,000	0·07150	46·100
5,000	0·08940	57·600

K.—Breaking Loads of Piano Wire.

Standard Wire Gauge No.	Inches.	Millimetres.	Breaking Load in Lbs.*
6	·1920	4·8770	7,134
7	1760	4·4700	5,994 ·
8	·1600	4·0640	4,955
9	·1440	3·6580	4,014
10	·1280	3·2510	3,171
11	·1160	2·9460	2,604
12	·1040	2·6420	2,091
14	·0800	2·0320	1,240
16	·0641	1·6260	792
18	·0480	1·2190	445
20	·0360	0·9144	251
22	·0280	0·7112	152
24	·0220	0·5588	94
26	·0180	0·4572	64
28	·0148	0·3759	42
30	·0124	0·3150	30

* These loads correspond with a breaking stress of 110 tons per square inch.

L.—Table of Relative Strengths for Weight.

Material.	Strength for Weight Number $= \dfrac{\text{Tensile str. in lbs. per sq. in.}}{\text{Weight per cu. ft. in lbs.}}$	
Mild steel	115	
Cast steel (unhardened)	140	
5 per cent. nickel steel (unhardened), 40 tons	183	
,, ,, ,, (oil-hardened), 80 tons	366	
Nickel Chrome (oil-hardened), 100 tons	457	
Chrome vanadium (oil-hardened), 115 tons ..	525	
Duralumin (rolled bar), 25 tons	320	
,, (rivet bar), 16 tons	204	
Aluminium (sheet), 12 tons	162	
Copper (sheet), 13 tons	53·4	
,, (wire), 26 tons	106·8	
Ash	322	200*
Birch	320	100*
Silver spruce	330	200*
Cedar (American)	308	170*
Mahogany (Honduras)	600	228*
Pine: white	322	148*
,, yellow..	406	166*
,, pitch	332	210*
Poplar	260	160*
Lancewood	350	
Hickory	330	220*
Walnut	170	120*

* Compression strengths.

APPENDIX II

TABLES OF WEIGHTS

A.—METALS.

B.—TIMBER.

C.—MISCELLANEOUS.

D.—STANDARD WIRE GAUGE: TABLE OF SIZES, WEIGHTS, AND LENGTHS OF STEEL WIRE.

E.—WEIGHTS OF DURALUMIN SHEETS AND RODS.

F.—STRAINER WEIGHTS.

G.—STRENGTH AND WEIGHT OF AEROPLANE CABLES.

H.—WEIGHTS AND DIMENSIONS OF METAL SHEETS.

I.—CALCULATED WEIGHTS IN POUNDS OF WHITWORTH'S STANDARD BOLTS AND NUTS.

J.—WEIGHT OF COPPER TUBES.

K.—WEIGHTS OF THREE-PLY BOARDS IN BIRCH.

A.—METALS.

Material.	Specific Gravity.	Weight per Cub. Ft. in Lbs.	Weight per Cub. In. in Lbs.
Duralumin	2·800	175·0	0·1015
Aluminium (rolled, sheet) ..	2·670	166·6	0·0960
,, (cast) ..	2·560	159·6	0·0920
Copper (sheet)	8·780	548·1	0·3160
,, (wire)	8·900	555·0	0·3210
Iron (cast)	7·230	451·0	0·2600
,, (wrought)	7·780	486·0	0·2800
Steel (mild)	7·852	489·6	0·2810
,, (cast)	7·848	489·3	0·2810
Brass (cast), average ..	8·280	517·0	0·2980
Gunmetal (10 copper to 1 tin) ..	8·464	528·4	0·3060
,, (8 copper to 1 tin) ..	8·459	528·0	0·3050
Tin (cast)..	7·291	455·0	0·2620
Zinc (cast)	7·000	437·0	0·2520
German silver	8·280	516·0	0·3000
Phosphor bronze (cast).. ..	8·600	536·8	0·3100
Aluminium bronze	7·680	475·0	0·2750

B.—Timber.

Material.				Specific Gravity.	Weight per Cu. Ft. in Lbs.	Weight per Cub. In. in Lbs.
Ash { from	..	..	..	0·690	43	0·025
{ to	..	..	..	0·760	47	0·027
Beech { from	..	..	..	0·690	43	0·025
{ to	..	..	..	0·700	43·5	0·025
Birch { fr m	..	..	..	0·710	44	0·026
{ too	..	..	..	0·730	45	0·026
Cork	..	..	..	0·250	15·5	0·009
Cedar: American			..	0·748	47	0·026
„ Indian ..			..	0·554	35	0·020
„ Lebanon			..	0·486	30	0·017
Elm: English ..		..	..	0·553	34	0·020
„ Canadian..			..	0·725	45	0·026
Hickory ..	..		..	0·690	43	0·025
Spruce (fir)	..	..	..	0·512	32	0·018
Larch { from	..	..	..	0·543	34	0·019
{ to	..	..	..	0·556	35	0·020
Maple ..	..		..	0·675	42	0·025
Mahogany: Honduras			..	0·560	35	0·020
„ Spanish			..	0·852	53	0·031
Pine: white { from			..	0·432	27	0·015
{ to ..			..	0·553	34	0·020
„ yellow	..	..	..	0·508	32	0·018
Poplar ..	..		..	0·390	24	0·014
Satinwood	..	..	..	0·960	60	0·034
Teak ..	..	..	..	0·800	50	0·030
English walnut ..		..	..	0·670	42	0·024

C.—Miscellaneous.

Material.	Specific Gravity.	Weight per Cub. Ft. in Lbs.	Weight per Cub. In. in Lbs.
Water: pure	1·000	62·280	0·0360
„ sea	1·027	64·000	0·0370
Petrol (average).. ..	0·700	43·600	0·0250
Oil (lubricating).. ..	0·900	57·980	0·0324
Glass (plate)	2·760	176·000	0·1000
Mica {from	2·780	179·000	0·1010
{to	3·150	202·100	0·1140
Rubber	0·930	58·000	0·0340
Vulcanite	1·520	82·200	0·0550
Vulcanized fibre.. ..	1·280	97·600	0·0460
Asbestos {from	2·100	135	0·0760
{to	2·800	180	0·1010
Celluloid	1·280	83	0·0480

$\frac{3}{16}$ ash 3-ply wood, weight per square foot = 0·66 pound.

1 inch wide Egyptian tape, 160 yards, weigh 1 pound.

D.—Standard Wire Gauge: Table of Sizes, Weights, and Lengths of Steel Wire.

Size on Standard Wire Gauge.	Diameter.		Sectional Area in Square Inches.	Approximate Weight of—		
	Decimal of an Inch.	Millimetres.		100 Feet.	Mile.	Kilometre.
				lbs.	lbs.	lbs.
7/0	·5000	12·700	·1963500	66·700000	3,522	2,188
6/0	·4640	11·800	·1691000	57·440000	3,033	1,885
5/0	·4320	11·000	·1465700	49·790000	2,629	1,634
4/0	·4000	10·200	·1256800	42·690000	2,254	1,400
3/0	·3720	9·400	·1086900	36·930000	1,950	1,211
2/0	·3480	8·800	·0951000	32·310000	1,706	1,060
1/0	·3240	8·200	·0824400	28·010000	1,479	919
1	·3000	7·600	·0706900	24·010000	1,268	788
2	·2760	7·000	·0598200	20·320000	1,073	667
3	·2520	6·400	·0498700	16·850000	895	556
4	·2320	5·900	·0422700	14·360000	758	471
5	·2120	5·400	·0353000	12·000000	633	393
6	·1920	4·900	·0289600	9·810000	518	323
7	·1760	4·500	·0243200	8·260000	436	271

STANDARD WIRE GAUGE—*continued*.

Size on Standard Wire Gauge.	Diameter.		Sectional Area in Square Inches.	Approximate Weight of—		
	Decimal of an Inch.	Milli-metres.		100 Feet.	Mile.	Kilometre.
				lbs.	lbs.	lbs.
8	·1600	4·100	·0201100	6·820000	360	224
9	·1440	3·700	·0162800	5·530000	292	182
10	·1280	3·300	·0128700	4·370000	231	143
11	·1160	3·000	·0105700	3·600000	190	118
12	·1040	2·600	·0085000	2·880000	152	95
13	·0920	2·300	·0066500	2·250000	119	74
14	·0800	2·000	·0050300	1·700000	90	56
15	·0720	1·800	·0040700	1·380000	73	45
16	·0640	1·600	·0032200	1·100000	58	36
17	·0560	1·400	·0024600	0·830000	44	27·5000
18	·0480	1·200	·0018100	0·610000	32·500	20·2000
19	·0400	1·000	·0012600	0·420000	22·540	14·0000
20	·0360	0·900	·0010200	0·340000	18·250	11·3400
21	·0320	0·800	·0008000	0·273000	14·420	8·9600
22	·0280	0·700	·0006200	0·209000	11·040	6·8600
23	·0240	0·600	·0004500	0·154000	8·110	5·0400
24	·0220	0·550	·0003800	0·129000	6·820	4·2400
25	·0020	0·500	·0003100	0·107000	5·630	3·5000
26	·0180	0·450	·0002500	0·086000	4·560	2·8400
27	·0164	0·400	·0002100	0·072000	3·790	2·3500
28	·0148	0·370	·0001700	0·058000	3·090	1·9200
29	·0136	0·350	·0001400	0·050000	2·610	1·6200
30	·0124	0·320	·0001200	0·041000	2·170	1·3500
31	·0116	0·280	·0001000	0·036000	1·890	1·1600
32	·0108	0·270	·0000910	0·031000	1·640	1·0200
33	·0100	0·254	·0000780	0·026000	1·400	0·8750
34	·0092	0·230	·0000660	0·022000	1·190	0·7440
35	·0084	0·203	·0000550	0·019000	0·901	0·5630
36	·0076	0·177	·0000450	0·015000	0·813	0·5080
37	·0068	0·172	·0000360	0·012000	0·651	0·4070
38	·0060	0·152	·0000280	0·009600	0·507	0·3170
39	·0052	0·127	·0000210	0·007200	0·380	0·2380
40	·0048	0·122	·0000180	0·006100	0·324	0·2020
41	·0044	0·112	·0000150	0·005100	0·272	0·1700
42	·0040	0·101	·0000120	0·004200	0·225	0·1400
43	·0036	0·091	·0000100	0·003400	0·182	0·1140
44	·0032	0·081	·0000080	0·002700	0·144	0·0900
45	·0028	0·071	·0000060	0·002100	0·110	0·0700
46	·0024	0·061	·0000040	0·001500	0·081	0·0500
47	·0020	0·050	·0000030	0·001060	0·056	0·0350
48	·0016	0·040	·0000020	0·000820	0·036	0·0225
49	·0012	0·030	·0000010	0·000266	0·020	0·0125
50	·0010	0·025	·0000007	0·000259	0·014	0·0097

E.—WEIGHTS OF DURALUMIN SHEETS AND RODS.

| | Sheets. | | | Rods. | |
| Thickness in Standard Wire Gauge. | Decimal Equivalent. | Weight in Lbs. per Sq. Ft. | Size. | Weight per Foot in Lbs. | |
				Round.	Square.
0	·3240	4·730	1/4	0·060	0·075
1	·3000	4·380	5/16	0·090	0·118
2	·2760	4·030	3/8	0·134	0·170
3	·2520	3·670	7/16	0·183	0·233
4	·2320	3·380	1/2	0·240	0·305
5	·2120	3·090	9/16	0·302	0·385
6	·1920	2·800	5/8	0·374	0·475
7	·1760	2·570	11/16	0·452	0·575
8	·1600	2·330	3/4	0·538	0·685
9	·1440	2·100	13/16	0·632	0·805
10	·1280	1·860	7/8	0·733	0·933
11	·1160	1·690	15/16	0·842	1·070
12	·1040	1·510	1	0·957	1·220
13	·0920	1·340	1 1/16	1·080	1·376
14	·0800	1·160	1 1/8	1·210	1·543
15	·0720	1·050	1 3/16	1·350	1·720
16	·0640	0·934	1 1/4	1·490	1·905
17	·0560	0·817	1 3/8	1·810	2·305
18	·0480	0·700	1 1/2	2·150	2·745
19	·0400	0·584	1 5/8	2·530	3·220
20	·0360	0·525	1 3/4	2·930	3·735
21	·0320	0·467	1 7/8	3·360	4·288
22	·0280	0·408	2	3·830	4·860
23	·0240	0·350	2 1/8	4·320	5·508
24	·0220	0·321	2 1/4	4·850	6·175
25	·0200	0·292	2 3/8	5·400	6·880
26	·0180	0·262	2 1/2	5·990	7·625
27	·0164	0·239	2 5/8	6·600	8·405
28	·0148	0·216			
29	·0136	0·200			
30	·0124	0·181			

F.—STRAINER WEIGHTS (HEWLETT AND BLONDEAU).

Diameter of Screw, over Thread, in Millimetres.	Weight in Ounces.	Breaking Load in Pounds.
2·5	0·125	480
3·0	0·200	700
3·5	0·400	1 000
4·0	0·600	1,180
4·5	1·000	1,515
5·0	2·000	1,900
6·0	2·660	2,315
7·0	3·750	3,680
8·0	5·750	4,670
10·0	6·500	7,530
12·0	8·660	11,000
14·0	13·250	15,200
16·0	14·250	19,970

G.—STRENGTH AND WEIGHT OF AEROPLANE CABLES (BULLIVANT).

Construction.		Size.				Approximate Breaking Load.		Approximate Weights.	
Number of Strands.	Wires per Strand.	Inches.		Millimetres.		Pounds.	Kilos.	Pounds per 1,000 Feet.	Kilos. per 100 Metres.
		Diam.	Circ.	Diam.	Circ.				
7	7	·068	3/16	1·7	5	500	227	8	1·2
7	7	·075	1/4	1·9	6	650	295	10	1·5
7	7	·088	9/32	2·2	7	1,120	500	14	2·1
7	7	·099	5/16	2·5	8	1,500	681	17	2·6
7	7	·110	11/32	2·8	9	1,680	762	20	3·0
7	7	·115	11/32	2·9	9	1,750	794	23	3·4
7	7	·130	13/32	3·3	10	2,300	1,043	30	4·5
7	7	·138	27/64	3·5	11	2,450	1,111	33	4·9
7	7	·140	7/16	3·6	11	2,600	1,179	36	5·3
7	7	·164	13/32	4·1	13	3,600	1,633	47	7·0
7	7	·180	9/16	4·6	15	4,500	2,041	55	8·2
7	7	·210	21/32	5·3	17	6,300	2,858	74	11·0

EXTRA FLEXIBLE.

7	12	·093	19/64	2·4	7	850	385	13	1·9
7	12	·105	5/16	2·7	8	1,200	544	18	2·7
7	14	·115	11/32	2·9	9	1,500	680	20	3·0
7	19	·126	13/32	3·2	10	2,000	907	27	4·0
7	19	·137	7/16	3·5	11	2,450	1,111	32	4·8
7	19	·150	1/2	3·8	12	2,900	1,315	38	5·7
7	19	·168	9/16	4·3	14	3,400	1,542	50	7·4
7	19	·182	11/16	4·6	15	4,200	1,905	56	8·3
7	19	·195	5/8	5·0	16	5,000	2,268	64	9·5
7	19	·218	11/16	5·5	17	5,500	2,495	80	11·9
7	19	·228	23/32	5·8	18	6,250	2,835	90	13·4
7	19	·239	3/4	6·1	19	7,250	3,288	100	14·9
7	19	·262	13/16	6·7	21	8,500	3,855	117	17·4
7	19	·270	27/32	6·9	22	9,600	4,356	124	18·4
7	19	·305	1	7·7	25	11,000	4,990	151	22·5

H.—Weights and Dimensions of Metal Sheets.

Standard Wire Gauge.	Thickness.		Weight : Lbs. per Square Foot.				
	Inch.	Millimetres.	Aluminium.	Brass.	Copper.	Steel.	Tin.
	·375	9·525	5·180	16·70	17·10	15·00	14·40
3/0	·372	9·449	5·140	16·50	17·00	14·90	14·30
2/0	·348	8·839	4·810	15·50	15·90	13·90	13·40
1/0	·324	8·229	4·480	14·40	14·80	13·00	12·50
	·312	7·937	4·310	13·90	14·20	12·50	12·00
1	·300	7·620	4·150	13·30	13·70	12·00	11·50
	·289	7·341	3·990	12·90	13·20	11·60	11·10
	·278	7·061	3·840	12·40	12·70	11·10	10·70
2	·276	7·010	3·810	12·30	12·60	11·00	10·60
	·270	6·858	3·730	12·00	12·30	10·80	10·40
3	·252	6·401	3·480	11·20	11·50	10·10	9·68
	·250	6·350	3·450	11·10	11·40	10·00	9·60
	·238	6·045	3·290	10·60	10·90	9·52	9·14
4	·232	5·893	3·200	10·30	10·60	9·28	8·91
	·216	5·486	2·980	9·61	9·86	8·64	8·31
5	·212	5·385	2·930	9·43	9·68	8·48	8·14
	·200	5·080	2·760	8·90	9·12	8·00	7·68
6	·192	4·877	2·650	8·54	8·76	7·68	7·37
	·187	4·762	2·580	8·32	8·53	7·48	7·18
	·182	4·623	2·520	8·10	8·31	7·28	6·99
7	·176	4·470	2·430	7·83	8·03	7·05	6·76
	·166	4·216	2·290	7·38	7·58	6·64	6·37
8	·160	4·064	2·210	7·12	7·30	6·40	6·15
	·150	3·810	2·070	6·67	6·85	6·00	5·76
9	·144	3·658	1·990	6·41	6·57	5·76	5·53
	·136	3·454	1·880	6·05	6·20	5·44	5·22
10	·128	3·251	1·770	5·69	5·84	5·12	4·92
	·125	3·175	1·730	5·56	5·70	5·00	4·80
	·124	3·150	1·710	5·52	5·66	4·96	4·76
11	·116	2·946	1·600	5·16	5·29	4·64	4·46
	·112	2·845	1·550	4·98	5·11	4·48	4·30
12	·104	2·642	1·440	4·63	4·75	4·16	3·99
	·100	2·540	1·380	4·45	4·57	4·00	3·84
13	·092	2·337	1·270	4·09	4·20	3·68	3·53
	·090	2·286	1·240	4·00	4·11	3·60	3·46
	·082	2·082	1·130	3·65	3·75	3·28	3·15
14	·080	2·032	1·110	3·56	3·65	3·20	3·07
	·077	1·956	1·070	3·43	3·52	3·08	2·96
15	·072	1·829	0·995	3·20	3·29	2·88	2·77
	·068	1·727	0·940	3·02	3·11	2·72	2·61
	·065	1·651	0·898	2·89	2·97	2·60	2·50

WEIGHTS AND DIMENSIONS OF METAL SHEETS—*continued*.

Standard Wire Gauge.	Thickness.		Weight : Pounds per Square Foot.				
	Inch.	Milli- metres.	Alu- minium.	Brass.	Copper.	Steel.	Tin.
16	·0640	1·626	·885	2·850	2·920	2·560	2·460
	·0630	1·600	·870	2·800	2·880	2·520	2·420
	·0620	1·587	·857	2·760	2·830	2·480	2·380
	·0600	1·524	·829	2·670	2·740	2·400	2·300
17	·0560	1·422	·774	2·490	2·560	2·240	2·150
	·0550	1·397	·760	2·450	2·510	2·200	2·110
	·0510	1·295	·705	2·270	2·330	2·040	1·960
18	·0480	1·219	·663	2·130	2·190	1·920	1·840
	·0470	1·194	·649	2·090	2·150	1·880	1·810
	·0420	1·067	·580	1·870	1·920	1·680	1·610
19	·0400	1·016	·552	1·780	1·830	1·600	1·540
	·0380	0·965	·525	1·690	1·740	1·520	1·460
20	·0360	0·914	·497	1·600	1·650	1·440	1·380
	·0350	0·889	·484	1·560	1·600	1·400	1·340
21	·0320	0·813	·442	1·420	1·460	1·280	1·230
	·0310	0·793	·429	1·380	1·420	1·240	1·190
22	·0280	0·711	·387	1·250	1·280	1·120	1·080
	·0270	0·686	·373	1·200	1·240	1·080	1·040
23	·0240	0·610	·332	1·070	1·100	0·960	0·921
	·0230	0·584	·318	1·020	1·050	0·920	0·883
24	·0220	0·559	·304	0·979	1·010	0·880	0·845
	·0210	0·533	·290	0·935	0·960	0·840	0·806
25	·0200	0·508	·276	0·890	0·914	0·800	0·768
	·0190	0·483	·262	0·846	0·868	0·760	0·730
26	·0180	0·457	·249	0·801	0·823	0·720	0·691
27	·0164	0·416	·227	0·730	0·750	0·656	0·630
	·0160	0·406	·221	0·712	0·731	0·640	0·614
	·0156	0·397	·215	0·694	0·713	0·624	0·599
28	·0148	0·376	·204	0·658	0·677	0·592	0·568
	·0140	0·356	·193	0·623	0·640	0·560	0·537
29	·0136	0·345	·188	0·605	0·622	0·544	0·522
30	·0124	0·315	·171	0·552	0·566	0·496	0·476
	·0120	0·305	·166	0·534	0·548	0·480	0·461
	·0105	0·267	·145	0·467	0·480	0·420	0·403
	·0090	0·229	·125	0·400	0·412	0·360	0·360
	·0080	0·203	·111	0·356	0·366	0·320	0·307
Specific gravity			2·670	8·620	8·820	7·740	7·400
Ratio of weights ..			1	3·230	3·300	2·900	2·780

I.—CALCULATED WEIGHTS IN POUNDS OF WHITWORTH'S STANDARD BOLTS AND NUTS: HEXAGONAL HEAD AND NUT.

Length* in Inches.	Diameter of Bolt in Inches.										
	¼	⅜	½	⅝	¾	⅞	1	1⅛	1¼	1⅜	1½
1	·042	·106	·222	0·376	0·612	—	—	—	—	—	—
1⅛	·044	·110	·229	0·387	0·628	—	—	—	—	—	—
1¼	·045	·114	·236	0·398	0·643	0·944	—	—	—	—	—
1⅜	·047	·118	·243	0·408	0·659	0·965	—	—	—	—	—
1½	·049	·122	·250	0·419	0·675	0·986	1·394	—	—	—	—
1⅝	·050	·126	·257	0·430	0·690	1·008	1·421	—	—	—	—
1¾	·052	·130	·264	0·441	0·706	1·029	1·449	1·966	—	—	—
1⅞	·054	·134	·271	0·452	0·722	1·050	1·477	2·001	—	—	—
2	·056	·138	·278	0·463	0·737	1·072	1·505	2·036	2·671	—	—
2¼	·059	·145	·292	0·484	0·769	1·114	1·561	2·107	2·758	—	—
2½	·063	·153	·305	0·506	0·800	1·157	1·616	2·177	2·845	3·572	—
2¾	·065	·161	·319	0·528	0·831	1·199	1·672	2·247	2·932	3·678	—
3	·069	·169	·333	0·549	0·862	1·242	1·727	2·318	3·019	3·783	4·766
3¼	·071	·177	·347	0·571	0·894	1·284	1·783	2·388	3·106	3·888	4·891
3½	·075	·185	·361	0·593	0·925	1·327	1·838	2·459	3·193	3·993	5·016
3¾	·079	·192	·375	0·615	0·956	1·369	1·893	2·529	3·280	4·098	5·142
4	·082	·200	·389	0·637	0·988	1·412	1·950	2·600	3·367	4·204	5·267
4¼	·085	·208	·403	0·658	1·019	1·455	2·005	2·670	3·454	4·309	5·392
4½	·089	·216	·417	0·680	1·050	1·497	2·061	2·740	3·541	4·414	5·517
4¾	·092	·224	·431	0·702	1·081	1·540	2·116	2·810	3·627	4·519	5·642
5	·096	·232	·445	0·724	1·113	1·583	2·172	2·881	3·714	4·624	5·767
5¼	·099	·240	·459	0·745	1·144	1·625	2·228	2·952	3·801	4·730	5·893
5½	·103	·247	·472	0·767	1·175	1·667	2·283	3·022	3·888	4·835	6·018
5¾	·106	·255	·486	0·789	1·207	1·710	2·339	3·092	3·975	4·940	6·143
6	·110	·263	·500	0·810	1·238	1·753	2·394	3·163	4·062	5·045	6·268
6½	·117	·279	·528	0·854	1·300	1·838	2·506	3·303	4·236	5·256	6·518
7	·124	·294	·556	0·897	1·363	1·923	2·617	3·444	4·410	5·466	6·769
7½	·130	·310	·584	0·941	1·425	2·008	2·728	3·585	4·584	5·676	7·019
8	·138	·326	·612	0·984	1·488	2·094	2·839	3·726	4·757	5·887	7·270
8½	—	·341	·639	1·028	1·550	2·179	2·950	3·867	4·931	6·097	7·520
9	—	·357	·667	1·071	1·613	2·264	3·062	4·008	5·105	6·308	7·770
9½	—	—	·695	1·115	1·676	2·349	3·173	4·149	5·279	6·518	8·021
10	—	—	·725	1·158	1·739	2·434	3·284	4·290	5·453	6·728	8·271
10½	—	—	—	1·202	1·801	2·519	3·396	4·430	5·627	6·939	8·521
11	—	—	—	1·245	1·863	2·605	3·507	4·571	5·800	7·149	8·772
11½	—	—	—	—	1·926	2·689	3·618	4·712	5·974	7·360	9·022
12	—	—	—	—	1·989	2·775	3·729	4·853	6·148	7·570	9·272
Nut†	·0134	·0345	·0757	·1394	·2164	·3203	·4611	·6379	·8511	1·075	1·391
Shank‡	·0139	·0313	·0557	·0869	·1252	·1703	·2225	·2817	·3477	·4208	·5007

* Of round portion of bolt, under head.
† Weight in pounds of one nut.
‡ Weight in pounds of shank per 1 inch of length.

J.—WEIGHT OF COPPER TUBES: POUNDS PER FOOT LENGTH.

Imp. Stand. Wire Gauge.	20	19	18	17	16	15	14	13	12	11	10	9	8		
Inch	0·036	0·040	0·048	0·056	0·064	0·072	0·080	0·092	0·104	0·116	0·128	0·144	0·160	0·176	0·192
Bore in Inches.															
¼	0·13	0·15	0·18	0·21	0·25	0·28	0·32	0·38	0·44	—	—	—	—	—	—
⅜	0·18	0·20	0·25	0·30	0·34	0·39	0·44	0·52	0·60	0·70	0·78	0·90	1·04	1·17	1·32
½	0·23	0·26	0·32	0·38	0·44	0·50	0·56	0·66	0·76	0·87	0·97	1·12	1·28	1·44	1·61
⅝	0·29	0·32	0·39	0·47	0·54	0·61	0·68	0·80	0·92	1·05	1·17	1·34	1·52	1·70	1·90
¾	0·34	0·38	0·47	0·55	0·63	0·72	0·80	0·94	1·08	1·22	1·37	1·56	1·77	1·97	2·19
⅞	0·40	0·44	0·54	0·64	0·73	0·82	0·93	1·08	1·23	1·40	1·56	1·78	2·01	2·25	2·48
1	0·45	0·51	0·61	0·72	0·83	0·93	1·04	1·21	1·39	1·58	1·76	2·00	2·26	2·51	2·79
1⅛	0·51	0·57	0·69	0·81	0·93	1·04	1·17	1·35	1·55	1·75	1·95	2·22	2·50	2·78	3·07
1¼	0·56	0·63	0·76	0·89	1·02	1·15	1·29	1·49	1·71	1·93	2·15	2·44	2·74	3·05	3·36
1⅜	0·61	0·69	0·83	0·98	1·12	1·26	1·42	1·63	1·87	2·11	2·34	2·66	2·98	3·32	3·66
1½	0·67	0·75	0·91	1·06	1·22	1·37	1·53	1·77	2·03	2·28	2·54	2·88	3·23	3·60	3·98
1⅝	0·73	0·81	0·98	1·15	1·32	1·48	1·65	1·91	2·18	2·46	2·75	3·10	3·47	3·85	4·25
1¾	0·79	0·87	1·05	1·23	1·41	1·59	1·77	2·05	2·34	2·63	2·93	3·31	3·72	4·12	4·53
1⅞	0·84	0·93	1·13	1·32	1·51	1·70	1·90	2·19	2·50	2·81	3·12	3·53	3·96	4·39	4·82
2	0·89	0·99	1·20	1·40	1·61	1·81	2·02	2·33	2·66	2·99	3·32	3·75	4·20	4·66	5·11
2¼	—	1·12	1·34	1·58	1·80	2·03	2·26	2·61	2·98	3·34	3·71	4·19	4·70	5·19	5·70
2½	—	1·24	1·49	1·76	2·00	2·25	2·50	2·89	3·30	3·70	4·10	4·63	5·18	5·73	6·28
2¾	—	1·36	1·63	1·91	2·19	2·47	2·75	3·17	3·61	4·05	4·48	5·08	5·70	6·26	6·88
3	—	—	—	2·08	2·38	2·68	3·00	3·45	3·93	4·40	4·87	5·50	6·15	6·80	7·46

K. Weights of Three-Ply Boards in Birch.

Thickness in Millimetres.	Weight per Superficial Square Foot in Ounces.
1·5	3·5
2·0	4·5
3·0	6·5
4·0	9·0
5·0	11·0
6·0	13·0

Note.—For *ash* ply-wood these weights should be increased by 5 per cent.

APPENDIX III

MISCELLANEOUS TABLES

A.—Tables for Aerodynamical Calculations.

B.—Tables of Horse-Powers, Speeds and Resistances.

C.—Table of Sines, Cosines, and Tangents.

D.—Diameters, Circumferences, and Areas of Circles.

E.—Principal Standards of Wire Gauge.

F.—International Metric Threads.

G.—British Association (B.A.) Screw-Threads.

H.—Whitworth's Standard Screw-Threads for Bolts.

J.—Whitworth's Threads for Gas and Water Pipes.

A.—TABLES FOR AERODYNAMICAL CALCULATIONS.

M.P.H.	Feet per Sec. (V).	V².	$\frac{V^2}{424}$.	$\frac{V}{550}$.	Pressure upon Normal Plane in Pounds.	
					For Small Plates, 0·00139 V².	For Large, over 2 Feet, 0·00148 V²
1	1·5	2·25	0·0053	·00273	0·00313	0·0032
2	2·9	8·41	0·0196	·00527	0·01169	0·0128
3	4·4	19·36	0·0457	·00801	0·02690	0·0288
4	5·9	34·81	0·0821	·01072	0·05300	0·0512
5	7·3	53·29	0·1260	·01327	0·07420	0·0800
6	8·8	77·44	0·1825	·01598	0·10770	0·1152
7	10·3	106	0·2500	·01873	0·14730	0·1567
8	11·7	137	0·3230	·02128	0·19050	0·2048
9	13·2	174	0·4110	·02400	0·24200	0·2590
10	14·7	216	0·5090	·02670	0·30050	0·3200
11	16·1	259	0·6120	·02930	0·36000	0·3870
12	17·6	310	0·7320	·03200	0·43150	0·4610
13	19·1	365	0·8610	·03470	0·50750	0·5410
14	20·5	420	0·9910	·03730	0·58400	0·6270
15	22·0	484	1·1400	·04000	0·67300	0·7200
16	23·5	552	1·3000	·04270	0·76800	0·8190
17	24·9	620	1·4600	·04530	0·86200	0·9250
18	26·4	697	1·6400	·04800	0·97000	1·0370
19	27·8	773	1·8200	·05060	1·07400	1·1550
20	29·3	858	2·0200	·05330	1·19300	1·2800
21	30·8	949	2·2400	·05600	1·32000	1·4110
22	32·3	1,043	2·4600	·05870	1·45000	1·5490
23	33·7	1,136	2·6800	·06130	1·57800	1·6930
24	35·2	1,239	2·9200	·06410	1·72200	1·8430
25	36·7	1,397	3·2900	·06670	1·94200	2·0000
26	38·1	1,452	3·4200	·06930	2·02800	2·1630
27	39·6	1,568	3·7000	·07210	2·18000	2·3330
28	41·1	1,689	3·9800	·07470	2·34800	2·5090
29	42·5	1,806	4·2600	·07730	2·51000	2·6910
30	44·0	1,936	4·5700	·08000	2·69000	2·8800
31	45·5	2,070	4·8900	·08280	2·88000	3·0750
32	46·9	2,200	5·1900	·08540	3·06000	3·2770
33	48·4	2,343	5·5400	·08820	3·26500	3·4850
34	49·9	2,490	5·8800	·09080	3·46500	3·6990
35	51·3	2,632	6·2100	·09330	3·66000	3·9200
36	52·8	2,788	6·5800	·09600	3·88000	4·1470
37	54·3	2,948	6·9600	·09880	4·10000	4·3810
38	55·7	3,102	7·3200	·10120	4·32000	4·6210
39	57·2	3,272	7·7200	·10380	4·55000	4·8670
40	58·7	3,446	8·1250	·10660	4·79000	5·1200
41	60·1	3,612	8·5200	·10910	5·02000	5·3970
42	61·6	3,795	8·9500	·11180	5·28000	5·6450
43	63·1	3,982	9·4000	·11460	5·54000	5·9170
44	64·5	4,160	9·8000	·11720	5·78000	6·1950
45	66·0	4,356	10·2600	·11980	6·06000	6·4800
46	67·5	4,556	10·7300	·12260	6·34000	6·7710
47	68·9	4,747	11·1800	·12530	6·60000	7·0680
48	70·4	4,956	11·6700	·12790	6·89000	7·3720
49	71·9	5,170	12·1800	·13060	7·20000	7·6830
50	73·3	5,373	12·6600	·13320	7·47000	8·0000
51	74·8	5,595	13·1800	·13580	7·78000	8·3230
52	76·3	5,821	13·7100	·13860	8·10000	8·6520

TABLES FOR AERODYNAMICAL CALCULATIONS—*continued.*

M.P.H.	Feet per Sec. (V).	V².	$\dfrac{V^2}{424}$	$\dfrac{V}{550}$	Pressure upon Normal Plane in Pounds.	
					For Small Plates, 0·00139 V².	For Large, over 2 Feet, 0·00148 V².
53	77·7	6,037	14·2200	·14110	8·39000	8·9890
54	79·2	6,273	14·7700	·14390	8·73000	9·3310
55	80·7	6,512	15·3300	·14660	9·06000	9·6800
56	82·1	6,740	15·8800	·14900	9·38000	10·0350
57	83·6	6,989	16·4600	·15180	9·72000	10·3970
58	85·1	7,242	17·0600	·15450	10·07000	10·7640
59	86·5	7,484	17·6300	·15720	10·41000	11·1390
60	88·0	7,744	18·2000	·15980	10·76000	11·5200
61	89·5	8,010	18·8500	·16260	11·13000	11·9070
62	90·9	8,263	19·3600	·16520	11·47000	12·3000
63	92·4	8,537	20·0800	·16780	11·86000	12·7010
64	93·9	8,817	20·7600	·17060	12·26000	13·1070
65	95·3	9,082	21·3400	·17320	12·63000	13·5200
66	96·8	9,370	22·0600	·17570	13·03000	13·9370
67	98·3	9,662	22·7400	·17850	13·43000	14·3640
68	99·7	9,940	23·4200	·18120	13·82000	14·7960
69	101·2	10,241	24·1600	·18380	14·24000	15·2370
70	102·7	10,547	24·8800	·18670	14·67000	15·6800
71	104·1	10,836	25·5800	·18930	15·08000	16·1300
72	105·6	11,151	26·2900	·19200	15·50000	16·5890
73	107·1	11,470	27·0200	·19480	15·93000	17·0520
74	108·5	11,772	27·7200	·19730	16·36000	17·5240
75	110·0	12,100	28·5400	·20000	16·83000	18·0000
76	111·5	12,432	29·3400	·20280	17·30000	18·4830
77	112·9	12,746	30·1000	·20540	17·72000	18·9720
78	114·4	13,087	30·8500	·20800	18·19000	19·4690
79	115·9	13,433	31·7000	·21100	18·69000	19·9710
80	117·3	13,759	32·4500	·21350	19·12000	20·4800
81	118·8	14,113	33·3000	·21620	19·62000	20·9970
82	120·3	14,472	34·1500	·21900	20·10000	21·5170
83	121·7	14,811	34·9500	·22100	20·60000	22·0450
84	123·2	15,178	35·8000	·22400	21·08000	22·5790
85	124·7	15,550	35·7000	·22680	21·62000	23·1200
86	126·1	15,901	37·5000	·22940	22·12000	23·6660
87	127·6	16,282	38·4000	·23200	22·65000	24·2210
88	129·1	16,667	39·3000	·23480	23·15000	24·7800
89	130·5	17,030	40·2000	·23740	23·70000	25·3490
90	132·0	17,424	41·1000	·24000	24·22000	25·9200
91	133·5	17,822	42·1000	·24300	24·76000	26·5010
92	134·9	18,198	42·9000	·24540	25·30000	27·0850
93	136·4	18,604	43·8000	·24800	25·88000	27·6780
94	137·9	19,016	45·2000	·25100	26·45000	28·2760
95	139·3	19,404	45·7500	·25350	26·70000	28·8810
96	140·8	19,824	46·7500	·25650	27·55000	29·4910
97	142·3	20,249	47·7500	·25900	28·15000	30·1090
98	143·7	20,649	48·7000	·26150	28·75000	30·7340
99	145·2	21,083	49·7000	·26400	29·34000	31·3600
100	146·7	21,520	50·7000	·26700	29·90000	32·0000
110	161·0	25,900	61·2000	·29300	36·00000	38·7000
120	176·0	31,000	73·2000	·32000	43·15000	46·1000
130	191·0	36,500	86·1000	·34700	50·75000	54·1000
140	205·0	42,000	99·1000	·37300	58·40000	62·7000
150	220·0	48,400	114·0000	·40000	67·30000	72·0000

B.—TABLE OF HORSE-POWERS, SPEEDS, AND RESISTANCES.

Resistance or Thrust in Pounds.

Power	Speed in Miles per Hour	10	20	30	40	50	60	70	80	90	100
1	375	3,750	7,500	11,250	15,000	18,750	22,500	26,250	30,000	33,750	37,500
5	75	750	1,500	2,250	3,000	3,750	4,500	5,250	6,000	6,750	7,500
10	37·50	375	750	1,125	1,500	1,875	2,250	2,625	3,000	3,375	3,750
15	25	250	500	750	1,000	1,250	1,500	1,750	2,000	2,250	2,500
20	18·80	188	375	562·5	750	937·5	1,125	1,312·5	1,500	1,687·5	1,875
25	15	150	300	450	600	750	900	1,050	1,200	1,350	1,500
30	12·50	125	250	375	500	625	750	875	1,000	1,125	1,250
35	10·71	107·1	214·3	321·4	428·6	535·7	642·8	750	857·1	964·3	1,071·4
40	9·38	93·8	187·5	281·3	375	468·8	562·5	656·3	750	843·8	937·5
45	8·33	83·3	166·7	250	333·3	416·7	500	583·3	666·7	750	833·3
50	7·50	75	150	225	300	375	450	525	600	675	750
60	6·25	62·5	125	187·5	250	312·5	375	437·5	500	562·5	625
70	5·36	53·6	107	160·7	214·3	267·9	321·4	375	428·6	482·1	535·7
80	4·69	46·9	93·8	140·6	187·5	234·4	281·3	328·3	375	421·9	468·8
90	4·17	41·7	83·3	125	166·7	208·3	250	291·7	333·3	375	416·7
100	3·75	37·5	75	112·5	150	187·5	225	262·5	300	337·5	375

C.—TABLE OF SINES, COSINES, AND TANGENTS.

Angle.	Radians.	Sine.	Tangent.	Co-tangent.	Cosine.		
0°	0	0	0	∞	1·0000	1·5708	90°
1	·0175	·0175	0·0175	57·2900	0·9998	1·5533	89
2	·0349	·0349	0·0349	28·6363	0·9994	1·5359	88
3	·0524	·0523	0·0524	19·0811	0·9986	1·5184	87
4	·0698	·0698	0·0699	14·3006	0·9976	1·5010	86
5	·0873	·0872	0·0875	11·4301	0·9962	1·4835	85
6	·1047	·1045	0·1051	9·5144	0·9945	1·4661	84
7	·1222	·1219	0·1228	8·1443	0·9925	1·4486	83
8	·1396	·1392	0·1405	7·1154	0·9903	1·4312	82
9	·1571	·1564	0·1584	6·3138	0·9877	1·4137	81
10	·1745	·1736	0·1763	5·6713	0·9848	1·3963	80
11	·1920	·1908	0·1944	5·1446	0·9816	1·3788	79
12	·2094	·2079	0·2126	4·7046	0·9781	1·3614	78
13	·2269	·2250	0·2309	4·3315	0·9744	1·3439	77
14	·2443	·2419	0·2493	4·0108	0·9703	1·3265	76
15	·2618	·2588	0·2679	3·7321	0·9659	1·3090	75
16	·2793	·2756	0·2867	3·4874	0·9613	1·2915	74
17	·2967	·2924	0·3057	3·2709	0·9563	1·2741	73
18	·3142	·3090	0·3249	3·0777	0·9511	1·2566	72
19	·3316	·3256	0·3443	2·9042	0·9455	1·2392	71
20	·3491	·3420	0·3640	2·7475	0·9397	1·2217	70
21	·3665	·3584	0·3839	2·6051	0·9336	1·2043	69
22	·3840	·3746	0·4040	2·4751	0·9272	1·1868	68
23	·4014	·3907	0·4245	2·3559	0·9205	1·1694	67
24	·4189	·4067	0 4452	2·2460	0·9135	1·1519	66
25	·4363	·4226	0 4663	2·1445	0·9063	1·1345	65
26	·4538	·4384	0 4877	2·0503	0·8988	1·1170	64
27	·4712	·4540	0·5095	1·9626	0·8910	1·0996	63
28	·4887	·4695	0·5317	1·8807	0·8830	1·0821	62
29	·5061	·4848	0·5543	1·8040	0·8746	1·0647	61
30	·5236	·5000	0·5774	1·7321	0·8660	1·0472	60
31	·5411	·5150	0·6009	1·6643	0·8572	1·0297	59
32	·5585	·5299	0·6249	1·6003	0·8480	1·0123	58
33	·5760	·5446	0·6494	1·5399	0·8387	0·9948	57
34	·5934	·5592	0·6745	1·4826	0·8290	0·9774	56
35	·6109	·5736	0·7002	1·4281	0·8192	0·9599	55
36	·6283	·5878	0·7265	1·3764	0·8090	0·9425	54
37	·6458	·6018	0·7536	1·3270	0·7986	0·9250	53
38	·6632	·6157	0·7813	1·2799	0·7880	0·9076	52
39	·6807	·6293	0·8098	1·2349	0·7771	0·8901	51
40	·6981	·6428	0·8391	1·1918	0·7660	0·8727	50
41	·7156	·6561	0·8693	1·1504	0·7547	0·8552	49
42	·7330	·6691	0·9004	1·1106	0·7431	0·8378	48
43	·7505	·6820	0·9325	1·0724	0·7314	0·8203	47
44	·7679	·6947	0·9657	1·0350	0·7193	0·8029	46
45	·7854	·7071	1·0000	1·0000	0·7071	0·7854	45
		Sine	Co-tangent	Tangent	Sine	Radians	Angle

12

THE DESIGN OF AEROPLANES

D.—Diameters, Circumferences, and Areas of Circles

Diameter.	Circumference.	Area.	Diameter.	Circumference.	Area.
1/32	0·0982	0·0008	5 1/4	16·493	21·647
1/16	0·1963	0·0031	5 3/8	16·886	22·690
1/8	0·3927	0·0122	5 1/2	17·278	23·758
3/16	0·5890	0·0276	5 5/8	17·671	24·850
1/4	0·7854	0·0490	5 3/4	18·064	25·967
5/16	0·9817	0·0767	5 7/8	18·457	27·108
3/8	1·1781	0·1104	6	18·849	28·274
7/16	1·3744	0·1503	6 1/4	19·635	30·679
1/2	1·5708	0·1963	6 1/2	20·420	33·183
9/16	1·7671	0·2485	6 3/4	21·205	35·784
5/8	1·9635	0·3068	7	21·991	38·484
11/16	2·1598	0·3712	7 1/4	22·776	41·282
3/4	2·3562	0·4418	7 1/2	23·562	44·178
13/16	2·5525	0·5185	7 3/4	24·347	47·173
7/8	2·7489	0·6013	8	25·132	50·265
15/16	2·9452	0·6903	8 1/4	25·918	53·456
1	3·1416	0·7854	8 1/2	26·703	56·745
1 1/8	3·5343	0·9940	8 3/4	27·489	60·132
1 1/4	3·9270	1·2271	9	28·274	63·617
1 3/8	4·3197	1·4848	9 1/4	29·059	67·200
1 1/2	4·7124	1·7671	9 1/2	29·845	70·882
1 5/8	5·1051	2·0739	9 3/4	30·630	74·662
1 3/4	5·4978	2·4052	10	31·416	78·540
1 7/8	5·8905	2·7611	10 1/4	32·201	82·516
2	6·2832	3·1416	10 1/2	32·986	86·590
2 1/8	6·6759	3·5465	10 3/4	33·772	90·762
2 1/4	7·0686	3·9760	11	34·558	95·033
2 3/8	7·4613	4·4302	11 1/4	35·343	99·402
2 1/2	7·8540	4·9087	11 1/2	36·128	103·860
2 5/8	8·2467	5·4119	11 3/4	36·913	108·430
2 3/4	8·6394	5·9395	12	37·699	113·090
2 7/8	9·0321	6·4918	12 1/4	38·484	117·860
3	9·4248	7·0686	12 1/2	39·270	122·710
3 1/8	9·8175	7·6699	12 3/4	40·055	127·680
3 1/4	10·2100	8·2957	13	40·840	132·730
3 3/8	10·6020	8·9462	13 1/4	41·626	137·890
3 1/2	10·9950	9·6211	13 1/2	42·411	143·130
3 5/8	11·3880	10·3200	13 3/4	43·197	148·490
3 3/4	11·7810	11·0440	14	43·982	153·930
3 7/8	12·1730	11·7930	14 1/4	44·767	159·480
4	12·5660	12·5660	14 1/2	45·553	165·130
4 1/8	12·9590	13·3640	14 3/4	46·338	170·870
4 1/4	13·3510	14·1860	15	47·124	176·710
4 3/8	13·7440	15·0330	15 1/4	47·909	182·650
4 1/2	14·1370	15·9040	15 1/2	48·694	188·690
4 5/8	14·5290	16·8000	15 3/4	49·480	194·830
4 3/4	14·9220	17·7202	16	50·265	201·060
4 7/8	15·3150	18·6650	16 1/4	51·051	207·390
5	15·7080	19·6350	16 1/2	51·836	213·820
5 1/8	16·1000	20·6290	16 3/4	52·621	220·350

DIAMETERS, CIRCUMFERENCES, AND AREAS OF CIRCLES—*continued*.

Diameter.	Circumference.	Area.	Diameter.	Circumference.	Area.
17	53·407	226·98	35	109·95	962·11
¼	54·192	233·70	½	111·52	989·80
½	54·977	240·52	36	113·09	1017·90
¾	55·763	247·45	½	114·66	1046·30
18	56·548	254·46	37	116·23	1075·20
¼	57·334	261·59	½	117·81	1104·50
½	58·119	268·80	38	119·38	1134·10
¾	58·905	276·12	½	120·95	1164·20
19	59·690	283·52	39	122·52	1194·60
¼	60·475	291·04	½	124·09	1225·40
½	61·261	298·64	40	125·66	1256·60
¾	62·046	306·35	½	127·23	1288·20
20	62·832	314·16	41	128·80	1320·30
¼	63·617	322·06	½	130·37	1352·70
½	64·402	330·06	42	131·94	1385·40
¾	65·188	338·16	½	133·51	1418·60
21	65·973	346·36	43	135·08	1452·20
¼	66·759	354·66	½	136·65	1486·20
½	67·544	363·05	44	138·23	1520·50
¾	68·329	371·54	½	139·80	1555·30
22	69·115	380·13	45	141·37	1590·40
¼	69·900	388·82	½	142·94	1626·00
½	70·686	397·60	46	144·51	1661·90
¾	71·471	406·49	½	146·08	1698·20
23	72·256	415·47	47	147·65	1734·90
¼	73·042	424·56	48	150·79	1809·60
½	73·827	433·73	49	153·93	1885·70
¾	74·613	443·01	50	157·08	1963·50
24	75·398	452·39	51	160·22	2042·80
½	76·969	471·43	52	163·36	2123·70
25	78·540	490·87	53	166·50	2206·20
½	80·110	510·70	54	169·64	2290·20
26	81·681	530·93	55	172·78	2375·80
½	83·252	551·54	56	175·92	2463·00
27	84·823	572·55	57	179·07	2551·80
½	86·394	593·95	58	182·21	2642·10
28	87·964	615·75	59	185·35	2734·00
½	89·535	637·94	60	188·49	2827·40
29	91·106	660·52	61	191·63	2922·50
½	92·677	683·49	62	194·77	3019·10
30	94·248	706·86	63	197·92	3117·20
½	95·818	730·61	64	201·06	3217·00
31	97·389	754·76	65	204·20	3318·30
½	98·968	779·31	66	207·34	3421·20
32	100·530	804·24	67	210·48	3525·70
½	102·100	829·57	68	213·62	3631·70
33	103·670	855·30	69	216·77	3739·30
½	105·240	881·41	70	219·91	3848·50
34	106·810	907·92	71	223·05	3959·20
½	108·380	934·82	72	226·19	4071·50

E.—Principal Standards for Wire Gauge used in the United States: Dimensions of Sizes in Decimal Parts of an Inch.

Number of Wire Gauge.	American, or Brown and Sharpe.	English, or Birmingham or Stubs'.	Washburn and Moen Manufacturing Co.	Number of Wire Gauge.
000000	—	—	·4600	000000
00000	—	—	·4300	00000
0000	·460000	·454	·3930	0000
000	·409640	·425	·3620	000
00	·364800	·380	·3310	00
0	·324860	·340	·3070	0
1	·289300	·300	·2830	1
2	·257630	·284	·2630	2
3	·229420	·259	·2440	3
4	·204310	·238	·2250	4
5	·181940	·220	·2070	5
6	·162020	·203	·1920	6
7	·144280	·180	·1770	7
8	·128490	·165	·1620	8
9	·114430	·148	·1480	9
10	·101890	·134	·1350	10
11	·090742	·120	·1200	11
12	·080808	·109	·1050	12
13	·071961	·095	·0920	13
14	064084	·083	·0800	14
15	057068	·072	·0720	15
16	·050820	·065	·0630	16
17	·045257	·058	·0540	17
18	·040303	·049	·0470	18
19	·035890	·042	·0410	19
20	·031961	·035	·0350	20
21	·028462	·032	·0320	21
22	·025347	·028	·0280	22
23	·022571	·025	·0250	23
24	·020100	·022	·0230	24
25	·017900	·020	·0200	25
26	·015940	·018	·0180	26
27	·014195	·016	·0170	27
28	·012641	·014	·0160	28
29	·011257	·013	·0150	29
30	·010025	·012	·0140	30
31	·008928	·010	·0135	31
32	·007950	·009	·0130	32
33	·007080	·008	·0110	33
34	·006304	·007	·0100	34
35	·005614	·005	·0095	35
36	005000	·004	·0090	36
37	·004453	—	·0085	37
38	·003965	—	·0080	38
39	·003531		·0075	39
40	·003144	—	·0070	40

F.—International Metric Threads: Angle of Thread,
60 Degrees.

Diameter.	Pitch.	Tapping-Hole.	Diameter.	Pitch.	Tapping-Hole.
mm.	mm.	mm.	mm.	mm.	mm.
3	0·55	2·35	14	2·00	11·60
	0·70	3·25	16	2·00	13·6ϛ
5	0·85	4·05	18	2·50	14·9ϛ
6	1·00	4·90	20	2·50	16·95
7	1·00	5·90	22	2·50	18·95
8	1·25	6·60	24	3·00	20·35
9	1·25	7·60	27	3·00	23·35
10	1·50	8·25	30	3·50	25·70
11	1·50	9·25	33	3·50	28·70
12	1·75	9·95	36	4·00	31·05

G.—British Association (B.A.) Screw Threads.

Number.	Nominal Dimensions in Thousandths of an Inch.		Threads per Inch.	Absolute Dimensions in Millimetres.	
	Diameter.	Pitch.		Diameter.	Pitch.
25	10	2·3	353	0·25	0·07
24	11	3·1	317	0·29	0·08
23	13	3·5	285	0·33	0·09
22	15	3·9	259	0·37	0·10
21	17	4·3	231	0·42	0·11
20	19	4·7	212	0·48	0·12
19	21	5·5	181	0·54	0·14
18	24	5·9	169	0·62	0·15
17	28	6·7	149	0·70	0·17
16	31	7·5	134	0·79	0·19
15	35	8·3	121	0·90	0·21
14	39	9·1	110	1·00	0·23
13	47	9·8	101	1·20	0·25
12	51	11·0	90·7	1·30	0·28
11	59	12·2	81·9	1·50	0·31
10	67	12·8	72·6	1·70	0·35
9	75	15·4	65·1	1·90	0·39
8	87	16·9	59·1	2·20	0·43
7	98	18·9	52·9	2·50	0·48
6	110	20·9	47·9	2·80	0·53
5	126	23·2	43·0	3·20	0·59
4	142	26·0	38·5	3·60	0·66
3	161	28·7	34·8	4·10	0·73
2	185	1·9	31·4	4·70	0·81
1	209	5·4	28·2	5·30	0·90
0	236	39·4	25·4	6·00	1·00

H.—Whitworth's Standard Screw Threads for Bolts.

Diameter of Bolt. Fractional Sizes.	Decimal Sizes.	Number of Threads per Inch.	Diameter at Bottom of Thread.	Distance across Flats.	Distance across Corners.	Thickness of Bolt Head.	Thickness of Nut.
$\frac{3}{16}$	0·1875	24	0·1341	0·4380	0·5015	0·1560	$\frac{3}{16}$
$\frac{1}{4}$	0·2500	20	0·1860	0·5250	0·6062	0·2187	$\frac{1}{4}$
$\frac{5}{16}$	0·3125	18	0·2414	0·6014	0·6944	0·2734	$\frac{5}{16}$
$\frac{3}{8}$	0·3750	16	0·2950	0·7094	0·8191	0·3281	$\frac{3}{8}$
$\frac{7}{16}$	0·4375	14	0·3460	0·8204	0·9473	0·3828	$\frac{7}{16}$
$\frac{1}{2}$	0·5000	12	0·3933	0·9191	1·0612	0·4375	$\frac{1}{2}$
$\frac{9}{16}$	0·5625	12	0·4558	1·0110	1·1674	0·4921	$\frac{9}{16}$
$\frac{5}{8}$	0·6250	11	0·5086	1·1010	1·2713	0·5468	$\frac{5}{8}$
$\frac{11}{16}$	0·6875	11	0·5711	1·2011	1·3869	0·6015	$\frac{11}{16}$
$\frac{3}{4}$	0·7500	10	0·6219	1·3012	1·5024	0·6562	$\frac{3}{4}$
$\frac{13}{16}$	0·8125	10	0·6844	1·3900	1·6050	0·7109	$\frac{13}{16}$
$\frac{7}{8}$	0·8750	9	0·7327	1·4788	1·7075	0·7656	$\frac{7}{8}$
1	1·0000	8	0·8399	1·6701	1·9284	0·8750	1
$1\frac{1}{8}$	1·1250	7	0·9420	1·8605	2·1483	0·9843	$1\frac{1}{8}$
$1\frac{1}{4}$	1·2500	7	1·0670	2·0483	2·3651	1·0937	$1\frac{1}{4}$
$1\frac{3}{8}$	1·3750	6	1·1616	2·2146	2·5571	1·2031	$1\frac{3}{8}$
$1\frac{1}{2}$	1·5000	6	1·2866	2·4134	2·7867	1·3125	$1\frac{1}{2}$
$1\frac{5}{8}$	1·6250	5	1·3689	2·5763	2·9748	1·4218	$1\frac{5}{8}$
$1\frac{3}{4}$	1·7500	5	1·4938	2·7578	3·1844	1·5312	$1\frac{3}{4}$
2	2·0000	4·500	1·7154	3·1491	3·6362	1·7500	2
$2\frac{1}{4}$	2·2500	4	1·9298	3·5460	4·0945	1·9687	$2\frac{1}{4}$
$2\frac{1}{2}$	2·5000	4	2·1798	3·8940	4·4964	2·1875	$2\frac{1}{2}$
$2\frac{3}{4}$	2·7500	3·500	2·3841	4·1810	4·8278	2·4062	$2\frac{3}{4}$
3	3·0000	3·500	2·6341	4·5310	5·2319	2·6250	3
$3\frac{1}{4}$	3·2500	3·250	2·8560	4·8500	5·6002	2·8430	$3\frac{1}{4}$
$3\frac{1}{2}$	3·5000	3·250	3·1060	5·1750	5·9755	3·0620	$3\frac{1}{2}$
$3\frac{3}{4}$	3·7500	3	3·3231	5·5500	6·4085	3·2810	$3\frac{3}{4}$
4	4·0000	3	3·5731	5·9500	6·8704	3·5000	4
$4\frac{1}{2}$	4·5000	2·875	4·0546	6·8250	7·8819	3·9370	$4\frac{1}{2}$
5	5·0000	2·750	4·5346	7·8000	9·0066	4·3750	5
$5\frac{1}{2}$	5·5000	2·625	5·0125	8·8500	10·2190	4·8120	$5\frac{1}{2}$
6	6·0000	2·500	5·4880	10·0000	11·5470	5·2500	6

J.—WHITWORTH THREADS FOR GAS AND WATER PIPES.

Internal Diameter of Pipe.	Diameter at Top of Thread.	Diameter at Bottom of Thread.	Number of Threads per Inch.	Internal Diameter of Pipe.	Diameter at Top of Thread.	Diameter at Bottom of Thread.	Number of Threads per Inch.
1/8	0·3830	0·3370	28	3 3/4	4·2000	4·0840	11
1/4	0·5180	0·4510	19	4	4·4500	4·3340	11
3/8	0·6560	0·5890	19	4 1/2	4·9500	4·8340	11
1/2	0·8250	0·7340	14	5	5·4500	5·3340	11
5/8	0·9020	0·8110	14	5 1/2	5·9500	5·8340	11
3/4	1·0410	0·9500	14	6	6·4500	6·3340	11
7/8	1·1890	1·0980	14	7	7·4500	7·3220	10
1	1·3090	1·1930	11	8	8·4500	8·3220	10
1 1/4	1·6500	1·5340	11	9	9·4500	9·3220	10
1 1/2	1·8820	1·7660	11	10	10·4500	10·3220	10
1 3/4	2·1160	2·0000	11	11	11·4500	11·2900	8
2	2·3470	2·2310	11	12	12·4500	12·2900	8
2 1/4	2·5870	2·4710	11	13	13·6800	13·5200	8
2 1/2	2·9600	2·8440	11	14	14·6800	14·5200	8
2 3/4	3·2100	3·0940	11	15	15·6800	15·5200	8
3	3·4600	3·3440	11	16	16·6800	16·5200	8
3 1/4	3·7000	3·5840	11	17	17·6800	17·5200	8
3 1/2	3·9500	3·8340	11	18	18·6800	18·5200	8

APPENDIX IV

TABLES OF EQUIVALENTS

A.—USEFUL INFORMATION.

B.—INCHES INTO MILLIMETRES.

C.—MILLIMETRES INTO INCHES.

D.—SQUARE INCHES INTO SQUARE CENTIMETRES.

E.—CUBIC INCHES INTO CUBIC CENTIMETRES.

F.—POUNDS INTO KILOGRAMMES.

G.—KILOGRAMMES INTO POUNDS.

H.—KILOGRAMMES PER SQUARE CENTIMETRE INTO POUNDS PER SQUARE INCH.

I.—POUNDS PER SQUARE INCH INTO KILOGRAMMES PER SQUARE CENTIMETRE.

J—KILOMETRES INTO MILES.

A.—USEFUL INFORMATION.

1 knot	=6,080 feet per hour = 1·689 feet per sec.
1 pound avoirdupois	=7,000 grains = 453·6 grams.
Weight of 1 pound	=445,000 dynes.
1 foot pound	=1·3562 × 10⁷ ergs.
1 horse-power	=33,000 foot-pounds per minute.
,,	=550 foot-pounds per sec. =746 watts.
,,	=1·0139 force de cheval.
1 radian	=57·296 degrees.
π· radians	=180 degrees.
π	=3·1415926.
π²	=9·869604.
√π	=1·772453.
Value of g at London	=32·182 feet per second, per second.
1 kilometre	=0·62137 mile.
1 mile per hour	−1·467 feet per second.
1 kilogrammetre	−7·233 foot-pounds.

Air.

1 cubic foot at 14·7 pounds pressure, and at 32° F. weighs 0·080728 pounds = 1·29 ounces.

Pressure of one atmosphere = 14·7 pounds per square inch.

,,	,,	,,	=2116·4 pounds per square foot.
,,	,,	,,	=1·0335 kilogrammes per sq. centimetre.
,,	,,	,,	=29·92 inches of mercury at 32° F.
,,	,,	,,	=76 centimetres of mercury at 32° F.
,,	,,	,,	=33·95 feet of water at 62° F.
1 pound per square inch			=2·035 inches of mercury at 32° F.
,,	,,	,,	=51·7 millimetres of mercury at 32° F.
,,	,,	,,	=2·31 feet of water at 62° F.

1 litre of air at atmospheric pressure and at 32° F. = 1·293 grammes.

1 pound of air at 62° F. = 13·141 cubic feet.

Variation of Density of Air with Temperature.

Temperature in Degrees Fah.	Cubic Feet per Pound.	Pounds per Cubic Foot.
0	11·583	0·08633
32	12·237	0·08073
40	12·586	0·07944
50	12·840	0·07788
60	13·141	0·07609
70	13·342	0·07495
80	13·593	0·07356
90	13·845	0·07223
100	14·096	0·07094
150	15·351	0·06515
200	16·606	0·06021

Skin Friction.

For a thin flat plate placed edgewise in the air-stream, the skin friction may be expressed as $F = 0.0000082 \ A^{0.93} \ v^{1.86}$ (Zahm), where F = force in lbs., v is the velocity in feet per second, and A the area of one surface of the plate; or $F = .0000316 \ A^{0.93}.V^{1.86}$ when V is in M.P.H.

An approximate rule for giving fairly accurate values from 0 to 100 miles per hour is (Berriman) $F = 0.000018 \ A.V^2$, where A is the area of the double surface, and V the velocity in feet per second.

This approximate formula gives results which are correct at 40 miles per hour, but which are about 10 per cent. too high at 100 miles per hour.

A useful figure to remember is that the skin friction per double square foot at 60 miles an hour is 0·06 pound, and that it varies approximately as the square of the velocity.

Skin Friction per Single Surface.

$$R = 0.0000082 \, A^{0.93} \, V^{1.86}.$$

v.	V.	R.	
Speed in Miles per Hour.	Speed in Feet per Second.	Plane 1 Foot in Length : Skin Friction in Pounds per Square Foot.	Plane 32 Feet in Length : Skin Friction in Pounds per Square Foot.
5	7·3	·000332	·000261
10	14·7	·001210	·000950
15	22·0	·002580	·002020
20	29·3	·004390	·003450
25	36·7	·006760	·005300
30	44·0	·009380	007370
35	51·3	·012540	009850
40	58·7	·015960	·012500
45	66·0	·019900	·015600
50	73·3	·024400	·019200
55	80·7	·029100	·022900
60	88·0	·034200	·026800
65	95·3	·039600	·031100
70	102·7	·045500	·035700
75	110·0	·051600	·040500
80	117·3	·058700	·046100
85	124·7	·065200	·051200
90	132·0	·072800	·057200
95	139·3	·080000	·062800
100	146·7	·087800	·068900
105	154·0	·096400	·075600
110	161·2	·105400	·082700
115	168·6	·113000	·088700
120	175·8	·122500	·096200
125	183·4	·132900	·104200
130	190·5	·142500	·111800
135	197·8	·149000	·116800
140	205·4	·163500	·128300
145	212·5	·175000	·137300
150	220·0	·187500	·147000

Wind Pressure upon Normal Flat Planes.

$$P = 0.00300 \, A \cdot V^2.$$
$$= 0.001392 \, A \cdot v^2.$$

Where V is the velocity of the air in miles per hour, v the velocity in feet per second, A the area in square feet, and P the pressure in pounds. [The value of the constant varies slightly with the size of the plane, and the above refers to areas of 2 sq. ft.   d above.]

Pressure upon Inclined Flat Plates.*

(Eiffel.) $P_\theta = \dfrac{\theta}{30}$. P for angles between 0° and 35° for square plates, where P_θ is the normal pressure at the inclination $\theta°$ to the direction of the air-flow, and P is the normal pressure at 90°.

Above 35° $P_\theta = P$ for square plates.

For plates with an aspect ratio = 6, $P_\theta = \dfrac{\theta}{45}$ P for angles up to 60°.

Over 60°, $P_\theta = P$.

It will be seen that the normal pressure between 45° and 60° exceeds the normal pressure at 90°.

Densities and Specific Heats of Gases.

Name of Gas.	Density in Pounds per Cubic Foot.	Cubic Feet per Pound.	Specific Heat at Constant Volume.	Specific Heat at Constant Pressure.
Air..	·08073	12·39	0·169	0·238
Hydrogen	·00559	178·80	2·410	3·405
Oxygen	·08950	11·18	0·156	0·218
Nitrogen	·07830	12·77	0·173	0·244
Carbon monoxide	·07830	12·77	0·173	0·244
Carbon dioxide ..	·12300	8·13	0·171	0·216
Methane	·04470	22·35	0·470	0·593
Ethylene	·07830	12·77	0·332	0·404
Steam	—	—	0·369	0·480

Linear Measure.

1 inch	= 25·400 millimetres.
1 foot	= 0·3048 metre.
1 yard	= 0·9144 metre
1 fathom	= 6 feet.
,,	= 1·8288 metres.
1 mile	= 1·6093 kilometres.

1 millimetre = 0·03937 inch.
1 metre   = 3·2809 feet,
,,   = 1·0936 yards.
1 kilometre = 0·6214 mile.

* Fuller information is given in " The Properties of Wing Sections and the Resistance of Bodies," in this Series.

Superficial Measure.

1 square inch	—6·4516 square centimetres.
1 square foot	—0·093 square metre.
1 square yard	—0·837 square metre.

1 square centimetre	=0·155 square inch.
1 square metre	—10·764 square feet.
1 square metre	—1·197 square yards.

Cubical Measure.

1 cubic inch	=16·387 cubic centimetre.
1 cubic foot	=0·0283 cubic metre.
1 cubic yard	=0·7645 cubic metre.

1 cubic centimetre	=0·0610 cubic inch.
1 cubic metre	—35·3147 cubic feet.
,, ,,	—1·3079 cubic yards.

1 gallon	=4·546 litres.
1 U.S.A. gallon	—231 cubic inches.
,, ,,	=0·83254 imperial gallon.
1 litre	=0·2199 gallon.

Weight.

1 ounce	=28·35 grammes.
1 pound	—0·4536 kilogramme.
1 cwt.	=50·80 kilogrammes.
1 ton	=1,016 kilogrammes.

1 American ton	—2,000 pounds.

1 kilogramme	=2·2046 pounds.
1 metric ton	=1,000 kilogrammes.
,, ,,	—2,204·6 pounds.

1 gallon of pure water weighs 10 pounds.

1 cubic foot of pure water weighs 62·32 pounds and =6¼ gallons.

1 cubic foot of sea water weighs 64 pounds.

Head of water × 0·4325 = pounds per square inch.

B.—EQUIVALENTS IN MILLIMETRES OF INCHES AND FRACTIONS OF AN INCH, ADVANCING BY 32NDS.

Inches.	0″.	1″..	2″.	3″.	4″.	5″.
	—	25·400	50·799	76·199	101·598	126·998
1/32	0·794	26·193	51·593	76·992	102·392	127·791
1/16	1·587	26·987	52·387	77·786	103·186	128·585
3/32	2·381	27·781	53·180	78·580	103·979	129·379
1/8	3·175	28·574	53·974	79·374	104·773	130·173
5/32	3·969	29·368	54·768	80·167	105·567	130·966
3/16	4·762	30·162	55·561	80·961	106·361	131·760
7/32	5·556	30·956	56·355	81·755	107·154	132·554
1/4	6·350	31·749	57·149	82·549	107·948	133·348
9/32	7·144	32·543	57·943	83·342	108·742	134·141
5/16	7·937	33·337	58·736	84·136	109·536	134·935
11/32	8·731	34·131	59·530	84·930	110·329	135·729
3/8	9·525	34·924	60·324	85·723	111·123	136·523
13/32	10·319	35·718	61·118	86·517	111·917	137·316
7/16	11·112	36·512	61·911	87·311	112·710	138·110
15/32	11·906	37·306	62·705	88·105	113·504	138·904
1/2	12·700	38·099	63·499	88·898	114·298	139·697
17/32	13·494	38·893	64·293	89·692	115·092	140·491
9/16	14·287	39·687	65·086	90·486	115·885	141·285
19/32	15·081	40·481	65·880	91·280	116·679	142·079
5/8	15·875	41·274	66·674	92·073	117·473	142·872
21/32	16·668	42·068	67·468	92·867	118·267	143·666
11/16	17·462	42·862	68·261	93·661	119·060	144·460
23/32	18·256	43·655	69·055	94·455	119·854	145·254
3/4	19·050	44·449	69·849	95·248	120·648	146·047
25/32	19·843	45·243	70·642	96·042	121·442	146·841
13/16	20·637	46·037	71·436	96·836	122·235	147·635
27/32	21·431	46·830	72·230	97·629	123·029	148·429
7/8	22·225	47·624	73·024	98·423	123·823	149·222
29/32	23·018	48·418	73·817	99·217	124·616	150·016
15/16	23·812	49·212	74·611	100·011	125·410	150·810
31/32	24·606	50·005	75·405	100·804	126·204	151·604

EQUIVALENTS IN MILLIMETRES OF INCHES AND FRACTIONS OF AN INCH, ADVANCING BY 32NDS—*continued.*

Inches.	6″.	7″.	8″.	9″.	10″.	11″.
0	152·397	177·797	203·196	228·596	253·995	279·395
	153·191	178·591	203·990	229·390	254·789	280·189
	153·985	179·384	204·784	230·183	255·583	280·982
	154·778	180·178	205·578	230·977	256·377	281·776
⅛	155·572	180·972	206·371	231·771	257·170	282·570
	156·366	181·765	207·165	232·565	257·964	283·364
	157·160	182·559	207·959	233·358	258·758	284·157
	157·953	183·353	208·752	234·152	259·552	284·951
¼	158·747	184·147	209·546	234·946	260·345	285·745
	159·541	184·940	210·340	235·739	261·139	286·539
	160·335	185·734	211·134	236·533	261·933	287·332
	161·128	186·528	211·927	237·327	262·727	288·126
⅜	161·922	187·322	212·721	238·121	263·520	288·920
	162·716	188·115	213·515	238·914	264·314	289·714
	163·510	188·909	214·309	239·708	265·108	290·507
	164·303	189·703	215·102	240·502	265·901	291·301
½	165·097	190·497	215·896	241·296	266·695	292·095
	165·891	191·290	216·690	242·089	267·489	292·888
	166·684	192·084	217·484	242·883	268·283	293·682
	167·478	192·878	218·277	243·677	269·076	294·476
⅝	168·272	193·672	219·071	244·471	269·870	295·270
	169·066	194·465	219·865	245·264	270·664	296·063
	169·859	195·259	220·659	246·058	271·458	296·857
	170·653	196·053	221·452	246·852	272·251	297·651
¾	171·447	196·846	222·246	247·646	273·045	298·445
	172·241	197·640	223·040	248·439	273·839	299·238
	173·034	198·434	223·833	249·233	274·633	300·032
	173·828	199·228	224·627	250·027	275·426	300·826
⅞	174·622	200·021	225·421	250·820	276·220	301·620
	175·416	200·815	226·215	251·614	277·014	302·413
	176·209	201·609	227·008	252·408	277·807	303·207
	177·003	202·403	227·802	253·202	278·601	304·001

C.—Equivalents of Millimetres in Inches.

Mm.	Inches.	Mm.	Inches.	Mm.	Inches.	Mm.	Inches.	Mm.	Inches.
1	0·039	41	1·614	81	3·189	121	4·764	161	6·339
2	0·079	42	1·654	82	3·228	122	4·803	162	6·378
3	0·118	43	1·693	83	3·268	123	4·843	163	6·417
4	0·157	44	1·732	84	3·307	124	4·882	164	6·457
5	0·197	45	1·772	85	3·346	125	4·921	165	6·496
6	0·236	46	1·811	86	3·386	126	4·961	166	6·535
7	0·276	47	1·850	87	3·425	127	5·000	167	6·575
8	0·315	48	1·890	88	3·465	128	5·039	168	6·614
9	0·354	49	1·929	89	3·504	129	5·079	169	6·654
10	0·394	50	1·969	90	3·543	130	5·118	170	6·693
11	0·433	51	2·008	91	3·583	131	5·158	171	6·732
12	0·472	52	2·047	92	3·622	132	5·197	172	6·772
13	0·512	53	2·087	93	3·661	133	5·236	173	6·811
14	0·551	54	2·126	94	3·701	134	5·276	174	6·850
15	0·591	55	2·165	95	3·740	135	5·315	175	6·890
16	0·630	56	2·205	96	3·780	136	5·354	176	6·929
17	0·669	57	2·244	97	3·819	137	5·394	177	6·969
18	0·709	58	2·283	98	3·858	138	5·433	178	7·008
19	0·748	59	2·323	99	3·898	139	5·472	179	7·047
20	0·787	60	2·362	100	3·937	140	5·512	180	7·087
21	0·827	61	2·402	101	3·976	141	5·551	181	7·126
22	0·866	62	2·441	102	4·016	142	5·591	182	7·165
23	0·906	63	2·480	103	4·055	143	5·630	183	7·205
24	0·945	64	2·520	104	4·095	144	5·669	184	7·244
25	0·984	65	2·559	105	4·134	145	5·709	185	7·284
26	1·024	66	2·598	106	4·173	146	5·748	186	7·323
27	1·063	67	2·638	107	4·213	147	5·787	187	7·362
28	1·102	68	2·677	108	4·252	148	5·827	188	7·402
29	1·142	69	2·717	109	4·291	149	5·866	189	7·441
30	1·181	70	2·756	110	4·331	150	5·906	190	7·480
31	1·220	71	2·795	111	4·370	151	5·945	191	7·520
32	1·260	72	2·835	112	4·409	152	5·984	192	7·559
33	1·299	73	2·874	113	4·449	153	6·024	193	7·598
34	1·339	74	2·913	114	4·488	154	6·063	194	7·638
35	1·378	75	2·953	115	4·528	155	6·102	195	7·677
36	1·417	76	2·992	116	4·567	156	6·142	196	7·717
37	1·457	77	3·032	117	4·606	157	6·181	197	7·756
38	1·496	78	3·071	118	4·646	158	6·221	198	7·795
39	1·535	79	3·110	119	4·685	159	6·260	199	7·835
40	1·575	80	3·150	120	4·724	160	6·299	200	7·874

13

EQUIVALENTS OF MILLIMETRES IN INCHES—*continued.*

Mm.	Inches.	Mm.	Inches.	Mm.	Inches.	Mm.	Inches.	Mm.	Inches.
201	7·913	241	9·488	281	11·063	321	12·638	361	14·213
202	7·953	242	9·528	282	11·102	322	12·677	362	14·252
203	7·992	243	9·567	283	11·142	323	12·717	363	14·291
204	8·032	244	9·606	284	11·181	324	12·756	364	14·331
205	8·071	245	9·646	285	11·221	325	12·795	365	14·370
206	8·110	246	9·685	286	11·260	326	12·835	366	14·410
207	8·150	247	9·724	287	11·299	327	12·874	367	14·449
208	8·189	248	9·764	288	11·339	328	12·913	368	14·488
209	8·228	249	9·803	289	11·378	329	12·953	369	14·528
210	8·268	250	9·843	290	11·417	330	12·992	370	14·567
211	8·307	251	9·882	291	11·457	331	13·032	371	14·606
212	8·347	252	9·921	292	11·496	332	13·071	372	14·646
213	8·386	253	9·961	293	11·536	333	13·110	373	14·685
214	8·425	254	10·000	294	11·575	334	13·150	374	14·725
215	8·465	255	10·039	295	11·614	335	13·189	375	14·764
216	8·504	256	10·079	296	11·654	336	13·228	376	14·803
217	8·543	257	10·118	297	11·693	337	13·268	377	14·843
218	8·583	258	10·158	298	11·732	338	13·307	378	14·882
219	8·622	259	10·197	299	11·772	339	13·347	379	14·921
220	8·661	260	10·236	300	11·811	340	13·386	380	14·961
221	8·701	261	10·276	301	11·850	341	13·425	381	15·000
222	8·740	262	10·315	302	11·890	342	13·465	382	15·040
223	8·780	263	10·354	303	11·929	343	13·504	383	15·079
224	8·819	264	10·394	304	11·969	344	13·543	384	15·118
225	8·858	265	10·433	305	12·008	345 ·	13·583	385	15·158
226	8·898	266	10·473	306	12·047	346	13·622	386	15·197
227	8·937	267	10·512	307	12·087	347	13·662	387	15·236
228	8·876	268	10·551	308	12·126	348	13·701	388	15·276
229	9·016	269	10·591	309	12·165	349	13·740	389	15·315
230	9·055	270	10·630	310	12·205	350	13·780	390	15·354
231	9·095	271	10·669	311	12·244	351	13·819	391	15·394
232	9·134	272	10·709	312	12·284	352	13·858	392	15·433
233	9·173	273	10·748	313	12·323	353	13·898	393	15·473
234	9·213	274	10·787	314	12·362	354	13·937	394	15·512
235	9·252	275	10·827	315	12·402	355	13·977	395	15·551
236	9·291	276	10·866	316	12·441	356	14·016	396	15·591
237	9·331	277	10·906	317	12·480	357	14·055	397	15·630
238	9·370	278	10·945	318	12·520	358	14·095	398	15·669
239	9·410	279	10·984	319	12·559	359	14·134	399	15·709
240	9·449	280	11·024	320	12·599	360	14·173	400	15·748

EQUIVALENTS OF MILLIMETRES IN INCHES—*continued*.

Mm.	Inches.	Mm.	Inches.	Mm.	Inches.	Mm.	Inches.	Mm.	Inches.
401	15·788	441	17·362	481	18·937	521	20·512	561	22·087
402	15·827	442	17·402	482	18·977	522	20·551	562	22·126
403	15·866	443	17·441	483	19·016	523	20·591	563	22·166
404	15·906	444	17·480	484	19·055	524	20·630	564	22·205
405	15·945	445	17·520	485	19·095	525	20·669	565	22·244
406	15·984	446	17·559	486	19·134	526	20·709	566	22·284
407	16·024	447	17·599	487	19·173	527	20·748	567	22·323
408	16·063	448	17·638	488	19·213	528	20·788	568	22·362
409	16·103	449	17·677	489	19·252	529	20·827	569	22·402
410	16·142	450	17·717	490	19·292	530	20·866	570	22·441
411	16·181	451	17·756	491	19·331	531	20·906	571	22·481
412	16·221	452	17·795	492	19·370	532	20·945	572	22·520
413	16·260	453	17·835	493	19·410	533	20·984	573	22·559
414	16·299	454	17·874	494	19·449	534	21·024	574	22·599
415	16·339	455	17·914	495	19·488	535	21·063	575	22·638
416	16·378	456	17·953	496	19·528	536	21·103	576	22·677
417	16·417	457	17·992	497	19·567	537	21·142	577	22·717
418	16·457	458	18·032	498	19·606	538	21·181	578	22·756
419	16·496	459	18·071	499	19·646	539	21·221	579	22·795
420	16·536	460	18·110	500	19·685	540	21·260	580	22·835
421	16·575	461	18·150	501	19·725	541	21·299	581	22·874
422	16·614	462	18·189	502	19·764	542	21·339	582	22·914
423	16·654	463	18·229	503	19·803	543	21·378	583	22·953
424	16·693	464	18·268	504	19·843	544	21·418	584	22·992
425	16·732	465	18·307	505	19·882	545	21·457	585	23·032
426	16·772	466	18·347	506	19·921	546	21·496	586	23·071
427	16·811	467	18·386	507	19·961	547	21·536	587	23·110
428	16·851	468	18·425	508	20·000	548	21·575	588	23·150
429	16·890	469	18·465	509	20·040	549	21·614	589	23·189
430	16·929	470	18·504	510	20·079	550	21·654	590	23·229
431	16·969	471	18·543	511	20·118	551	21·693	591	23·268
432	17·008	472	18·583	512	20·158	552	21·732	592	23·307
433	17·047	473	18·622	513	20·197	553	21·772	593	23·347
434	17·087	474	18·662	514	20·236	554	21·811	594	23·385
435	17·126	475	18·701	515	20·276	555	21·851	595	23·424
436	17·166	476	18·740	516	20·315	556	21·890	596	23·464
437	17·205	477	18·780	517	20·355	557	21·929	597	23·503
438	17·244	478	18·819	518	20·394	558	21·969	598	23·543
439	17·284	479	18·858	519	20·433	559	22·008	599	23·582
440	17·323	480	18·898	520	20·473	560	22·047	600	23·622

EQUIVALENTS OF MILLIMETRES IN INCHES—*continued*.

Mm.	Inches.	Mm.	Inches.	Mm.	Inches.	Mm.	Inches.	Mm.	Inches.
601	23·662	641	25·236	681	26·811	721	28·386	761	29·961
602	23·701	642	25·276	682	26·851	722	28·425	762	30·000
603	23·740	643	25·315	683	26·890	723	28·465	763	30·040
604	23·780	644	25·355	684	26·929	724	28·504	764	30·079
605	23·819	645	25·394	685	26·969	725	28·544	765	30·118
606	23·858	646	25·433	686	27·008	726	28·583	766	30·158
607	23·898	647	25·473	687	27·047	727	28·622	767	30·197
608	23·937	648	25·512	688	27·087	728	28·662	768	30·236
609	23·977	649	25·551	689	27·126	729	28·701	769	30·276
610	24·016	650	25·591	690	27·166	730	28·740	770	30·315
611	24·055	651	25·630	691	27·205	731	28·780	771	30·355
612	24·095	652	25·670	692	27·244	732	28·819	772	30·394
613	24·134	653	25·709	693	27·284	733	28·859	773	30·433
614	24·173	654	25·748	694	27·323	734	28·898	774	30·473
615	24·213	655	25·788	695	27·362	735	28·937	775	30·512
616	24·252	656	25·827	696	27·402	736	28·977	776	30·551
617	24·292	657	25·866	697	27·441	737	29·016	777	30·591
618	24·331	658	25·906	698	27·481	738	29·055	778	30·630
619	24·370	659	25·945	699	27·520	739	29·095	779	30·670
620	24·410	660	25·984	700	27·559	740	29·134	780	30·709
621	24·449	661	26·024	701	27·599	741	29·173	781	30·748
622	24·488	662	26·063	702	27·638	742	29·213	782	30·788
623	24·528	663	26·103	703	27·677	743	29·252	783	30·827
624	24·567	664	26·142	704	27·717	744	29·292	784	30·866
625	24·607	665	26·181	705	27·756	745	29·331	785	30·906
626	24·646	666	26·221	706	27·796	746	29·370	786	30·945
627	24·685	667	26·260	707	27·835	747	29·410	787	30·985
628	24·725	668	26·299	708	27·874	748	29·449	788	31·024
629	24·764	669	26·339	709	27·914	749	29·488	789	31·063
630	24·803	670	26·378	710	27·953	750	29·528	790	31·103
631	24·843	671	26·418	711	27·992	751	29·567	791	31·142
632	24·882	672	26·457	712	28·032	752	29·607	792	31·181
633	24·921	673	26·496	713	28·071	753	29·646	793	31·221
634	24·961	674	26·536	714	28·110	754	29·685	794	31·260
635	25·000	675	26·575	715	28·150	755	29·725	795	31·299
636	25·040	676	26·614	716	28·189	756	29·764	796	31·339
637	25·079	677	26·654	717	28·229	757	29·803	797	31·378
638	25·118	678	26·693	718	28·268	758	29·843	798	31·418
639	25·158	679	26·733	719	28·307	759	29·882	799	31·457
640	25·197	680	26·772	720	28·347	760	29·922	800	31·496

EQUIVALENTS OF MILLIMETRES IN INCHES—*continued*.

Mm.	Inches.	Mm.	Inches.	Mm.	Inches.	Mm.	Inches.	Mm.	Inches.
801	31·536	841	33·111	881	34·685	921	36·260	961	37·835
802	31·575	842	33·150	882	34·725	922	36·300	962	37·874
803	31·614	843	33·189	883	34·764	923	36·339	963	37·914
804	31·654	844	33·229	884	34·803	924	36·378	964	37·953
805	31·693	845	33·268	885	34·843	925	36·418	965	37·992
806	31·733	846	33·307	886	34·882	926	36·457	966	38·032
807	31·772	847	33·347	887	34·922	927	36·496	967	38·071
808	31·811	848	33·386	888	34·961	928	36·536	968	38·111
809	31·851	849	33·425	889	35·000	929	36·575	969	38·150
810	31·890	850	33·465	890	35·040	930	36·615	970	38·189
811	31·929	851	33·504	891	35·079	931	36·654	971	38·229
812	31·969	852	33·544	892	35·118	932	36·693	972	38·268
813	32·008	853	33·583	893	35·158	933	36·733	973	38·307
814	32·048	854	33·622	894	35·197	934	36·772	974	38·347
815	32·087	855	33·662	895	35·237	935	36·811	975	38·386
816	32·126	856	33·701	896	35·276	936	36·851	976	38·426
817	32·166	857	33·740	897	35·315	937	36·890	977	38·465
818	32·205	858	33·780	898	35·355	938	36·929	978	38·504
819	32·244	859	33·819	899	35·394	939	36·969	979	38·544
820	32·284	860	33·859	900	35·433	940	37·008	980	38·583
821	32·323	861	33·898	901	35·473	941	37·048	981	38·622
822	32·362	862	33·937	902	35·512	942	37·087	982	38·662
823	32·402	863	33·977	903	35·552	943	37·126	983	38·701
824	32·441	864	34·016	904	35·591	944	37·166	984	38·741
825	32·481	865	34·055	905	35·630	945	37·205	985	38·780
826	32·520	866	34·095	906	35·670	946	37·244	986	38·819
827	32·559	867	34·134	907	35·709	947	37·284	987	38·859
828	32·599	868	34·174	908	35·748	948	37·323	988	38·898
829	32·638	869	34·213	909	35·788	949	37·363	989	38·937
830	32·677	870	34·252	910	35·827	950	37·402	990	38·977
831	32·717	871	34·292	911	35·866	951	37·441	991	39·016
832	32·756	872	34·331	912	35·906	952	37·481	992	39·055
833	32·796	873	34·370	913	35·945	953	37·520	993	39·095
834	32·835	874	34·410	914	35·985	954	37·559	994	39·134
835	32·874	875	34·449	915	36·024	955	37·599	995	39·174
836	32·914	876	34·488	916	36·063	956	37·638	996	39·213
837	32·953	877	34·528	917	36·103	957	37·677	997	39·252
838	32·992	878	34·567	918	36·142	958	37·717	998	39·292
839	33·032	879	34·607	919	36·181	959	37·756	999	39·331
840	33·071	880	34·646	920	36·221	960	37·796	1000	39·370

D.—EQUIVALENTS OF SQUARE CENTIMETRES IN SQUARE INCHES.

1 SQUARE CENTIMETRE = 0·155059 OR 1 SEE CM.

Square Centimetres	.0	.1	.2	.3	.4	.5	.6	.7	.8	.9
1	591	0·17051	0·18601	0·20151	0·21701	0·23251	0·24801	0·26351	0·27901	0·29451
2	0·31001	0·32551	0·34101	0·35651	0·37201	0·38751	0·40301	0·41852	0·43402	0·44952
3	0·46502	0·48052	0·49602	0·51152	0·52702	0·54252	0·55802	0·57352	0·58902	0·60452
4	0·62002	0·63552	0·65102	0·66652	0·68203	0·69753	0·71303	0·72853	0·74403	0·75953
5	0·77503	0·79053	0·80603	0·82153	0·83703	0·85253	0·86803	0·88353	0·89903	0·91453
6	0·93004	0·94554	0·96104	0·97654	0·99204	1·00754	1·02304	1·03854	1·05404	1·06954
7	1·08504	1·10054	1·11604	1·13154	1·14704	1·16254	1·17804	1·19355	1·20905	1·22455
8	1·24005	1·25555	1·27105	1·28655	1·30205	1·31755	1·33305	1·34855	1·36405	1·37955
9	1·39505	1·41055	1·42605	1·44156	1·45706	1·47256	1·48806	1·50356	1·51906	1·53456
10	1·55006	1·56556	1·58106	1·59656	1·61206	1·62756	1·64306	65856	1·67406	1·68956

E. EQUIVALENTS OF SQUARE INCHES IN SQUARE CENTIMETRES.

1 SQ. IN. = 6·451367 SQUARE CENTIMETRES.

Square Inches.	.0	.1	.2	.3	.4	.5	.6	.7	.8	.9
1	6·4514	7·0965	7·7416	8·3868	9·0319	9·6770	10·3222	10·9673	11·6125	12·2576
2	12·9027	13·5479	14·1930	14·8381	15·4833	16·1284	16·7736	17·4187	18·0638	18·7090
3	19·3541	19·9992	20·6444	21·2895	21·9346	22·5798	23·2249	23·8701	·252	25·1603
4	25·8055	26·4506	27·0957	27·7409	28·3860	·292	29·6763	30·3214	30·9666	31·6117
5	32·2568	32·9020	33·5471	34·1922	34·8374	35·4825	36·1277	36·7728	·179	38·0631
6	38·7082	39·3533	3985	990	41·2887	41·9339	42·5790	43·2242	43·8693	44·5144
7	45·1596	45·8047	46·4498	990	47·7401	48·3853	49·0304	49·6755	·997	·998
8	51·6109	52·2561	5912	3263	·915	54·8366	55·4818	56·1269	56·7720	·172
9	58·0623	58·7074	59·3526	·997	60·6428	61·2880	61·9331	62·5783	63·2234	63·8685
10	64·5137	65·1588	65·8039	66·4491	67·0942	67·7394	68·3845	69·0296	69·6748	70·3199

F. EQUIVALENTS OF CUBIC INCHES IN CUBIC CENTIMETRES.

1 CUBIC INCH = 16·386176 CUBIC CENTIMETRES.

Cubic Inches.	·0.	·1.	·2.	·3.	·4.	·5.	·6.	·7.	·8.	·9.
1	16·386	18·025	19·663	21·302	2941	24·579	26·218	27·856	2995	31·134
2	32·772	34·411	36·050	37·688	39·327	40·965	42·604	1443	45·881	47·520
3	49·158	50·797	52·436	54·074	55·713	57·352	58·990	60·629	6267	63·906
4	6545	67·183	68·822	70·461	72·099	73·738	75·376	77·015	78·654	80·292
5	81·931	809	898	86·847	88·485	90·124	91·763	9401	95·040	96·678
6	98·317	99·956	101·594	103·233	104·872	106·510	108·149	109·787	111·426	113·065
7	114·703	116·342	1980	119·619	121·258	122·896	124·535	126·174	127·812	129·451
8	131·089	132·728	134·367	136·005	137·644	139·282	140·921	142·560	144·198	145·837
9	147·476	149·114	150·753	152·391	154·030	155·669	157·307	158·946	160·585	162·223
10	163·862	165·500	167·139	168·778	170·416	172·055	173·693	175·332	176·971	178·609

G.—Pounds in Kilogrammes.

Lbs.	Kilo-grammes.	Lbs.	Kilo-grammes.	Lbs.	Kilo-grammes.	Lbs.	Kilo-grammes.
1	0·454	26	11·793	51	23·133	76	34·473
2	0·907	27	12·247	52	23·587	77	34·927
3	1·361	28	12·701	53	24·040	78	35·380
4	1·814	29	13·154	54	24·494	79	35·834
5	2·268	30	13·608	55	24·948	80	36·287
6	2·722	31	14·061	56	25·401	81	36·741
7	3·175	32	14·515	57	25·855	82	37·195
8	3·629	33	14·969	58	26·308	83	37·648
9	4·082	34	15·422	59	26·762	84	38·102
10	4·536	35	15·876	60	27·252	85	38·555
11	4·989	36	16·329	61	27·669	86	39·009
12	5·443	37	16·783	62	28·123	87	39·463
13	5·897	38	17·236	63	28·576	88	39·916
14	6·350	39	17·690	64	29·030	89	40·370
15	6·804	40	18·144	65	29·483	90	40·823
16	7·257	41	18·597	66	29·937	91	41·277
17	7·711	42	19·051	67	30·391	92	41·731
18	8·165	43	19·504	68	30·844	93	42·184
19	8·618	44	19·958	69	31·298	94	42·638
20	9·072	45	20·412	70	31·751	95	43·091
21	9·523	46	20·865	71	32·205	96	43·545
22	9·979	47	21·319	72	32·659	97	43·998
23	10·433	48	21·772	73	33·112	98	44·452
24	10·886	49	22·226	74	33·566	99	44·906
25	11·340	50	22·680	75	34·019	100	45·359

H.—KILOGRAMMES IN POUNDS.

Kilos.	Pounds.	Kilos.	Pounds.	Kilos.	Pounds.	Kilos.	Pounds.
1	2·205	26	57·320	51	112·436	76	167·551
2	4·409	27	59·525	52	114·640	77	169·756
3	6·614	28	61·729	53	116·845	78	171·900
4	8·818	29	63·934	54	119·049	79	174·165
5	11·023	30	66·139	55	121·254	80	176·370
6	13·228	31	68·343	56	123·459	81	178·574
7	15·432	32	70·548	57	125·663	82	180·779
8	17·637	33	72·752	58	127·868	83	182·983
9	19·842	34	74·957	59	130·073	84	185·118
10	22·046	35	77·162	60	132·277	85	187·393
11	24·251	36	79·366	61	134·482	86	189·597
12	26·455	37	81·571	62	136·486	87	191·802
13	28·660	38	83·776	63	138·891	88	194·010
14	30·865	39	85·980	64	141·096	89	196·211
15	33·069	40	88·185	65	143·300	90	198·416
16	35·274	41	90·389	66	145·505	91	200·620
17	37·479	42	92·594	67	147·710	92	202·825
18	39·683	43	94·799	68	149·914	93	205·030
19	41·888	44	97·003	69	152·119	94	207·234
20	44·092	45	99·208	70	154·323	95	209·439
21	46·297	46	101·413	71	156·528	96	211·644
22	48·502	47	103·617	72	158·733	97	213·848
23	50·706	48	105·822	73	160·937	98	216·053
24	52·911	49	108·026	74	163·142	99	218·275
25	55·115	50	110·231	75	165·347	100	220·462

I.—Equivalents of 1 Kilogramme per Square Centimetre in Pounds per Square Inch.

1 Kilogramme per Square Centimetre = 14·22282 Pounds per Square Inch.

Kilos. per Sq. Centimetre.	·0.	·1.	·2.	·3.	·4.	·5.	·6.	·7.	·8.	·9.
1	14·223	15·645	17·067	18·490	19·912	21·334	22·757	24·179	25·601	27·023
2	28·446	29·868	31·290	32·712	34·135	35·557	36·979	38·402	39·824	41·246
3	42·668	44·091	45·513	46·935	48·358	49·780	51·202	52·624	54·047	55·469
4	56·891	58·314	59·736	61·158	62·580	64·003	65·425	66·847	68·270	69·692
5	71·114	72·536	73·959	75·381	76·803	78·226	79·648	81·070	82·492	83·915
6	85·337	86·759	88·181	89·604	91·026	92·448	93·871	95·293	96·715	98·137
7	99·560	100·982	102·404	103·827	105·249	106·671	108·093	109·516	110·938	112·360
8	113·783	115·205	116·627	118·049	119·472	120·894	122·316	123·739	125·161	126·583
9	128·005	129·428	130·850	132·272	133·695	135·117	136·539	137·961	139·384	140·806
10	142·228	143·650	145·073	146·495	147·917	149·340	150·762	152·184	153·606	155·029

J.—EQUIVALENTS OF POUNDS PER SQUARE INCH IN KILOGRAMMES PER SQUARE CENTIMETRE.

1 POUND PER SQUARE INCH = 0·07030954 OF A KILOGRAMME PER SQUARE CENTIMETRE.

Pounds per Sq. Inch.	·0	·1	·2	·3	·4	·5	·6	·7	·8	·9
1	·070310	·077340	·084371	·091402	·098433	·105464	·112495	·119526	·126557	·133588
2	·140619	·147650	·154681	·161712	·168743	·175774	·182805	·189836	·196867	·203898
3	·210929	·217960	·224991	·232021	·239052	·246083	·253114	·260145	·267176	·274207
4	·281238	·288269	·295300	·302331	·309362	·316393	·323424	·330455	·337486	·344517
5	·351548	·358579	·365610	·372641	·379672	·386702	·393733	·400764	·407795	·414826
6	·421857	·428888	·435919	·442950	·449981	·457012	·464043	·471074	·478105	·485136
7	·492167	·499198	·506229	·513260	·520291	·527322	·534353	·541383	·548414	·555445
8	·562476	·569507	·576538	·583569	·590600	·597631	·604662	·611693	·618724	·625755
9	·632786	·639817	·646848	·653879	·660910	·667941	·674972	·682003	·689033	·696064
10	·703095	·710126	·717157	·724188	·731219	·738250	·745281	·752312	·759343	·766374

K.—Conversion of Miles into Kilometres.

Kilos.	*Miles.*	*Kilos.*	*Miles.*	*Kilos.*	*Miles.*	*Kilos.*	*Miles.*	*Kilos.*	*Miles.*
1	⅝	16	10	31	19¼	46	28⅝	60	37¼
2	1¼	17	10⅝	32	19⅞	47	29¼	70	43½
3	1⅞	18	11¼	33	20½	48	29⅞	80	49¾
4	2½	19	11¾	34	21⅛	49	30½	90	55⅞
5	3⅛	20	12⅜	35	21¾	50	31⅛	100	62⅛
6	3¾	21	13	36	22⅜	51	31¾	200	124¼
7	4⅜	22	13⅝	37	23	52	32¼	300	186⅜
8	5	23	14¼	38	23⅝	53	32⅞	400	248½
9	5⅝	24	14⅞	39	24¼	54	33½	500	310¾
10	6¼	25	15½	40	24⅞	55	34⅛	600	372⅞
11	6⅞	26	16⅛	41	25½	56	34¾	700	435
12	7½	27	16¾	42	26⅛	57	35⅜	800	497⅛
13	8⅛	28	17⅜	43	26¾	58	36	900	559¼
14	8¾	29	18	44	27⅜	59	36⅝	1,000	621⅜
15	9⅜	30	18⅝	45	28				

BIBLIOGRAPHY

THE reader is referred for fuller information upon questions connected with aeroplane design to the following books and papers:

A.—BOOKS.

1. " Aerodynamics ": *Aerial Flight.* By F. W. Lanchester. (Published by Constable and Co.)

2. " Aerodonetics." By same author.

3. " The Mechanics of the Aeroplane." By Captain Duchêne. Translated by J. Lebeboer and T. O'B. Hubbard.

4. " Elementary Aeronautics." By Thurston. (Published by Whittaker and Co.)

5. " Essais d'Aerodynamique." By A. de Gramont. (Paris: Hachette.)

6. " Étude Raisonnée de L'Aeroplane. By J. Bordeaux, Paris.

7. The *Aeronautical Journals,* 1910 to date (the organ of the Aeronautical Society of Great Britain, 11, Adam Street, Adelphi, W.C.)

8. " The Resistance of the Air and Aviation." By G. Eiffel. Translated by J. C. Hunsaker. (Published by Constable and Co., 1913.)

9. " New Researches on the Resistance of the Air and Aviation, made in the Auteuil Laboratory." By G. Eiffel, Paris. (Published by H. Dunod and E. Pinat, Paris.)

10. " The Technical Reports of the Advisory Committee for Aeronautics," 1909-10, 1910-11, 1911-12, 1912-13, to date. (Published by H.M. Stationery Office, and obtainable from Wyman and Sons, Fetter Lane, E.C.)

11 " Bulletins de l'Institut Aerodynamique de Koutchino," fascicules 1. to v. (Moscou : Imprimerie, I. N. Kouchnereff and Co., 1914.)

12. " Practical Aeronautics." By C. C. Hayward. Amercian School of Correspondence, 1912.

13. " Aéro Manuel," 1914. By Ch. Favoux and G. Bonnet. (Paris: Dunod et Pinat.)

14. " Cours d'Aeronautique." By Marchis. (Published by Dunot et Pinat, Paris.)

15. " Revue Générale de L'Aeronautique." Tomes I. to V.

16. " Causeries technique sans formules sur l'aeroplane." Capt. Duchêne.

B.—REFERENCES, PAPERS, ETC.

1. The Howard Lecture: " Aeronautics." By Professor Petavel. Published in the *Journal of the Society of Arts*, October 31 to November 14, 1913.

2. " The Flying Machine from an Engineering Standpoint." By F. W. Lanchester. Read before the Institute of Civil Engineers, May 5, 1914. Reprinted in *Flight*, May 9 to July 17, 1914.

3. " Aeroplane Design." Paper by F. S. Barnwell, read before the Engineering Society of Glasgow University. Reprinted in *The Aeroplane*, January 20 to February 17, 1915.

4. " Modern Developments of Aeroplane Theory." By A. R. Low. Read before the Junior Institution of Engineers, May, 1913.

5. " The Rational Design of Aeroplanes." By A. R. Low, *Aeronautical Journal*, April, 1914.

6. " The Laws of Similitude." By L. Bairstow, *Aeronautical Journal*, July, 1913.

7. " The Comparison of Monoplanes and Biplanes." By F. Handley Page. *Aeronautical Journal*, April, 1913.

8. " Problems relating to Aircraft." By Mervyn O'Gorman. London: Institution of Automobile Engineers, 1911.

9. " Stresses in Wings." The R.F.A. Method of Estimating. *Flight*, October 18, 1913.

10. The " Dynamics of the Flying Machine." By James S. Stephens. Chicago: Western Society of Engineers, 1911.

11. Military Aeroplane Competition, 1912. Report of the Judges' Committee. London: Wyman and Sons.

12. " Tests on Wing Spars." By Alex. Ogilvie. *Flight*, July 19, 1913.

INDEX

THE END

BILLING AND SONS, LTD., PRINTERS, GUILDFORD, ENGLAND

FLIGHT

Eighth Year

The Premier
and First
Aero Weekly
in the World.

 **D.**

Illustrations

a

Feature.

<u>EVERY</u>

<u>FRIDAY</u>

Whittaker's Practical Handbooks

ATKINS, E. A. .	**Practical Sheet and Plate Metal Work.** 6s. net.
BARR, J. R. . .	**Direct Current Electrical Engineering.** 10s. net.
BARR & ARCHIBALD	**Design of Alternating Current Machinery.** 12s. 6d net.
GARRARD, A. .	**Gas, Oil, and Petrol Engines.**
GASTER & DOW .	**Modern Illuminants and Illuminating Engineering.** 12s. 6d. net.
HAWKINS & WALLIS	**The Dynamo: Its Theory, Design, and Manufacture.** Two Vols. Vol. I., 10s. 6d net ; Vol. II, 10s. 6d. net.
HIBBERT, W.	**Magneto and Electric Ignition.** 2s. net.
HOBART, H. M.	**Continuous-Current Dynamo Design.** 7s. 6d. net.
.. . . .	**Electric Motors—Continuous, Polyphase, and Single Phase Motors.** 18s. net.
HORNER, J. G.	**Principles of Fitting.** 5s. net.
	Metal Turning. 3s. 6d. net.
MARCHANT, W. H.	**Wireless Telegraphy.** A Practical Handbook for Operators and Students. 5s. net.
MAYCOCK, W. P. .	**Electric Lighting and Power Distribution.** Vol. I., 6s. net; Vol. II., 6s. 6d. net.
	Alternating-Current Work. 6s. net.
	Electric Wiring, Fittings, Switches, and Lamps. 6s. net.
MURDOCH & OSCHWALD	**Electrical Instruments in Theory and Practice.** 10s. 6d. net.
OULTON & WILSON	**Practical Testing of Electrical Machines.** 4s. 6d. net.
PENDRY, H. W.	**Elementary Telegraphy.** 2s. 6d. net.
POOLE, J.	**Practical Telephone Handbook.** 6s. net.
PULL, E.	**Engineering Workshop Exercises.** With a chapter on Screw Cutting and Notes on Materials. 2s. net.
WALKER, S. F.	**Electricity in Homes and Workshops.** 5s. net.
WHITTAKER'S	**Arithmetic of Electrical Engineering.** 1s. 6d. net.
	Electrical Engineer's Pocket Book. 5s. net.
	Mechanical Engineer's Pocket Book. 3s. 6d. net.
WIGHT, J. T.	**Elementary Graphic Statics.** 4s. net.
WHITE, W. J.	**Wireless Telegraphy and Telephony.** 2s. 6d. net.

Catalogue of Books on Electricity, Engineering, etc., Post Free.

WHITTAKER & CO., 2, WHITE HART STREET, LONDON, E.C.

CPSIA information can be obtained
at www.ICGtesting.com
Printed in the USA
LVOW01s1554111115
462082LV00020B/1117/P